THE FATHERS
OF THE CHURCH

A NEW TRANSLATION

VOLUME 107

THE FATHERS OF THE CHURCH

A NEW TRANSLATION

EDITORIAL BOARD

Thomas P. Halton
The Catholic University of America
Editorial Director

Elizabeth Clark
Duke University

Robert D. Sider
Dickinson College

Joseph T. Lienhard, S.J.
Fordham University

Michael Slusser
Duquesne University

Frank A. C. Mantello
The Catholic University of America

Cynthia White
The University of Arizona

Kathleen McVey
Princeton Theological Seminary

Robin Darling Young
The University of Notre Dame

David J. McGonagle
Director
The Catholic University of America Press

FORMER EDITORIAL DIRECTORS

Ludwig Schopp, Roy J. Deferrari, Bernard M. Peebles,
Hermigild Dressler, O.F.M.

Joel Kalvesmaki
Staff Editor

ST. GREGORY OF NAZIANZUS
SELECT ORATIONS

Translated by

MARTHA VINSON
Indiana University
Bloomington, Indiana

THE CATHOLIC UNIVERSITY OF AMERICA PRESS
Washington, D.C.

Copyright © 2003
THE CATHOLIC UNIVERSITY OF AMERICA PRESS
All rights reserved
Printed in the United States of America

The paper used in this publication meets the minimum requirements of the American National Standards for Information Science—Permanence of Paper for Printed Library Materials, ANSI z39.48—1984. ∞

LIBRARY OF CONGRESS CATALOGING-IN-PUBLICATION DATA

Gregory, of Nazianzus, Saint.
  [Orations. English. Selections]
  Select orations / translated by Martha Vinson.
    p. cm. — (The fathers of the church ; v. 107)
  Includes bibliographical references and indexes.
  ISBN 0-8132-0107-1 (alk. paper)
  ISBN 9787-0-8132-2769-6 (pbk.)
  1. Sermons, Greek. 2. Speeches, addresses, etc.,
Greek. I. Vinson, Martha Pollard. II. Title. III. Series.
BR60.F3 G68
[BR65.G62]
270 s—dc21
[252/.0

                    2002154383

CONTENTS

Abbreviations   vii
Select Bibliography   ix
Introduction   xiii

SELECT ORATIONS

Oration 6	3
Oration 9	21
Oration 10	26
Oration 11	30
Oration 13	36
Oration 14	39
Oration 15	72
Oration 17	85
Oration 19	95
Oration 20	107
Oration 22	117
Oration 23	131
Oration 24	142
Oration 25	157
Oration 26	175
Oration 32	191
Oration 35	216
Oration 36	220
Oration 44	230

INDICES

General Index	241
Index of Holy Scripture	244

ABBREVIATIONS

DOP   Dumbarton Oaks Papers. Cambridge, Mass.: Harvard University Press.
KJV   Bible: King James Version.
LSJ   *Greek-English Lexicon. With a Revised Supplement.* 9th ed. Ed. H. G. Liddell - R. Scott - H. S. Jones, et al. Oxford: The Clarendon Press, 1996.
LXX   Septuagint.
PG   Patrologiae Cursus Completus: Series Graeca. Ed. J.-P. Migne. Paris, 1857–86. 161 vols.
PGL   *A Patristic Greek Lexicon.* Ed. G. W. H. Lampe. Oxford: The Clarendon Press, 1961.
RSV   Bible: Revised Standard Version.
SC   Sources Chrétiennes. Paris: Cerf, 1941– .

SELECT BIBLIOGRAPHY

Critical Editions

Calvet-Sébasti, M.-A. *Grégoire de Nazianze. Discours 6–12.* SC 405. Paris: Cerf, 1995.
Moreschini, C., ed. and P. Gallay, trans. *Grégoire de Nazianze. Discours 32–37.* SC 318. Paris: Cerf, 1985.
Mossay, J. with Guy Lafontaine. *Grégoire de Nazianze. Discours 20–23.* SC 270. Paris: Cerf, 1980.
Mossay, J. with Guy Lafontaine. *Grégoire de Nazianze. Discours 24–26.* SC 284. Paris: Cerf, 1981.

Translations

Collier, J. A. *Panegyrick upon the Maccabees by St. Gregory Nazianzen.* London: G. Strahan, 1716.
Haeuser, P., trans. and M. Kertsch, ed. *Gregor von Nazianz, Reden: Über die Liebe zu den Armen.* Munich: Kösel, 1983.
The Liturgy of the Hours. Vol. 2. New York: Catholic Book Publishing Company, 1976.
Phan, P. C. *Social Thought.* Wilmington, Del.: Michael Glazier, 1984.
Toal, M. F., trans. and ed. *The Sunday Sermons of the Great Fathers.* Vol. 4, *From the Eleventh Sunday after Pentecost to the Twenty-fourth and Last Sunday after Pentecost.* Chicago: Henry Regnery, 1963. Reprint, Swedesboro, N.J.: Preservation Press, 1996.

Secondary Literature

Bernardi, J. *La prédication des pères cappadociens. Le prédicateur et son auditoire.* Paris: Presses Universitaires de France, 1968.
Calvet-Sébasti. M.-A. "L'évocation de l'affaire de Sasimes par Gregoire de Nazianze." In *L'historiographie de l'église des premiers siècles*, ed. B. Pouderon and Y. M. Duval. Paris: Beauchesne, 2001: 481–97.
Constantelos, D. J. *Byzantine Philanthropy and Social Welfare.* New Brunswick: Rutgers University Press, 1968.

Coulie, B. *Les richesses dans l'oeuvre de Saint Grégoire de Nazianze. Étude littéraire et historique.* Louvain-la-Neuve: Catholic University of Louvain, 1985.
Delehaye, H. "Cyprien d'Antioche et Cyprien de Carthage." *Analecta Bollandiana* 39 (1921): 314–32.
Frangeskou, V. "The Indirect Tradition of Gregory Nazianzen's Texts in the Acts of the Ecumenical Councils." *Le Muséon* 112 (1999): 381–416.
Gallay, P. *La vie de Saint Grégoire de Nazianze.* Paris: Emmanuel Vitte, 1943.
Hauser-Meury, M.-M. *Prosopographie zu den Schriften Gregors von Nazianz.* Bonn: Peter Hanstein, 1960.
Holman, S. R. *The Hungry are Dying. Beggars and Bishops in Roman Cappadocia.* Oxford: Oxford University Press, 2001.
Kertsch, M. *Bildersprache bei Gregor von Nazianz. Ein Beitrag zur spätantiken Rhetorik und Popularphilosophie.* Grazer Theologischen Studien 2. Graz: RM Druck- und Verlagsgesellschaft, 1980.
Macé, C. and C. Sanspeur. "Nouvelles perspectives pour l'histoire du texte des Discours de Grégoire de Nazianze. Le cas du Discours 6 en grec et en arménien." *Le Muséon* 113 (2000): 377–416
McGuckin, J. *Saint Gregory of Nazianzus. An Intellectual Biography.* Crestwood, New York: St. Vladimir's Seminary Press, 2001.
Moreschini, C. *Filosofia e letteratura in Gregorio di Nazianzo.* Milan: Vita e Pensiero, 1997.
Mossay, J. "Le *Discours 10* de Grégoire de Nazianze. Notes et Controverses." *Byzantion* 70 (2000): 447–55.
———. "Note sur Héron-Maxime, écrivain ecclésiastique." *Analecta Bollandiana* 100 (1982): 229–36.
———. "Gregor von Nazianz in Konstantinople (379–381)." *Byzantion* 47 (1977): 223–38.
Norris, F. W., intro. and comm. Trans. L. Wickham and F. Williams. *Faith Gives Fullness to Reasoning: The Five Theological Orations of Gregory of Nazianzen.* Leiden: E. J. Brill, 1991.
Ruether, R. R. *Gregory of Nazianzus. Rhetor and Philosopher.* Oxford: Clarendon, 1969.
Russell, D. A. and N. G. Wilson. *Menander Rhetor.* Oxford: Clarendon, 1981.
Sharf, A. "The Eighth Day of the Week." In *Kathegetria. Essays Presented to Joan Hussey for her 80th Birthday,* ed. J. Chrysostomides, 27–50. Camberley, Surrey: Porphyrogenitus, 1988.
Sinko, T. "De Gregorii Nazianzeni laudibus Macchabaeorum." *Eos* 13 (1907): 1–29.

SELECT BIBLIOGRAPHY

Snee, R. "Gregory Nazianzen's Anastasia Church: Arianism, the Goths, and Hagiography." *DOP* 52 (1998): 158–64.

Somers, V. *Histoire des collections complètes des Discours de Grégoire de Nazianze*. Publications de l'Institut Orientaliste de Louvain 48. Leuven: Peeters, 1997.

Trisoglio, F. "San Gregorio Nazianzeno 1966–1993." *Lustrum* 38 (1996): 7–361.

———. "Reminiscenze e consonanze classiche nell XIV orazione di San Gregorio Nazianzeno." *Atti della Academia delle Scienze di Torino* 99 (1964–65): 129–204.

Van Dam, R. *Families and Friends in Late Roman Cappadocia*. Philadelphia: University of Pennsylvania Press, 2003.

———. "Emperor, Bishops, and Friends in Late Antique Cappadocia." *Journal of Theological Studies*, n.s., 37 (1986): 53–76.

Vinson, M. P. "Rhetoric and Writing Strategies in the Ninth Century." In *Writing Byzantium*, ed. E. Jeffreys. Aldershot: Ashgate, 2003.

———. "Gregory Nazianzen's Homily 15 and the Genesis of the Christian Cult of the Maccabean Martyrs." *Byzantion* 64 (1994): 166–92.

———. "Gregory Nazianzen's Homily 36: A Socratic Response to Christian Persecution." *Classica et Mediaevalia* 44 (1993): 255–66.

Winslow, D. F. "The Maccabean Martyrs: Early Christian Attitudes." *Judaism* 23 (1974): 78–86.

INTRODUCTION

The sermons translated here represent those omitted from the *Select Library of Nicene and Post-Nicene Fathers of the Christian Church*.[1] Since *Orations* 4 and 5, *Against Julian*, are easily accessible in the translation of C. W. King,[2] they have not been included in the present volume. Of the remaining nineteen sermons, although a few, notably *Orations* 14 and 15, *On Love for the Poor* and *In Praise of the Maccabees* respectively,[3] have been previously translated, most are appearing here in English for the first time. These sermons span all the phases of Gregory's ecclesiastical career, beginning with his service as a parish priest assisting his father, the elder Gregory, in his hometown of Nazianzus in the early 360's, to his stormy tenure as bishop of Constantinople from 379–81, to his subsequent return to Nazianzus and role as interim caretaker of his home church (382–83). The subject matter is similarly diverse and ranges from the purely theological to the deeply personal, but throughout Gregory stands revealed as an individual deeply engaged in the pursuit of social and political justice, whether this pursuit is conducted in an overt or covert manner. Finally, Gregory expresses himself in a variety of rhetorical formats such as the *lalia* and encomium.

In comparison to most of his contemporaries, Gregory led a

---

1. *Select Orations of Saint Gregory Nazianzen*, trans. C. G. Browne and J. E. Swallow in *A Select Library of Nicene and Post-Nicene Fathers of the Christian Church*, ed. P. Schaff and H. Wace, 2d series, vol. 7 (1894; reprint, Peabody, Mass.: Hendrickson, 1995), pp. 203–434.
2. C. W. King, *The Emperor Julian* (London, 1888), pp. 1–121.
3. M. F. Toal trans. and ed., *The Sunday Sermons of the Great Fathers*, vol. 4 (Chicago and New York: Regnery, 1963; reprint, Swedesboro, N.J.: Preservation Press, 1996), pp. 43–64. There is also a partial translation of *Homily* 14 in Peter C. Phan, *Social Thought* (Wilmington, Del.: Michael Glazier, 1984), pp. 122–26 and in *The Liturgy of the Hours*, vol. 2 (New York: Catholic Book Publishing Co., 1976), pp. 96–97. J. Collier, *A Panegyrick upon the Maccabees by St. Gregory Nazianzen* (London, 1716).

very privileged existence. Born to wealthy, landowning parents around 329, he received the best education money could buy, beginning at home in Nazianzus, then on to Caesarea, the provincial capital of Cappadocia, before proceeding abroad for graduate work in rhetoric in Alexandria and Athens, where he studied with the Christian Prohaeresius. The friendships that Gregory made during his student days with Basil, the future bishop of Caesarea, and Julian, who was to become an important treasury official, were enduring ones. And Gregory's lifelong love of learning and devotion to the authors of classical antiquity such as Homer and Plato stand as a testament to the dedication of the teachers who inspired him.

Indeed, Gregory seems to have been on the verge of becoming a perennial student when he decided to return home in 358–59 and was subsequently ordained a priest against his will by his own father in 361. This tyrannical exercise of paternal prerogative not only ensured that Gregory would stay close to home at least until his parents' deaths in 374, but also freed his younger brother, Caesarius, to pursue a secular career as a physician at the imperial court in Constantinople. Gregory never got over the sense of betrayal or his resentment that the choice between the contemplative and active life had been taken completely out of his hands. These negative feelings only intensified ten years later when his best friend Basil, now bishop of Caesarea, acting in collusion with the elder Gregory, consecrated him bishop of Sasima in 372 in order to further his own ecclesiastical ambitions. Although Gregory never failed in his duty as a pastor or a bishop, he also never forgot the treachery of those closest to him and from time to time withdrew from active participation in worldly affairs to practice philosophy, that is, solitary contemplation.

The sermons from the first phase of Gregory's career (361–79) reveal the influence that these events had on him both personally and professionally. Yet however much Gregory may have longed for monastic life, he nonetheless remained in the world and, despite his protestations of indifference, fully engaged in worldly affairs. Worldly affairs, both then and now, included politics, local as well as national. For Gregory, the central event during this formative period was the reign of Julian the Apostate (361–63), who attempted to restore traditional Greco-Roman religion to its former prominence. *Oration* 15, *On the Maccabees,* given in December 362, although ostensibly a simple Sunday sermon, is actually a powerful political manifesto that responds to Julian's attempt to separate Christianity from its Hellenic and Jewish roots by introducing the cult of the Maccabean martyrs into the Christian calendar.[4] Similarly, *Oration* 14, *On Love for the Poor,* which was prompted by the construction of a hospital complex in Caesarea in 368–72 and describes the plight of lepers in eloquent and moving terms, should also be seen in the context of a rivalry between pagans and Christians over the delivery of social services, as noted for example in Julian's letter to Arsacius, the high priest of Galatia.[5] Also belonging to the period shortly after his ordination is *Oration* 6, which was delivered in Nazianzus most probably in 364 upon the resolution of a conflict between the local monastic community and Gregory's father, who had inadvertently instigated the crisis by signing a document of questionable Orthodoxy while his son was visiting his friend Basil in Pontus.

Gregory's consecration as bishop of Sasima provided the occasion for a cluster of sermons, *Orations* 9, 10, 11, and 13, written in 372.[6] Basil's betrayal of his friend was in turn a response to a new imperial policy implemented by the emperor Valens, who during 371–72 subdivided the province of Cappadocia into two new administrative districts, Cappadocia Prima and Cappacocia Secunda, with the capitals of Caesarea and Tyana respectively. The difficulty arose over whether the new boundaries applied to ecclesiastical administration. Anthimus, who as bishop of Tyana had formerly been Basil's subordinate, thought that the redistricting gave him jurisdiction over the new province and he acted accordingly by, for example, seizing rev-

---

4. See further M. Vinson, "Gregory Nazianzen's Homily 15 and the Genesis of the Christian Cult of the Maccabean Martyrs," *Byzantion* 64 (1994): 166–92.
5. *Ep.* 22 (Wright); 84 (Bidez).
6. See J. Mossay, "Le *Discours 10* de Grégoire de Nazianze. Notes et Controverses," *Byzantion* 70 (2000): 447–55, for a different approach to the date and circumstances of *Oration* 10.

enues that had formerly gone to the bishop of Caesarea. Basil responded by creating the new bishoprics of Sasima and Nyssa in Cappadocia Secunda and placing his best friend and brother, both named Gregory, in the new posts. Gregory never took up the position, but the appointment would come back to haunt him in later years. Instead, Gregory remained in Nazianzus, where he took an increasingly active role in church administration. *Oration* 17, *To the Frightened Citizens of Nazianzus and the Irate Prefect*, is the last sermon to refer to Gregory's father as being present in the audience and has traditionally been assigned to late 373 or early 374. Shortly thereafter, *Oration* 19, *On his Sermons and to the Tax Adjuster Julian*, along with his *Letters* 67–69, reveal Gregory's active involvement in local politics on behalf of his congregation. Following the death of his parents in 374, Gregory withdrew to the monastery of St. Thecla in Seleucia for a period of several years.

In 379, Gregory accepted an invitation to lead the Orthodox community at the church of the Anastasia in Constantinople,[7] which at the time was largely Arian and still reeling from the Gothic invasions that resulted in the death of the Emperor Valens at Adrianople on August 9, 378. Most of the remaining sermons in this volume were delivered here prior to his consecration as bishop of Constantinople on November 27, 380. *Oration* 20, *On Theology and the Office of Bishops*, is grouped with the five *Theological Orations* (27–31), delivered in the Anastasia church during the summer or fall of 380.[8] The chronological sequence of *Orations* 22 and 23, as well as their relationship to *Oration* 6, the *First Oration on Peace*, is in dispute. The most recent editor, J. Mossay,[9] follows the manuscript tradition in identifying *Oration* 22 as the *Third Homily on Peace* and *Oration* 23 as the *Second Homily on Peace;* this order is inverted in the Maurist edition published in the *Patrologia Graeca*. *Oration* 24, *In Praise of*

---

7. See R. Snee, "Gregory Nazianzen's Anastasia Church: Arianism, the Goths, and Hagiography," *DOP* 52 (1998): 158–64.

8. F. W. Norris, *Faith Gives Fullness to Reasoning. The Five Theological Orations of Gregory Nazianzen*, introduction and commentary by F. W. Norris with a translation by Lionel Wickham and Frederick Williams (Leiden: Brill, 1991).

9. J. Mossay, *Grégoire de Nazianze. Discours 20–23*, SC 270 (1980).

Cyprian, delivered in October 379, conflates two Cyprians, one the bishop of Carthage who was martyred in 258 under Valerian, and the other, Cyprian of Antioch in Pisidia who was martyred in 304 under Diocletian. In its erotic content and the disproportionate length of its narrative portion, this sermon displays an affinity with Hellenistic novels.

Oration 25, *In Praise of Hero the Philosopher*, and Oration 26, *On Himself upon Returning from the Country after the Maximus Affair*, both from 380, concern another unpleasant chapter in Gregory's life, this one involving Maximus, a Cynic convert to Christianity, who ingratiated himself with Gregory and then betrayed his trust by attempting to have himself consecrated bishop of Constantinople in Gregory's own church. These sermons are particularly interesting for the light they shed on the personal, cultural, and international dimensions of the internecine conflict within the Orthodox community in the capital. Oration 32, *On Discipline in Theological Discourse*, delivered in 379, is noteworthy for its references to the ancient philosophical tradition. Oration 36, *On Himself and to Those Who Claim That It Was He Who Wanted the See of Constantinople*, was written in 380 and provides a response to those who opposed Gregory's consecration as bishop of Constantinople by using literary allusions to Plato's early dialogues to portray himself as a victim of unjust persecution in the manner of Socrates.[10] Oration 44, *On New Sunday*, dated 382–83, belongs to the last phase of Gregory's career after he returned to Nazianzus. The unfinished and spurious *Oration 35, On the Holy Martyrs and Against the Arians* is included here for the sake of completeness.

Despite, or rather because of his extensive rhetorical training, Gregory's sermons remain accessible to a diverse audience that included his peers among the intellectual elite as well as those who have traditionally been denied the benefits of higher education, such as women and the economically disadvantaged, to whom frequent reference is made throughout the corpus by means of apostrophe. Gregory employs various strategies in or-

---

10. M. Vinson, "Gregory Nazianzen's Homily 36: A Socratic Response to Christian Persecution," *Classica et Mediaevalia* 44 (1993): 255–66.

der to communicate effectively and persuasively with a diverse audience.[11] Among them is the choice of rhetorical form. One of the most frequently used formats in the Gregorian corpus is the *lalia* or talk, a particularly flexible and informal type of discourse, which receives extensive treatment in the late antique treatise on epideictic oratory by Menander Rhetor.[12] Menander finds the genre "extremely useful to the sophist" and suggests that it falls under two kinds of rhetoric, the deliberative and the epideictic:

If we wish to praise a ruler, it yields abundant store of encomia: we can indicate his justice, wisdom, and other virtues in the form of a talk. We can also easily give advice in this form to the whole city and all our audience and (if we wish) to a governor who attends the delivery of the speech. Nor is there anything to prevent one revealing to the audience in a "talk" some anger or pain or pleasure of one's own. It is possible also to give the whole thought a special slant by making a jest of it or trying to satirize (?) someone's character or finding fault with his way of life, or something like that.[13]

Menander goes on to suggest "the insertion of examples making the speaker's intentions clear, and by the choice of stories which are very agreeable to the audience to learn, e.g., stories about the gods, showing how their nature is to take thought for mankind."[14] One should urge the audience "to bring themselves together in mutual goodwill.... You should often ridicule or find fault, but without mentioning names, sketching the personality, if you so wish, and criticizing the character."[15] Further, "a 'talk' does not aim to preserve a regular order as other speeches do, but allows the treatment to be disorderly."[16] Plutarch's *Lives* are recommended because "they are full of stories, apophthegms, and proverbs."[17] The style "should be simple, plain, and unadorned."[18]

---

11. See further M. Vinson, "Rhetoric and Writing Strategies in the Ninth Century," in *Writing Byzantium,* ed. E. Jeffreys (Aldershot: Ashgate, 2003).
12. D. A. Russell and N. G. Wilson, *Menander Rhetor,* (Oxford: Clarendon, 1981), pp. 115–26.
13. Ibid., p. 115.
14. Ibid. p. 117.
15. Ibid., p. 119.
16. Ibid., p. 121.
17. Ibid., p. 123.
18. Ibid., p. 125.

INTRODUCTION

Oration 14 provides a good example of how these directions could be closely followed but at the same time adjusted to meet Christian needs. The heroes of old and the episodes illustrating their achievements are now biblical. Instead of the Platonic cardinal virtues that pagan epideictic regularly invoked to catalogue and celebrate moral excellence we have now in sections 1–8 a catalogue of Christian ideals. The goodwill that shaped the sentiment of the pagan paragons now becomes Christian philanthropy. Instead of general truths drawn from secular folk wisdom (though Gregory uses such elsewhere) we are given quotations from the Psalms and Proverbs. The pampered rich and all those insensitive to the sufferings of their fellow citizens are attacked more than once, but as a class, without naming names. Nor does the sermon show the tight structure of an ancient oration. The disorder that Menander prescribes is evident in the ease with which Gregory passes from one theme to another, carried along, as it were, by the free association of his thoughts as he moves through tragic scene, social appeal, personal meditation, and theological judgment, all culminating in the drum roll of ethical demand in the form of accumulated biblical citations at the end of the sermon (section 36 *ad fin.*). Finally, the directness of the language, the often literal descriptions, the general absence of metaphor, the use of repetition to enforce inescapable message, the fictitious interlocutor (sections 29, 36), the rapid fire questions (sections 7, 11, 13, 15, 18, 19, 21, 23), all reflect the kind of style Menander recommends.

Behind such types of address as the *lalia* lies an older phenomenon, the Hellenistic diatribe. Its origins are a matter of dispute, but it seems clear that it has at least partial connections with the Platonic dialogue both in method and content, and that it describes in part a technique of the Hellenistic philosophical schools. The debate of the Hellenistic classroom, acute and more doctrinal than its classical source, becomes now theological instruction and exhortation within the new classroom, the Christian church. Indeed, a residue of philosophical interest may be seen in the discussion (sections 32–33) of the pagan view of providence. The mode, however, had also another setting. Developed, to a degree independently, by itinerant Cynic preachers it eventually yielded the sharper harangue that we know as the Cynic-Stoic diatribe, a genre that came to influence the New Testament as well in important ways. In this more public environment emotion acquires a special importance and a more compelling prominence as the speaker presses not only for persuasion but for allegiance. As a result, psychological stratagems acquire a special importance. Accordingly, they are particularly in evidence in the second part of the homily, in rhetorical parlance, the *narratio* (διήγησις), the portion according to Aristotle (*Rhetoric* 1417a16–19) where moral purpose is revealed. Aristotle also points out that in epideictic, narration is not continuous but intermittent (1416b16–18) and should make use of the traits of emotion (1416a35). Gregory's method is in keeping with these observations. Since he is dealing not with a story but with the unremitting distress of the lepers his design is to elaborate a poignant recital of the victims' singular misery, which he illuminates again and again by a series of scenes strongly pictorial in their impact. This tableau of related images, which draws its power from the interaction of literary and visual device so characteristic of his style in general, helps to burn his message more deeply and forcefully upon our sensibilities.

Such multiple reference is an expression of one of the most fundamental habits of all rhetorical discourse, and especially of epideictic, the technique of enlargement of a theme (*amplificatio*, αὔξησις).[19] In a Christian sermon, where the object is the adoption of a course of action and the rejection of its opposite, it is an especially potent force. In our case the steady prick and relentless intimacy of detail, made even more stark through keenly delineated contrasts and the resulting immediacy of tone, are part of its method and effect. The interplay of persuasion and dissuasion is in point of fact a main structural frame of the text, as benefaction toward the unfortunate is placed in opposition to indifference, commitment to withdrawal, orthodoxy to heresy, which is itself a denial. One notes as well the frequent

---

19. Aristotle, *Rhetoric* 1417b31.

use of satire (sections 23–25, 29, 33), a mode that works by setting moral value against human failing. This strong sense of contrast may, however, have roots deeper within the Gregorian psyche itself. It is possible to see here an analogue with the "geometry" of Gregory's own career of retreat and return and may also be reflected in the ease with which he passes between social and personal concerns (sections 6, 8, 19–21, 30–33), both aspects for him of a common reality. Nor can one ignore his poetic gift. He is the only one among the Greek church fathers to have left us so large a legacy of poetry. Besides being an outlet *per se* of his individuality that differs from the more public forum of his orations, his verses are extensively given over to autobiography,[20] but an autobiography regularly interlarded with social and theological commentary, and as such reflecting the ingredients of our own sermon. For the literary historian he can stand as forerunner to the even fuller self-revelation of an Augustine in the next generation.

Amplification works best within a pattern of quickening tempo and rising intensity. The procedure appears already in the prologue. Once the orator establishes a rapport with his audience by calling them his friends, he gives his words the widest possible sanction by drawing from a biblical base. Prologues are usually short. In our case, the prologue extends through several sections (1–8), in which the long list of Christian virtues culminates and combines into the love for the poor. Accumulation is made to work hand in hand with scriptural support in a rising tide. Further, the scriptural citations in this early portion describe for the most part events from the Judaic or Christian past and serve to confirm moral prescription with historical rationale. Then, as we move towards the peroration, the biblical passages, now in greater and greater profusion, derive more from Psalms, Proverbs, and the prophetic books (sections 36–38). They sing now a timeless and generalizing crescendo to the theme, issuing finally in a roster of New Testament figures, who are cited as mirroring, however imperfectly, the union of faith and good works, a call that echoes throughout the homily as a

---

20. Cf. *Poema De Vita Sua*, PG 37.1029A–1166B, et al.

whole. In short, amplification, in an apt alliance of style and substance, acts as the linguistic expression of God's own plenitude.

Oration 14 stands as one of Gregory's most distinctive and successful productions. It illustrates in extensive detail both the breadth and depth of Gregory's intellectual interests as well as his commitment to social justice. Gregory's skill in translating the diverse store of knowledge that formed the intellectual and spiritual basis of his faith into a comprehensive course of action involving the entire community helps us to understand the attraction he held as a friend, ally, and leader. Yet at the same time, his uncompromising vision of how the world should be and his unremitting efforts to make that vision a reality also explain the disappointment and failure that he experienced over the long course of his career. Within the context of late antiquity, these difficulties shed light on the tension between active involvement in public life and withdrawal from it that affected Gregory and others like him. This tension, however, was by no means an exclusive phenomenon of the late antique period. In fifth century Athens, for example, the title character of Euripides' play, *Ion*, lines 596–601, articulates very clearly the quandary that decent and intelligent people of every age encounter:

But if I push myself forward to the front rank of the state and try to be somebody I shall be hated by the incompetent crowd, for superiority is always odious. Then there are those honest and able men who in their wisdom keep quiet and do not rush into the limelight—with them I should get the reputation of being a silly fool, because I would not hold my peace in a city full of disquiet.[21]

It is hoped that the present volume will contribute to an appreciation of the complexity of the circumstances in which Gregory produced these sermons and a vindication, if any is needed, of the choices that he made.

This volume has been many years in the making. It began as a collaborative venture with George L. Kustas, now professor emeritus of Classics at the State University of New York at Buffa-

---

21. *Ten Plays by Euripides,* trans. M. Hadas and J. McClean (Toronto: Bantam Books, 1981), p. 147.

lo, who initiated the project and oversaw its early stages. Dr. Kustas withdrew from the project in 1993 after coordinating the revision of the translation and contributing the notes and introductory material for several homilies, notably *Orations* 14, 24, and 25. The preparation of the volume for publication, including the final revision of the translation and the completion of the annotation and introduction, has fallen to me. We are most grateful to our editor, Dr. Michael Slusser, for his thoughtful and learned reading of our manuscript. In addition, the University of Louisville and Debbie Purcell provided clerical assistance for which I remain grateful.

The base text used for the translation is that of Migne, *Patrologia Graeca*. Where available, the *Sources chrétiennes* series has been consulted and significant differences between PG and SC are indicated in the notes.

For biblical citations of the Old and New Testaments, we have used the Revised Standard Version and for the Aprocrypha, *The Apocrypha of the Old Testament. Revised Standard Version. Expanded Edition Containing the Third and Fourth Books of the Maccabees and Psalm 151*, ed. Bruce M. Metzger (New York: Oxford University Press, 1965, 1977). Where the RSV does not accurately reflect Gregory's text, we have also used the King James Version of the Bible and for the Old Testament, *The Septuagint Version of the Bible*, translated by Sir Lancelot Lee Brenton (1844; reprint, Peabody, Mass.: Hendrickson, 1986). These departures from the RSV are indicated in the notes by KJV and LXX, respectively.

SELECT ORATIONS

ORATION 6

First Oration on Peace. On the occasion of the reconciliation of the monks after his silence, delivered in the presence of his father.[1]

N ARDENT SENSE of purpose unfetters my tongue, and because of the law of the Spirit I turn my back on the law of men, and to peace I offer my words, which up to now I have granted to no one.[2] Some time ago, when its members were in revolt against us and the great and venerable body of Christ was being split and torn apart so that our bones were nearly strewn *at the mouth of Sheol*[3] like a thick clod of earth broken by the plow and strewn over the land, and the Evil One had ripped to shreds the *coat*, indivisible and *woven throughout*,[4] and appropriated it for himself, achieving through us what he had not the power to do through those who crucified Christ—it was then that I set a bridle on my lips,[5] which were not in any case inclined to speak, because I thought that the priorities of the Spirit were first to purify myself through the philosophy that resides in action; next, to open the mouth of my mind and draw in the Spirit; then to utter *a goodly theme*,[6] and to speak God's perfect *wisdom among them that are perfect*.[7] And just as *for every*

---

1. PG 35.721A–52A. Delivered in Nazianzus ca. 364.
2. This sermon is the first of three (*Or.* 6, 22, 23) that the later tradition entitled *Orations on Peace*. It was delivered in Nazianzus most probably in 364 upon the resolution of a conflict between the local monastic community and their bishop, the father of our author. The breach occurred when Gregory the Elder signed a document of questionable orthodoxy while his son was visiting his friend Basil in Pontus; the monks responded by dissociating themselves from their bishop and resorting to the ordination of priests not by him but by others. See also *Or.* 9 and 11.
3. Ps 141.7 (LXX 140.7).
4. Jn 19.23 KJV.
5. Ps 39.1 (LXX 38.2).
6. Ps 45.1 (LXX 44.2).
7. 1 Cor 2.6–7 KJV.

matter both great and small *there is a season*—Solomon's adage is profoundly true—so I came to realize that, just as for anything else, *there is a time to speak and a time to keep silence.*[8]

2. This is why *I was dumb, and humbled myself,* retiring far away from every comfort, and a cloud, as it were, had stolen over my heart and cast its shadow over the bright ray of my words, and night and day *my grief was renewed.*[9] And everything served to fuel the memory of the division among my brothers: vigils; fasts; prayers; tears; calloused knees; beatings of the breast; groans welling from the heart; standing the night long in devotion; the mind's transport to God; soft sobs in prayer that move those who hear them to compunction by their spell; singers of psalms; singers of doxologies; those who meditate on the law *of the Lord day and night;*[10] those who bear *the high praises of God in their throats;*[11] as well as these beautiful tokens and prefigurements of the life in God: silent heralds; hair dirty and unwashed; feet bare in imitation of the Apostles;[12] a body dead to sin;[13] hair properly cropped; dress that chastens vanity; a belt, elegant in its inelegance, that girds up a tunic only slightly and almost not at all; a serene gait; a tempered gaze; a gentle smile, or rather the hint of a smile inhibiting petulant laughter; thoughtful discourse; silence more precious than words; praise *seasoned with salt*[14] and designed not for flattery but as a guide to betterment; criticism more coveted than compliment; cheer and melancholy in moderation and their harmonious blend; kindliness coupled with fervor and severity with compassion, not so as to be mutually destructive but so that one enhances the other; a middle ground between involvement in society and withdrawal from it, the one educating others to the world, the other to the mysteries of the Spirit, the one preserving solitude in the midst of community, the other fraternity and fellowship amid the solitary life; and, still nobler and more uplifting than these, riches in poverty; firm tenure in transience; glory in abasement; power

---

8. Eccl 3.1, 7.
9. Ps 39.2 (LXX 38.3) LXX.
10. Ps 1.2.
11. Ps 149.6.
12. Mt 10.10.
13. The literal meaning is "bearing nothing dead." Cf. Rom 8.10.
14. Col 4.6.

in frailty, fecundity in celibacy (for things that are born of God are superior to the issue of the flesh); those who feast on abstinence; those who lower themselves for the sake of the blessings on high; those who are nothing in the world and so transcend it; those who abandon the flesh while in it, whose portion is the Lord;[15] those poor for the sake of the kingdom, who for their poverty are kings.

3. These are the people, my substance, my noble delight, who both when present made me radiant and when absent cast me down. These are the things that distressed, these that troubled my soul; these that caused me to walk *bowed down and in mourning;*[16] these the reason why I rejected speech along with everything else that gave me pleasure; because my beloved *kicked*[17] and *turned their back to me, and not their face,*[18] and became a flock with greater liberty, not to say license, than their shepherd; because the true vine turned bitter for me, though it had been so beautifully pruned by its noble gardener to produce a noble vintage for the wine presses of God; because *my friends and my neighbors drew near before me and stood still; and my nearest of kin stood afar off;*[19] because we tore apart Christ, we who love God and Christ so well, and deceived one another in the name of truth, and in the name of love fostered hatred and for the sake of *the cornerstone*[20] were crushed, and *of the rock*[21] rent asunder; because in the name of peace we warred more than honor allowed, and in the name of him who was raised on the cross we were brought low, and in the name of him who was buried and resurrected we embraced death.

4. Such was our former state. But why would anyone on a joyous occasion rake over past unpleasantness and dwell on painful events horrible to experience and repellent to recall? Silence is mightier than words. It clothes the wreckage that befalls us in the deep folds of forgetfulness unless someone stirs up the painful memories for the sole purpose of edifying us by example and, as with illnesses, of helping us avoid the causes that led

---

15. Ps 16.5 (LXX 15.5).
17. Dt 32.15.
19. Ps 38.11 (LXX 37.12) LXX.
21. 1 Cor 10.4; Lk 6.48.

16. Ps 35.14 (LXX 34.14).
18. Jer 2.27.
20. Eph 2.20.

us to them. But now that *sorrow and pain and groaning have fled away,*[22] when we of the One have become one; we of the Trinity like in nature and same in heart and in honor; we of the Logos above unreason; we of the Spirit *aglow*[23] with, not against, one another; we of the Truth[24] *of the same mind*[25] and voice; we of the Wisdom[26] conscientious and wise; we of the Light[27] *honest as in the day;*[28] we of the Way[29] all straight in our course; we of the Door[30] all inside; we of the Lamb[31] and the Shepherd[32] gentle and share the same fold and a single shepherd, not one who uses the implements of *a worthless shepherd*[33] in his shepherding or ravages the sheep in his flock or abandons them to the wolves and the precipices, but one most solicitous and able; when we of him who suffered the Passion for our sake have become compassionate and lighten one another's *burdens;*[34] we of the Head joined as one body and knit together, unified completely in the Spirit;[35] when he *who makes all things and changes them*[36] to our greater advantage has turned our mourning into joy and replaced our *sackcloth with gladness.*[37] now finally the time has come for me to part with my silence and along with it the events of the past and offer my words to the present occasion and to you, or rather, to God, as a most fitting sacrifice, a gift purer than gold, more valuable than precious stones, more precious than woven robes, more holy than the sacrifice of the Law, more sacred than the offering of the first-born, *more* pleasing to God *than a* young *bull,*[38] its horns, hooves, and senses undeveloped, than incense, than burnt offering, than countless fat lambs with which the rude Law controlled the still infant Israel, prefiguring by its blood sacrifices the sacrifice to come.

5. This is what I offer to God; this do I dedicate, my sole re-

22. Is 35.10 LXX.
23. Rom 12.11.
24. Jn 14.6.
25. Phil 2.2; Rom 12.16, 15.5; 2 Cor 13.11.
26. 1 Cor 1.30.
27. Jn 8.12; 9.5.
28. Rom 13.13 KJV.
29. Jn 14.6.
30. Jn 10.7, 9.
31. Jn 1.29.
32. Jn 10.11.
33. Zec 11.15.
34. Gal 6.2.
35. Col 2.19.
36. Am 5.8 LXX.
37. Ps 30.11 (LXX 29.12).
38. Ps 69.31 (LXX 68.32).

maining possession, my sole wealth.[39] The rest I have made over to the commandment and the Spirit, and in exchange for all I once had I have taken the *pearl of great value*[40] and become a rich merchant, or rather, hope to be such, trading things small and altogether corruptible for the great and everlasting; and as devotee of the word I cling to the Word alone and would never willingly neglect this possession, but on the contrary honor it and embrace it and take more pleasure in it than in all other things combined that delight the multitude; and I make it the partner of my whole life and my good counselor and companion, and my guide on the road to heaven and my eager confederate; and because I reject all gratification here below, this is what, after God, or rather, in addition to him, receives all my outpoured affection; for it is the Logos, he alone, who through our mind makes God accessible to us and through whom God is apprehended in his truth and is cherished and grows within us. I have said that *wisdom* was *my sister;*[41] and I have honored and embraced her to the extent of my ability; and for my head I seek a *crown of graces*[42] and delight, the gifts of wisdom and of the Logos who illumines the faculty of reason within us and lights our steps on the path of God.

6. With this I curb incontinent anger; with this I quiet corrosive envy; with this again I quell grief that shackles the heart; with this I restrain effusive pleasure; with this I moderate hatred, but not love: the one we should moderate, the other, know no limit. It is this that makes me unassuming when I prosper and generous when poor; this that impels me to keep pace with the swift of foot and to extend my hand to the fallen; to share the afflictions of the weak[43] and the ebullience of the strong. With this as my companion, home and abroad are the same to me, and likewise, changes of location affect others, not me. It is this that sets apart two worlds for me, drawing me away from the one and uniting me to the other; this that both leads me forth *with the weapons of righteousness for* my *right hand,* yet I do not exalt myself, and when life is too harsh and sinister[44] it encourages

39. I.e., his sermon.
40. Mt 13.45–46.
41. Prv 7.4.
42. Prv 1.9 LXX.
43. 1 Cor 9.22.
44. 2 Cor 6.7.

and consoles me by joining me to the hope that does not disappoint[45] and by lightening the present with the future. It is with this that I welcome on this special occasion my friends and brothers and set before them a *table* of the Logos and an everflowing bowl of the Spirit,[46] not the dainties of an earthly table that pander to the belly, which is doomed to destruction[47] and impervious to cure.

7. *I have been silent; shall I also always be silent? I have endured like a travailing woman.*[48] Shall I endure forever? John's birth puts an end to Zacharias's silence;[49] indeed, the father of the Voice, once it had issued forth, could not rightly remain silent, but just as it had tied his tongue in disbelief, so, when it came forth, it could properly set free the father to whom the glad tidings had been given and be born the Voice and the Lamp, forerunner of the Logos[50] and the Light.[51] As for me, it is the present boon that frees my tongue and lifts my voice like a trumpet, as well as this most beautiful spectacle, *the children of God who are scattered abroad* gathered *into one*[52] and *settling under the same wings*[53] and walking to *God's* house *in fellowship*[54] and attuned in a single harmony, that of the Spirit and the good; when we no longer have at one another, we who were so much the victims of the Devil's lies and abuse, and whose reason, clouded by a darkness that he himself produced, was the target of his deadly barbs, so as—how should I say it?—both to rejoice in one another's misfortunes and to fail to recognize our severance from one another as a detriment to the whole; when Judah and Israel *appoint for themselves one head*[55] and Jerusalem and Samaria are gathered together into one Jerusalem on high, and we no longer belong to Paul or Apollos or Cephas,[56] on whose account and in whom we felt pride, but belong all now to Christ.

8. And now that you have both me and my words and have lovingly imposed your will upon me (though I did not object), I

45. Rom 5.5.
46. Prv 9.2.
47. 1 Cor 6.13.
48. Is 42.14 LXX.
49. Lk 1.20.
50. Jn 1.1.
51. Jn 8.12, 9.5.
52. Jn 11.52.
53. Mt 23.37; Lk 13.34.
54. Ps 55.14 (LXX 54.15).
55. Hos 1.11.
56. 1 Cor 3.4.

shall do as you ask and speak, albeit with difficulty, and the words I shall speak will be ones of thanks and admonition. My thanks then, are of this sort: *Who will utter the mighty doings of the Lord?*[57] Who will declare to all ears the praise that all share? because *both* have become *one* and *the dividing wall of hostility* has been broken down;[58] because you kept us from being *a byword among the nations, a laughingstock among the peoples;*[59] because you afflicted us to such a degree as to have us recognize through our dissension the blessing of peace, and, after you subjected us to suffering, once again restored us—O, the wonder of the healing art! You disciplined us to peace as quickly as possible through our instinctive hatred of hatred, effecting opposite through opposite and driving us so far apart that we raced all the more fervently towards one another, just like those plants that, bent back by the force of our hands and then released, recover and snap back, displaying in the process their original true nature, in that, though bent back by force, they right themselves without force—because the hand no longer scorns the eye, nor *the eye* the hand; because *the head* is no longer at cross purposes with the feet, and *the feet,* no longer at odds with the head,[60] become not the agents of harm but rather the victims of it through that lack of order and regulation that confounds and dissolves the whole; instead, the members have *the same care for one another*[61] in accordance with the order and bond of nature that has bound and preserves all things through one another, and we have come forth *one body and one Spirit, just as* we have been called *to the one hope that belongs to our call.*[62]

9. *Therefore the poor people,* indigent before and become rich, *shall bless thee*[63] because you have wondrously shown *thy steadfast love*[64] towards us and a new chapter has been added to the stories of old. For *where sin increased, grace abounded all the more;*[65] because I sowed a grain and reaped an ear of wheat; because I grieved for my flock and found shepherds for them; and I do not doubt that I shall add to their number the most venerable

57. Ps 106.2 (LXX 105.2).
58. Eph 2.14.
59. Ps 44.14 (LXX 43.14).
60. 1 Cor 12.21.
61. 1 Cor 12.25.
62. Eph 4.4.
63. Is 25.3 LXX.
64. Ps 17.7 (LXX 16.7).
65. Rom 5.20.

of shepherds even if, for spiritual reasons, he postpones the assumption of his pastoral duties.[66] For although he has been entrusted with the Spirit and the investment of the talents[67] and care of his flock, and has received the chrism of his consecration as priest, he still wisely defers the responsibilities of office and keeps his light under a bushel (in a short while he will put it *on a stand*[68] to illumine the whole soul of the Church and be *a light to our path*),[69] surveying for now his valleys and mountains and streams and devising snares for the wolves who ravage souls so that in due time he may also take up his staff and with the true Shepherd shepherd this spiritual flock, making it to dwell *in green pastures* amid the ever-blossoming words of God and nourishing it *beside still waters,*[70] that is, the Spirit. This, then, is what we both hope and pray for. And now is the right time for me to add to my thanksgiving an admonition as well. This too I shall make as short as possible, since most of the lesson you have already drawn from the events themselves: those schooled by experience do not require too many words.

10. My brothers, we should neither have been divided in the first place, nor should we have suffered the devastating loss of our status and distinction of old, thanks to which I regarded our flock, though too small to be included among the congregations of great account, equal to the largest and most important, and I even treasured it above some others in the power of the Spirit. In truth, each congregation was distinguished to a greater or lesser degree; but the special characteristic of our flock was that it was impregnable and free from faction, so much so, in fact, as even to be on many occasions called Noah's ark for being the only one to have ridden out the deluge of the whole world and to keep safe in it the seeds of piety.[71] But since we proved all too human and did not completely succeed in avoiding the Devil's envy, nor manage to overcome the disease

---

66. The identification of this shepherd remains uncertain, but the possibilities include Basil, an unnamed cleric, and even Gregory himself. See the discussion by M.-A. Calvet-Sebasti in SC 405, pp. 16–18 and 142–43, n. 1.
67. Mt 25.15.   68. Mt 5.15.
69. Ps 119.105 (LXX 118.105).   70. Ps 23.2 (LXX 22.2).
71. Gn 7.23; Wis 14.6.

that gripped the whole world, but on the contrary both ourselves caught a part of the common calamity and failed to preserve to the end the fair inheritance of our fathers, the blessing of concord, yet even here we were vouchsafed no small advantage over the rest (if it is at all proper for those who trust in Christ to go so far as to exult over our enmity): we were both the last to be afflicted and the first to recover. To fall ill belongs to our common nature and our human frailty, which affects us all, even the very vigorous of body and of mind; but to be cured so as once again to espouse one another belongs to reason and grace, which justly and fairly has given us the victory even in excess of our prayers and the expectations of others.

11. For we on our part graciously welcomed the leaders who had been assigned to the separated portion on the grounds that their novel secession was prompted by piety with the object of helping the struggle of orthodox doctrine, and we did not reject them as enemies but embraced them as brothers who for a short time had contested our paternal inheritance, though in a brotherly, not a malicious way. Though we did not welcome their opposition, we respected their zeal. Disagreement motivated by piety is superior to concord held together by sentiment. That is why we converted their withdrawal to our increment, dispelling their suspicions by an act of charity and reversing the usual order to such a degree that instead of grace following their election, election followed grace, and we accepted to this end the consecration by alien hands, anticipated to a degree by the Spirit. You for your part laid aside your misgivings based on the letter and sought reassurance in the spirit,[72] and, although disappointed with our naive interpretation of the text, you did not attribute it to impiety, because you knew that our view of the Trinity is as stable and unchanging as its very nature, and that for us circumscribing or dissociating any one of its members is tantamount to destroying the whole and to making a barefaced assault on all of Divinity. Moreover, the fact that despite our differences we defend one another on various occasions and before various persons most assuredly provides the

---

72. Cf. Rom 2.29; 2 Cor 3.6.

greatest confirmation that neither does truth succumb to the pressures of the moment nor does enmity utterly extinguish the spark of love that is within us; so that, even in our quarrels we were sustained by that greatest of all blessings, our unanimity in matters of doctrine, as well as by the awareness that, where the truth was concerned, we were neither mismated[73] or opposed to one another, but molded by the same impress of faith and our primal hope.[74]

12. Indeed, for those whose faith in God is pure there is no greater stimulus to unanimity than using the same words when we speak of him; nor is anything more conducive to division than disagreement on this score. A person who is extremely tolerant in all other respects becomes quite heated when it comes to this matter, and *the timid* becomes *a* true *warrior*[75] when he sees that his forbearance is causing him to lose God, or rather, that his transgression is a loss to God, who enriches and is enriched by us. Hence, as I have said, even our discord so tended toward moderation that our very unity was more noteworthy than our dissension, and right conduct on both sides has almost overshadowed what intervened. But since the swift restoration of peace does not guarantee its stability unless also a sermon come forth to uphold it, and God, from whom all blessings both originate and reach fruition, appear as its ally, come now, let us secure it both with our prayers and with our thoughts as best we can, reflecting first of all that God is the fairest and most exalted of the things that exist, unless one prefers to think of him as even transcending all being or to place the sum total of existence in him, from whom also it flows to everything else; and second, that of all those beings that derive first from God and make up his court, I mean the angelic and heavenly hosts that, drawing first from the first light and illumined by the word of truth, are light and themselves effulgences of perfect light, nothing is so characteristic as the absence of conflict and faction. For not only is there no discord in Godhead and, as a re-

---

73. 2 Cor 6.14.
74. The reference is to baptism; cf. 1 Pt 1.3, 21, 3.21.
75. Jl 3.11 LXX.

ORATION 6

sult, no dissolution, since dissolution is the child of discord, but so great is the element of harmony both internally and in relation to the secondary beings that this is the very virtue that joins, indeed, takes precedence over, the other forms of address that find favor with God. For he is called *peace*[76] and *love*[77] and the like, and through these designations inspires us to adopt the virtues they represent because they are his own.

13. The one angel who dared revolt and rise above his station, hardening his neck against the Lord almighty[78] and, as the prophet says, intent upon the throne beyond the clouds,[79] received the punishment he deserved for his mad deeds, condemned to be darkness instead of light or, more accurately, become so by his own hand; but the rest remain in their station, of which the prime mark is peacefulness and freedom from faction, and draw their unity, as indeed their radiance, from the honored and holy Trinity. For this too both is, and is believed in faith to be, one God, as much for its inner harmony as for its identity of substance; so that all those who openly embrace the blessing of peace and loathe and despise its contrary, strife, are close to God and things divine, while in the opposite group are all those who are bellicose in character and pursue popularity through innovation and make a display of their own shamelessness; for the Devil too, thanks to his fickle and vicious passions, is both in revolt against himself and as *a murderer* and hater of the good *from the beginning*[80] produces this same effect in others in order that he might shoot *in the dark at*[81] the common body of the Church, concealing himself, to my way of thinking, in the murk of faction; and he uses his constantly varied tricks and devices to insinuate himself into each of us and by his cunning opens up, as it were, a place for himself in our persons so that he may attack us with all his might, just as a champion warrior does an army when there has been a breach in the fortifications or battle-line.

14. The one great and indispensable requirement for una-

76. Eph 2.14.
78. Jb 15.25.
80. Jn 8.44.
77. 1 Jn 4.8, 16.
79. Is 14.14.
81. Ps 11.2 (LXX 10.2).

nimity and concord is this, the imitation of God and of things divine. It is to these alone that the soul, created in God's image, must steadfastly gaze in order that, by gravitating toward them and becoming as much like them as possible, it may preserve to the greatest extent its noble status; and second, let us heed the divine voice and *look up to the heaven above and the earth below*[82] and gain an understanding of the laws of creation, to wit, that heaven and earth and sea and this whole cosmos, the great and celebrated sign of God, by which God is heralded in silent proclamation, so long as it enjoys tranquility and is at peace within itself and stays within the confines of its own nature and nothing contends against anything else or oversteps the bonds of good will, bonds with which Logos the artificer has bound together the whole, is both a cosmos, just as it is called, and an unmatchable object of beauty, and one could never imagine anything more splendid or majestic than it; but the very moment it ceases to be at peace, it ceases to be a cosmos as well. Or do you think that the sky, when in its good order it imparts a portion of its light to the air and its rains to the earth, is not guided by the law of good will, and that the earth and air, in making their respective gifts of food and breath, hence maintaining life in all living things, are not faithful imitations of parental love?

15. And the seasons gently and gradually merging and succeeding one another and easing the harshness of their extremes by the interval between them: does it not seem that it is peace that fitly gives them their direction with a view at the same time both to pleasure and to utility? And what of day and night and their respective circuits, equally measured and distributed between them, the one rousing us for work, and the other giving us rest? What of sun and moon and the beautiful throng of stars rising and setting in order? And do not sea and land, placidly overlapping and through a gracious process of giving and receiving in turn, lovingly nurture man by supplying him with their fruits in lavish abundance? What of the rivers that stream through mountains and plains and do not overflow their banks without good reason or alter their course to flood

---

82. Is 8.21–22; 51.6 LXX.

the earth? And the compounds and mixtures of elements, and the proportions and compatibility of the parts of the body? And the animals with their sustenance and propagation and assigned habitats? And the fact that some things command and others are commanded and that some are subject to us and others are free? All these things being so and guided and directed in accordance with the first causes of harmony, or rather of conflux and conspiration,[83] what else could they ever be seen to be but proclamations of love and concord, teaching mankind unanimity through their example?

16. And when matter divides against itself and becomes intractable and intent on destruction through discord, or when God disturbs a measure of the harmony in order to terrify and punish sinners, whether by tidal wave or earthquake, or freak torrential storms or solar eclipse, or by prolonging a season or by conflagration, then there is turmoil and fear for the universe and the blessing of peace is shown through the disruption. And I shall pass over peoples and cities and kingdoms as well as assemblies and armies and households and ships' crews and married couples and brotherhoods, which are held together by peace and dissolved through discord, and proceed instead to treat of Israel, reminding you of her sufferings and dispersion and wandering, which both continues to this day and will continue for the longest time, as the prophecies regarding them convince me; and after that I shall put the question to you, since you know very well, What was the cause of these troubles? in order that we may learn the lesson of concord through the misfortunes of others.

17. While they were at peace both among themselves and with God, pressured by the iron furnace that was Egypt and drawn together by their common suffering—for sometimes even this very thing, suffering, has therapeutic value for salvation—they came to be known as a holy nation and the *Lord's portion* and *a royal priesthood*.[84] Nor was this distinction a nominal

---

83. Cf. Hippocrates, *On Nutriment* 23, where the terms *conflux* and *conspiration* characterize the cooperative relationship existing between the parts of the body.
84. Ex 19.6; Dt 32.9; 1 Pt 2.9.

one and out of keeping with the facts. Indeed, they were led by generals who were led by God and were guided night and day by a pillar of fire and of cloud;[85] and the sea parted for them in their flight,[86] and heaven showered them with food in their hunger,[87] and a rock gushed forth for them in their thirst,[88] and in war [Moses'] outstretched hands took the place of multitudes, erecting trophies through prayer and opening the way ahead;[89] and rivers subsided[90] in imitation of their kinsman, the sea, and heavenly bodies stood still,[91] and walls came crashing down with trumpets.[92] And what need is there to mention the blows inflicted on the Egyptians on their behalf,[93] and the voice of God heard on the mountain,[94] and the legislation with two meanings,[95] one in the letter, the other in the spirit, and all the other honors that in time past Israel received in excess of her deserts? And when corruption set in and madness against one another took hold and they were split into numerous factions—it was the Cross that helped drive them to their final ruination and the insanity that they directed against our God and Savior in refusing to recognize the God-in-man—and they brought down upon themselves the *rod of iron*[96] that had long threatened them (I refer to the imperial government that now holds sway), what was the result? What happened to them?

18. Jeremiah grieves over their former sufferings and laments their captivity in Babylon, for those events, too, were truly worthy of dirges and lamentations. And how could they not be of the most poignant sort? Walls razed to the ground; city

---

85. Ex 13.21.   86. Ex 14.22.
87. Ex 16.13.   88. Ex 17.6.
89. Ex 17.11. The trophies or monuments put up by the ancient Greeks on the field of battle consisted of a suit of enemy armor erected on a stake and thus resembled a figure with arms outstretched in prayer.
90. Jos 3.14–17.   91. Jos 10.12–13.
92. Jos 6.20.   93. Ex 7.11–12.30.
94. Ex 19.16–25.
95. Ordinarily this would refer to the Mosaic Law and Christian Gospel, but in the present instance Gregory's emphasis on the distinction between literal and spiritual meaning both here and in section 11 may have been motivated by the predicament in which his father found himself by signing a document that had a significance quite different from what he intended.
96. Ps 2.9.

ORATION 6   17

levelled; sanctuary stripped; votive offerings carried off; profane feet and hands trampling hallowed ground and fingering the forbidden; prophets mute; priests taken captive; elders ruthlessly treated; maidens raped; boys corrupted; fire set by foreign enemies; rivers of blood in place of holy fire and holy blood; Nazarites dragged off; voices raised not in hymn but in lamentation; and, to cite a phrase from Jeremiah's Lamentations directly, *The precious sons of Zion,* worth their weight in gold,[97] the pampered ones and strangers to evils, trodding an unfamiliar road, and, *The roads to Zion* mourning *for none come to the appointed feast*,[98] and, just before, *hands of compassionate women* not feeding their children because a siege was in force, but tearing them apart for food and curing their hunger with those dearest to them.[99] These things, how are they not dreadful, and beyond dreadful, not only for those exposed to them at the time, but to those who hear them even now? For myself, whenever I pick up this book and give myself over to Lamentations (which I do whenever I want through the reading to dampen excessive optimism), my voice chokes, and I dissolve in tears, and the suffering comes vividly before my eyes, as it were, and I join the lamenter in his lament. And as for the final blow and their migration, and the yoke of slavery that now presses upon them, and their celebrated humiliation at the hands of the Romans, caused by nothing so much as discord, who among those skilled in composing lamentations and matching words to suffering will do them justice? What books can accommodate these horrors? One monument stands to them of their disaster: the entire world throughout which they have been scattered, and the cessation of their worship, and the scarcely recognizable ground of Jerusalem itself. Presenting themselves for a single day to lament its desolation constitutes their sole access to it and sole opportunity to bask in their former glory.[100]

97. Lam 4.2.   98. Lam 1.4.
99. Lam 4.10.
100. After crushing the revolt of Bar Kochba (132–35 AD), the emperor Hadrian issued a decree forbidding Jews to enter Jerusalem and its environs although this ban was subsequently modified to allow one visit a year, on 9 Ab, to

19. Yet, although discord is so terrible a thing and a source of such enormous suffering as both the foregoing illustrates and we can learn from numerous other examples, far more terrible it is that those who have laid pettiness aside and had a taste of the blessings of peace should succumb once more to the same disorder and, as the saying goes, return to their own *vomit*,[101] having learned nothing from experience, as even fools do. For in fact I note that it is not those whose misconduct is constant that we consider empty-headed and foolish, but rather those who vacillate and change between concord and strife without compunction like shifting winds or tides alternating in narrow straits or the fitful waves of the sea. And I observe this too, that the mere hope of concord instils a more compliant spirit in those who are always at strife and lightens in very great part the burden of their misfortune; for it is in the hope of change and the glimpse of a better tomorrow that the unfortunate find their greatest succor; while those who have often joined in accord but have constantly shifted back into evil ways lie stripped, along with everything else, of the hope of improvement as well, since they are always apprehensive of concord and of strife alike and take no heart in either because of the instability and uncertainty in both.

20. But let no one imagine me to mean that all peace is desirable. I am equally aware of a beneficial kind of strife as well as a harmful type of concord; but what I have in mind is the noble sort, undertaken for a noble purpose, and linking us to God. If a distinction between the two is in order, here in brief are my views: it is not good to be either too compliant or too contentious, with the result that one is either so uncritical that he obliges everyone or so volatile that he cuts himself off from everyone. Lack of discrimination is just as unproductive as inconstancy is socially irresponsible. But wherever acts of impiety come to light we must turn and grapple with fire and sword and unfavorable circumstance and authorities and everything rather than participate in the evil ferment; and we must make

---

commemorate the city's fall. See Eusebius, *Ecclesiastical History* 4.6.3 and E. M. Smallwood, *The Jews under Roman Rule* (Leiden: Brill, 1976), 460.

101. Prv 26.11.

common cause with the unfortunate and of all things fear nothing so much as fearing anything before God and thereby in the service of truth betraying the doctrine of the true faith. When, on the other hand, it is suspicion and unfounded fear that gall, patience is preferable to haste and magnanimity to selfishness, and it is more effective and advantageous by far to stay within the common body and join together as members of one another and be joined rather than to try and impose a solution by decree after prejudging the issue by defection and vacating one's moral claim by disengagement. This is how tyrants behave, not brothers.

21. In this knowledge, my brothers, let us clasp one another; let us embrace; let us truly become one; let us imitate him who broke down *the dividing wall of hostility*[102] and *by* his *blood* united and reconciled *all things;*[103] let us say to this father we have in common,[104] the gray head that we revere, our kind and gentle shepherd, Do you see the fruit of forbearance? *Lift up your eyes round about, and see* your children gathered, just as you have fervently been wishing and the only thing you have been praying night and day to gain, that you might end the sojourn of your life in happy old age. Behold, all have come[105] to you and nestle *under* your *wings.*[106] They who left in tears now come forward eagerly in gladness and stand round their altar. Come, hail and rejoice, best and most devoted of fathers, because you are vestured and arrayed in them all, like a bride in her finery. Declare before us, you also, *Behold, I and the children whom the Lord has given me,*[107] and add also another most appropriate exclamation of the Lord, those that *thou hast given me I have guarded* and I have lost *none of them.*[108]

22. Yes, let no one be lost, but let us all abide *in one spirit, with one mind striving side by side for the faith of the gospel,*[109] *being in full accord and of one mind*[110] armed with the shield *of faith, loins* gird-

---

102. Eph 2.14.
103. Col 1.20.
104. Gregory's father, also named Gregory, was the spiritual father of the congregation at Nazianzus.

105. Is 60.4.   106. Mt 23.37; Lk 13.34.
107. Is 8.18.   108. Jn 17.12.
109. Phil 1.27.   110. Phil 2.2.

ed about *with truth*,[111] acknowledging one war alone, that against the Devil and his minions, fearing not those who can *kill the body* but cannot take the soul,[112] but fearing the Lord of both soul and body; guarding *the truth*[113] that we have received from our fathers, reverencing Father and Son and Holy Spirit; knowing the Father in the Son, the Son in the Holy Spirit, in which names we have been baptized, in which we believe, and under which we have been enlisted, dividing them before combining them and combining them before dividing them, and not regarding the three as a single individual (for they are not without individual reality nor do they comprise a single reality, as though our treasure lay in names and not in actual fact), but rather believing the three to be a single entity. For they are a single entity not in individual reality but in divinity, a unity worshipped in Trinity and a Trinity summed up into unity, venerable as one whole, as one whole royal, sharing the same throne, sharing the same glory, above space, above time, uncreated, invisible, impalpable, uncircumscribed, its internal ordering known only to itself, but for us equally the object of reverence and adoration, and alone taking possession of the Holy of Holies and excluding all of creation, part by the first veil, and part by the second. The first veil separates the heavenly and angelic realm from the Godhead, and the second, our world from that of the heavens. These things, my brothers, let us do, and such let our devotion be; and as for those who disagree, let us regard them as a plague against the truth and make every effort to help them and heal them; but if they are not receptive to cure let us turn away from them lest they infect us with their affliction before we give them of our own health. And *the God of peace*,[114] which passes *all understanding*,[115] will be with us, in Jesus Christ our Lord. Amen.

111. Eph 6.14, 16.
112. Mt 10.28.
113. 2 Tm 1.14.
114. 2 Cor 13.11.
115. Phil 4.7.

ORATION 9

Apologia to his father Gregory, in the presence of Basil, when he was consecrated bishop of Sasima.[1]

PIRIT AND CHRISM upon me again; and again I make my way *bowed down and in mourning*.[2] You are, perhaps, surprised. Isaiah himself, before seeing the glory of God and the high and exalted throne with the Seraphim around it, does not speak this way nor is he affected by either fear or despair. On the contrary, he rages against Israel while exempting himself and denying his complicity. But when he saw these marvels and heard the holy and mystical voice, then, as if with a greater awareness of his own involvement, he says, *Woe is me, for I am lost*[3]—I avoid the blasphemy of his subsequent remarks. I also adduce one of the judges of old, the famous Manoah, and, later, Peter, the pillar of the Church, the one declaring Woman, we are undone; *we have seen God*,[4] after he had experienced a vision that transcended his human capacity, while the other was unable to endure the presence and power that the Savior had revealed to him and his companions while they were fishing. Although the experience filled him with wonder, he nevertheless besought Christ to leave the boat, claiming himself unworthy of divine visitation and company.[5]

2. And whenever I hear the Gospel story of the centurion who, though he asked for the power, yet declined the actual presence because his roof could not contain the divine dignity and grandeur,[6] I cannot fault my own reluctance and melan-

---

1. PG 35.820A–25D. Written on the occasion of Gregory's consecration as bishop of Sasima in 372.
2. Ps 35.14 (LXX 34.14).
3. Is 6.5.
4. Jgs 13.22.
5. Lk 5.8.
6. Lk 7.3–6; cf. Mt 8.5–8.

choly. For just as the sun testifies to the weakness of the eye, God by his presence testifies to the infirmity of the soul. To some he is light; to others fire, depending on our own individual make-up and character. How are we to understand the example of Saul? He was anointed, received the Spirit, and was thereupon undeniably spiritual, in my opinion. Indeed, he even became a prophet, and so surpassed any reasonable expectation that that miracle in fact gave rise to the proverb that is still repeated to this very day, *Is Saul also among the prophets?*[7] But inasmuch as he did not surrender himself fully to the Spirit he was also not changed purely *into another man*,[8] as had been foretold, but retained something of the old spark of wickedness and of the evil seed and was subject to a conflict between spirit and flesh. Why should I give a tragic recital of all the calamities that befell him? You know the story of the evil spirit and the singer who charmed him.[9] His experience, then, provides further proof that, even if grace does not affect the unworthy or for that matter any instrument that is completely worthless and fit for nothing—for I personally believe that *wisdom* is correctly said not to *enter a deceitful soul*[10]—still, I say, owing to the manifold inconstancies of human nature and habit, maintaining one's worthiness and moral fitness is just as difficult as the possession of these qualities in the first place. Consequently, even grace itself, to mention the strangest and worst of our own misfortunes, by implanting delusion and false hopes, frequently creates a distance between God and those who have not come to him in the right spirit, and we are cast down *when* we *were lifted up*,[11] *that sin might be shown to be sin, working death in me through what is good.*[12]

3. It is the dread of this misfortune that has filled me with anguish and depression. My experience is somewhat akin to what children feel when they see lightning—a mixture of terror and delight: I have come at the same time to love and to fear the Spirit. I needed time to collect my thoughts and compose myself, to regain my strength and self-confidence, in order that, once what troubled me fell away, like tares in the sowing, and

---

7. 1 Sm 10.12.
8. 1 Sm 10.6.
9. 1 Sm 16.14–23.
10. Wis 1.4.
11. Ps 73.18 (LXX 72.18) LXX.
12. Rom 7.13.

my mean thoughts yielded to better ones, the Spirit might prevail and keep me safely in its grasp for its service and ministry, for the strengthening of this people, for the governance of souls, for teaching through word, deed, and example, *with the weapons of righteousness for the right hand and for the left,*[13] for the effective exercise of my pastoral office, which tears them away from the world, leads them to God, exhausts their body, adds them to the Spirit, turns away from the darkness, glories in the light, drives away predators, draws together the fold, guards against precipices and desert solitudes, helps it reach the mountains and high places. This is what I think the venerable Micah means when he speaks about leading us from the plain down below up to the heights reserved for us: *Draw ye near to the everlasting mountains. Arise thou, and depart; for this is not thy rest,*[14] even though some think it lies in an existence that grovels and turns to the ground.

4. This is the pastoral duty I would have you teach me, my dear ones, whom I shall henceforth call pastors and fellow-pastors. The insignia of this vocation bestow upon me, both you, our common father, who has trained and outstripped many a pastor in years gone by, and you, the rigorous arbiter of my life in grace.[15] And yet—graciously hear what I have to say—can we really provide pastoral care and nurture in a conscientious way when we are being pulled hither and yon by a roaring tempest?[16] I hope you will not be offended by my observation that you showed more kindness when, as members of a flock, we fed together on pagan learning than you do now when, as two shepherds, we have been summoned to spiritual pasture. You have us, as you desired, in your hands; you have prevailed over the unconquerable. And lo! along with everything else, you have my sermon too, which you kept asking for although you already heard it and which, inadequate though it is, you have continued to shower with frequent and copious praise.

5. But I have also a bone to pick with my friend. Who among

---

13. 2 Cor 6.7.   14. Mi 2.9–10 LXX.
15. I.e., Gregory, our Gregory's father, and Basil.
16. I.e., the difficult personal and political circumstances that attended Gregory's consecration.

the friends we have in common will serve as judge on my behalf? Who will be the impartial referee who will give a just decision and not, as most people do, take sides? Would you have me state my complaint? Do you promise not to hurl a retort at me? You of all people, admirable man, did something unspeakable to me, something truly unspeakable and incredible and, what is more, something previously unheard of in our relationship. We were not persuaded; we were forced. How strange! How oddly everything has changed! How great the gap that has arisen between us! Would you have me attribute it to *the throne* or to the magnitude *of grace*?[17] However it may be, lead and *in your majesty ride forth victoriously*[18] and shepherd us, your shepherds. How ready we are to follow the lead of your lofty and inspired shepherd's soul! We will tell the truth even if our affection has made us presumptuous. Teach us your love for your flocks, your blend of diligence and good judgment, your solicitude, your vigilance, your withdrawal from the flesh to make way for the Spirit, your shining countenance as you labor for your flock, the zeal expressed in gentleness, the peace and serenity shown in action—a rare virtue with few examples—the campaigns on behalf of your flock, and the victories you have won in Christ.

6. Tell us what pastures we are to seek, what springs draw near, and what pastures or streams to avoid. Whom are we to shepherd with the staff, whom with the pipe? When lead them to and when recall them from pasture? How do we combat the wolves and avoid combat with the shepherds, especially at the present time when *shepherds are stupid* and have scattered the flocks of the fields, to use the same sad expression as the holy prophets?[19] *How will I strengthen* the weak and raise the fallen and bring back the *strayed* and seek out *the lost* and *watch over the strong*? How am I both to master and uphold this code in the true pastoral way, your way? No; let me not prove a bad shepherd, feeding on the milk and clothing myself *with the wool* and slaughtering or selling off the fattest of the flock while abandoning the rest to the cliffs and *wild beasts*, thus benefiting as a

17. Heb 4.16.   18. Ps 45.4 (LXX 44.5).
19. Jer 10.21.

shepherd not the sheep but myself, the very behavior that the old leaders of Israel used to censure.[20] This is the knowledge I would have you impart to me; these the words I would have you use to strengthen me; these the precepts by which I would have you shepherd me and help me to shepherd others. Preserve me and this holy flock by your instruction as well as your prayers, bringing assurance in this way to me and rejoicing to yourselves on the day of the coming and revelation of our great God and Chief Shepherd,[21] Jesus Christ, through whom and with whom glory be to the Almighty Father together with the Holy and life-giving Spirit both now and forever and ever. Amen.

20. Ezek 34.3–10.
21. Phil 2.16; Ti 2.13; 1 Pt 5.4.

ORATION 10

On himself and to his father and Basil the Great after the return from exile.[1]

NOTHING IS MIGHTIER than old age and nothing more venerable than friendship. It is by these that I, *a prisoner* in Christ,[2] have been led to you, bound not in chains of iron but by the indissoluble bonds of the Spirit. Up to now I thought of myself as a strong and indomitable person and—what foolishness!—I refused to indulge in conversation with even these my beloved friends and brothers so that I might have the freedom and peace to live quietly as an ascetic, leaving all my worldly affairs to those who want them while I communed with myself and the Spirit. My thoughts kept turning to Elias on Mt. Carmel, to John in the desert, and to the other world of those who pursue such a way of wisdom, and I came to regard life on this earth as a kind of storm, and I was ever on the lookout for some rock, or covert, or walled spot where I might take cover. Let others exert themselves and obtain recognition, I used to say; let others fight the battles and win the trophies. As for myself, let me be content to live my life as I can, rejecting the field of battle in favor of inner contemplation, crossing, as it were, a small expanse of sea on a flimsy raft and securing a small place in heaven by the poverty of my life here

---

1. PG 35.828A–32A. J. Mossay, "Le *Discours 10* de Grégoire de Nazianze. Notes et Controverses," *Byzantion* 70 (2000): 447–55, has recently attempted to resolve the difficulties concerning this homily's place and date of delivery (i.e., whether at Nazianzus, Sasima, or Caesarea either before, after, or during his consecration as bishop of Sasima) by proposing that it was written at Karvali at the end of Gregory's life. The homily has traditionally been associated with *Or.* 9, 11, and 13, all written on the occasion of Gregory's consecration as bishop of Sasima in 372.
2. Eph 3.1; Phlm 1.1.

on earth. This way of thinking is perhaps characteristic of those who set their sights too low and who prefer the safety of avoiding equally both the peak and the valley.

2. This was my cast of mind while I could still make up shadows and dreams and enjoy the entertainment of an idle imagination. And now what? Friendship has brought me round, and a father's white hair has vanquished me: old age, with its fullness of life, wisdom, its now secure haven, and friendship with a man who, through being rich in the Lord, enriches others. My anger is now a thing of the past—*let the afflicted hear and be glad*[3]—and I look kindly upon the hand that played the tyrant, and I laugh in the Spirit, and my heart is at peace, and good judgment has returned, and friendship, like a flame that has died down and gone out, has been rekindled from a tiny spark and springs back to life once again. My soul refused to be comforted[4] and *my spirit faints within me.*[5] Never again, I said, will I put my faith in friendship. Why should I place my trust in a mortal creature when *every* man *goes about as a slanderer* and *every brother supplants his neighbor*[6] and, coming all from the same earthen lump[7] and having tasted of the same tree of evil, each of us adopts a mask more specious than the next? What benefit, I kept asking, did I derive from that enviable and celebrated friendship which started in the world and advanced to the Spirit? What indeed from sharing the same roof and table? Or teachers and schooling? What indeed from feeling closer than brothers and later on experiencing a true oneness of heart, since I was not allowed even this much, the option of retaining my humble station in a time of power and eminence, when most strive to achieve the reverse: a share in the power and participation in the prosperity of their friends?

3. Why should I mention all the feelings of sorrow and despair, of what I call the dark side, that the mind can imagine? They did exist, and so did others more absurd (I shall deliberately incriminate myself, whether the charge be that of madness

---

3. Ps 34.2 (LXX 33.3).
4. Ps 77.2 (LXX 76.3).
5. Ps 143.4 (LXX 142.4).
6. Jer 9.4.
7. Gn 2.7; 1 Cor 5.6–7.

or stupidity). Now, however, I am different, with an attitude far more realistic than before as well as more worthy of us. And in order that you may appreciate the sincerity of my change of heart, my admirable friend,[8] not only do you break down the silence that you reproved and criticized so much, but these very words stand as your confirmation, reflecting as they clearly do our mutual regard and the presence of the Spirit within us. Of what does this confirmation consist? If I am wrong, do correct me, as you have often done in the past. You refused to prefer our friendship to the Spirit: although you favor us over anyone else, still, in your eyes, the Spirit is far more precious than we. You refused to let the talent lie buried and hidden in the ground.[9] You refused to let the *lamp,* by which you mean my light and my mission in life, remain concealed under *the bushel* for long.[10] You sought someone to play Barnabas to your Paul.[11] You sought a Titus to complement Silvanus and Timotheus[12] in order that your charism might course[13] through those who are genuinely concerned for you and you might fully preach *the Gospel from Jerusalem and as far round as Illyricum.*[14]

4. This is why you bring me back into the world and, despite my reluctance, take my hand and seat me next to you. This, you will say, is the grievance for which you make me share your burdens as well your laurels. This is why you anoint me high priest, dress me in the robe, and place the mitre upon my head; why you escort me to the altar of the spiritual offering, offer the calf of ordination,[15] and consecrate my hands in the Spirit; why you lead me to the Holy of Holies for initiation and make me a minister of *the true tent, which is set up not by man but by the Lord.*[16] But whether I am worthy, both of you who anoint me and of him for whose sake and in whose name I am anointed, this the Father of the real and truly Anointed One knows, whom he *has anointed*

---

8. I.e., Basil.   9. Mt 25.18.
10. Lk 11.33.   11. Gal 2.1.
12. Elias, the Byzantine scholiast, explains that Paul is Basil, Barnabas and Titus Gregory of Nazianzus, and Silvanus and Timotheus Basil's two brothers, Gregory of Nyssa and Peter of Sebaste, but the latter identification has been challenged. See M.-A. Calvet-Sebasti in SC 405, p. 324, n. 1.
13. Cf. 2 Thes 3.1.   14. Rom 15.19.
15. Ex 29.   16. Heb 8.2.

with the oil of gladness above his *fellows*,[17] anointing humanity with divinity so as to make *both one;*[18] and our Lord and God himself, Jesus Christ, *through whom* we have received *our reconciliation;*[19] and the Holy Spirit, which has charged us with this ministry in which we now take our place, jubilant *in the hope of sharing the glory*[20] of our Lord Jesus Christ, to whom be the glory forever and ever. Amen.

17. Ps 45.7 (LXX 44.8).
19. Rom 5.11.
18. Eph 2.14.
20. Rom 5.2.

ORATION 11

By the same to Gregory of Nyssa, the brother of Basil the Great, who arrived after the consecration.[1]

HERE IS NOTHING in this world *so precious as a faithful friend* and *no scales can measure his excellence. A faithful friend is a sturdy shelter,* a fortified palace. A faithful friend is a living treasure.[2] A faithful friend is *more than gold and much precious stone.*[3] A faithful friend is *a garden locked, a fountain sealed,*[4] to be opened and enjoyed in season. A faithful friend is a haven of refreshment, and if he excels also in understanding, how great a boon that is! And if a paragon of learning too, both ours and what was once ours, how much more splendid! And if he is besides a child *of light,*[5] or a man *of God,*[6] or draws near to God,[7] or a *man greatly beloved,*[8] or merits any of the kinds of epithets that Scripture applies to those distinguished by their holiness, dignity, and eminence, this is truly a gift from God and clearly more than we deserve. And if besides he comes to us from a friend whose goodness and devotion to us are no less, that is still more delightful and gratifying, and more fragrant than the ointment that graces the *beard* of the priest and *the collar of his robes.*[9]

2. Have I said enough? Have my words adequately depicted the man to you? Or should we, like those painstaking artists, keep adding colors so that the picture we present to you might be more complete? Well, then, we shall depict him to you with

---

1. PG 35.832B–42B. Written on the occasion of Gregory's consecration as bishop of Sasima in 372.
2. Sir 6.14–15.
3. Ps 19.10 (LXX 18.11) LXX.
4. Song 4.12.
5. Jn 12.36; Eph 5.8.
6. Dt 33.1; 2 Kgs 1.9.
7. Ex 24.2; Ezek 43.19.
8. Dn 9.23.
9. Ps 133.2 (LXX 132.2).

ORATION 11

greater fullness and clarity. Who is the most famous lawgiver? Moses. Who the holiest priest? Aaron. They were brothers no less in their piety than in their persons.[10] One was *a god to Pharaoh*,[11] and leader and lawgiver of Israel, who went into the cloud, initiate and initiator in the divine mysteries, and architect *of the true tent, which is set up not by man but by the Lord.*[12] Yet both alike were priests. *Moses and Aaron were among his priests,* says Scripture.[13] Moses was ruler of rulers and priest of priests, using Aaron as his *mouth*, and being *to him as God*,[14] while Aaron was next after him but far above the rest in worth and closeness to God; both the scourge of Egypt, parting the sea, leading forth the people of Israel, drowning their enemies, drawing bread from heaven, miraculously making water gush forth in the desert on one occasion and sweetening it on another, both vanquishing Amalek by the reach of their holy hands and prefigurement of a higher mystery,[15] both eagerly leading the way to the promised land. Is any illustration more familiar than this? Has not the portraying word sketched for you in clear outline my namesake and soul-mate?

3. Of these men one anointed us, bringing us out of hiding into the world. I know not what incident or impulse motivated him to act so unworthily of the Spirit within him (my words are admittedly somewhat harsh, but I will say them nevertheless: friendship is a patient listener that will accept all things). The other has come to commiserate with me and to restore harmony by reconciling us to the Spirit. It is a great thing for me that you are here even now, very great indeed, inasmuch as I have held you up as the model of my whole life. My only criticism is that you have come after I needed you. What good is an alliance, my dearest of friends and allies, after the attack and defeat? The pilot after the storm? The medicine after the scar? Was it because, professing as you do a brother's love, you were embarrassed by your high-handedness? Perhaps as my superior

---

10. The brothers Basil the Great and Gregory of Nyssa were both in the audience. Basil is being depicted as Moses to Gregory's Aaron.
11. Ex 7.1.
12. Heb 8.2.
13. Ps 99.6 (LXX 98.6).
14. Ex 4.16.
15. Ex 17.8–13.

you personally resented my insubordination? Which brother do you indict and which absolve from blame? I shall quote to you one of Job's remarks to his friend, however unlike you he was, because I too am in pain, though not with the same affliction: To *whom dost thou attach thyself, or whom art thou going to assist? Is it not he that has much strength? Is it not to him who has much wisdom and knowledge?*[16] I observe this behavior in many of our current judges: they find it easier to excuse the gravest offenses in the mighty than the slightest in inferiors. You probably have knowledge of this yourself. It is not my place to call attention to any misstep on your part, for I regard you as the exemplary model of perfect morality, and besides, I am admonished by Scripture not to be hasty in judgment.[17] For my part I am prepared in the name of friendship to justify to you or anyone at all my, as some would have it, insubordination, or rather, as I am myself convinced, cautious prudence, so that you might know that your friend is not altogether ignorant or foolish, but rather one more capable than the mass of the broad view, confident where confidence is warranted, but given to fear where there is reason to fear and where it would be even more frightening for sensible men not to be afraid.

4. What, then, is the better course of action in your opinion? Would you have us render an account of ourselves right now? You do not consider the present occasion inappropriate? This is, after all, a festal assembly, not a court of law. Or should we defer to another time and assembly? The fact is, our oral defense is longer than present circumstances allow. But what can we say to you that will be in keeping with the festivities? It would not do for us to send you away hungry, especially since we are the hosts.

Let us purify ourselves, brethren, through the martyrs;[18] or rather, through him through whom they too were purified in blood and truth. Let us free ourselves *from every defilement of body and spirit.*[19] Let us wash; let us become *clean;*[20] yea, let us present

---

16. Jb 26.2–3 LXX.   17. Mt 7.1; 1 Cor 4.5.
18. The sermon contains no clue that would allow the identification of the martyrs whose feast is being celebrated.
19. 2 Cor 7.1.   20. Is 1.16.

our very *bodies* and souls *as a living sacrifice, holy and acceptable to God, which is* our *spiritual worship*[21] and petition. For nothing is so precious to the Pure as purity and purification. Let us enter the lists for the sake of the athletes; let us be victorious for the victors; let us witness to the truth for the witnesses. The contribution that we should make to their achievements is this, that we ourselves too win the crown of victory and claim as our inheritance the same glory that we have bestowed upon them here and that is reserved for them in heaven, of which the visible world around us is but a shallow hint and impress. Let us struggle *against the principalities, against the powers,* against lurking tyrants and persecutors, *against the world rulers of this present darkness, against the spiritual hosts of wickedness in the heavenly places*[22] and among the celestial beings, against the war which goes on even within ourselves among the passions, against the daily onslaught of external events.

5. Let us handle our anger as if it were a ferocious beast and our tongue as a sharp sword, and let us extinguish our love of pleasure like a flame. Let us place shutters over our ears that can be duly opened and closed; and let us curb our roving eye; let us control our wanton touch and ravenous taste lest death come up *into* our *windows*[23] (this means, I believe, our senses); and let us scorn inordinate laughter. Let us not bow a *knee to Baal*[24] out of want, nor worship the golden *image* out of fear.[25] Our one and only fear should be fearing anything more than God and in our wickedness defiling his image. Let us in all things take *the shield of faith* and let us deflect *all the darts of the evil one.*[26] Dread is this war too and mighty this line of battle; mighty too are the spoils. If this is the purpose of our meeting and assembly, then our festival truly is in Christ; we truly have done honor to the martyrs, or shall do so; we truly have cause for triumphal celebration. But if we are here to gratify the pleasures of the belly and to indulge passing delights and ingest what is voided, and if we think this is a place for carousing rather than sobriety, an opportunity for transactions and trade instead

21. Rom 12.1.
23. Jer 9.21; see also *Or.* 27.7.
25. Dn 3.18.
22. Eph 6.12.
24. 1 Kgs 19.18; Rom 11.4.
26. Eph 6.16.

of ascent or, if I may be so bold, deification, of which the martyrs are the intercessors, I do not even accept the occasion in the first place. For what has chaff to do with wheat?[27] Bodily indulgence with a martyr's struggle? The one is to be found in the theaters, the other in my congregations; the one among the pleasure-seekers, the other among men of restraint; the one among devotees of the flesh, the other among those who free themselves from the body. I am tempted to follow up my remarks with even stronger language, but out of respect for the day I refrain from anything inauspicious. Besides, this is not what the martyrs require of us, to put it mildly.

6. Let us not, then, my brethren, perform our holy rites with impurity, our high solemnities in lowly fashion, our observances of honor dishonorably, nor, in short, our matters of the spirit in the ways of the flesh. The Jew also observes holy days, but according to the letter of the law; the Hellene too has his celebrations, but as pleases the gods. With us, on the other hand, since everything is spiritual—our actions, deportment, will, words, even the way we walk and dress and nod agreement—because reason reaches into all things and brings man, made in God's image, into step with him, such too are both our holidays and our expressions of gladness. Certainly I do not disallow relaxation; I do censure excess. If we bear these things in mind as we gather to celebrate, we shall—marvelous to say—both obtain the same rewards and inherit the same glory ourselves. For *what no eye has seen nor ear heard* nor mind of man conceived,[28] which imagines blessedness as best it can, these rewards we believe are in store for those who have been washed in the blood and have imitated Christ's sacrifice; the splendor of the holy martyrs, however, we shall certainly see—itself no small reward, in my estimation—and we shall come into the joy of the same Lord and shall be illumined more brightly and more purely, I know it well, by the light of the blessed and sovereign Trinity in which we have put our faith, which we worship, and which we confess before God and man with no fear and no shame, not before the

27. Cf. Mt 3.12.
28. Is 64.4; 1 Cor 2.9.

foe from without, not before the false Christs and enemies of the Spirit within our midst. And it is my hope that up to our last breath we shall continue to confess fully and freely the sacred trust[29] of the holy fathers, who were closer to Christ and the origins of our Faith, the confession that we first uttered and that has been our companion from childhood and with which may we end our days, taking with us from this world piety, this, if nothing else.

7. The God of peace, who *through the cross* has reconciled to himself us who through sin became his enemies; who preached *peace to those who were near* and to those who were far off,[30] to those under the Law and those outside it; the father of love, *love itself*,[31] for these are the forms of address that please him above all others so that he may, by his very names, endow brotherly love with the authority of his law; who gave a *new commandment* that we love *one another* as much as we have been loved;[32] who has provided scope for virtuous action both in the exercise of absolute authority and in the submission to it out of fear, in yielding when reason demands it and again with reason making bold; who strengthens the large flocks and increases the small through his grace: yea, this very one, may he in the abundance of his goodness, comfort us with much comfort and lead us forward, helping us in the task of tending and preserving the flock; and you may he strengthen for every *good work*[33] and bring you to honor the martyrs with spiritual celebration and find you worthy of the joys of heaven, where is *the dwelling of all those that rejoice*[34] and, when you appear *in righteousness*,[35] fill you with his own glory seen in Jesus Christ our Lord, to whom be the power and the glory, the honor and the worship, forever and ever. Amen.

29. Cf. 2 Tm 1.14.
30. Eph 2.16–17.
31. 1 Jn 4.16.
32. Jn 13.34.
33. Phil 1.6.
34. Ps 87.7 (LXX 86.7) LXX.
35. Ps 17.15 (LXX 16.15).

ORATION 13

Homily delivered on the occasion of the consecration of Eulalius as bishop of Doara.[1]

CCEPT WHAT I HAVE TO SAY, my brethren, although in its brevity my sermon falls far short of what the occasion demands. Yet the Lord knows how to balance mercy with fairness.[2] He accepts both Paul's planting because it is Paul's, but also Apollos's watering;[3] he accepts as well the widow's *two copper coins*,[4] and the publican's humility,[5] and Manasseh's confession.[6] Accept my newly created sermon for a newly created pastor. Accept a voice raised in thanksgiving for the marvels before our eyes. We ourselves are lowly, the least among the children of Israel, but there is nothing to keep even the lowly from richly giving thanks. The more perfect, of course, will render more perfect praise to God. We, however, shall do the best we can today. And so, *Sing to the Lord a new song, for he has done marvelous things*.[7] We were caught up in a mael-

---

1. PG 35.852A–56C. Written on the occasion of Gregory's consecration as bishop of Sasima in 372. It is generally agreed that the bishop whose consecration is being celebrated here cannot be Gregory's cousin and eventual successor at Nazianzus, Eulalius, who, in contrast to the secular savvy ascribed to the new bishop of Doara in section 4, is characterized in nearly contemporary documents (Gregory Nazianzen, *Ep*. 14 and 15) by his lack of worldly experience and devotion to philosophy, i.e., monastic life. P. Gallay, *La vie de Saint Grégoire de Nazianze* (Lyon, 1943), p. 123, n. 3, attempted to resolve the question of identity by arguing that the Eulalius in the title was the editor of the sermon rather than its subject and that consequently the new bishop of Doara was neither Gregory's cousin nor another man with the same name but an anonymous third party. The problem with this identification, which has been widely accepted, is that the dative case is not normally used to indicate personal agency. Thus, the phrase that forms the basis of Gallay's argument, ὁμιλία ἐκδοθεῖσα Εὐλαλίῳ ἐπισκόπῳ, will not mean a homily "edited by" but rather "given for" Eulalius.

2. Is 28.17.
3. 1 Cor 3.6.
4. Lk 21.2.
5. Lk 18.13.
6. 2 Chr 33.12–13.
7. Ps 98.1 (LXX 97.1).

strom; we were afflicted with war; we were being forcibly expelled. Some of these calamities were already upon us; others were still to come. But who calmed the storm *into a gentle breeze?*[8] Who *broke the shield, the sword, and the weapons of war?*[9] Who welcomed us when we were driven away and cast off?[10] Was it not you, our God, who performed this?[11] *The Lord strong and mighty, the Lord mighty in battle!*[12]

2. He it was who parted the sea; who fed a nation of exiles by showering them with a curious kind of rain; who made the rock gush forth; who defeated Amalek through a strange and mystical gesture of hands[13]—this is what the hands of the priest, raised in an attitude of prayer on a mountain top could do and countless thousands could not; who shattered walls without war or battle;[14] lastly, who brought down Goliath, the arrogant and swaggering descendant of giants, when he dared to challenge the mighty David.[15] Let us then sing all together, *Blessed be the Lord, who has not given us as prey to their teeth! The flood would have swept us away. We have escaped as a bird from the snare of the fowlers;*[16] and all else that a soul joyously proclaims amid God's bounty. We have come to bring, not the sword, but peace.[17] We have not come to dishonor the great shepherd who presides over a magnificent city.[18] We consider him venerable; we acknowledge him as our head; we call him holy even though we are the victims of his injustice. Only let him be devoted to his children and provide for the whole Church. We have directed our efforts toward increasing, not reducing, the number of priests; towards confounding heretics, not decimating the ranks of the orthodox.

3. What do you say, son of Dathan and Abiram,[19] you, the unprincipled mastermind of the revolt against Moses,[20] who

---

8. Ps 107.29 (LXX 106.29) LXX.
9. Ps 76.3 (LXX 75.4).
10. Mi 4.6.
11. Is 41.4.
12. Ps 24.8 (LXX 23.8).
13. Ex 14.21; 16.13–15; 17.11–12.
14. Jos 6.20.
15. 1 Sm 17.49.
16. Ps 124.6, 4, 7 (LXX 123.6, 4, 7).
17. Cf. Mt 10.34.
18. The "great shepherd" is most likely Basil of Caesarea, the capital of Cappadocia Prima, who committed the "injustice" of appointing Gregory bishop of Sasima. See also *Or.* 9 and 10.
19. The identity of this individual remains unknown, but he apparently was a partisan of Anthimus who, as bishop of Tyana, the capital of the newly created province of Cappadocia Secunda, rejected Basil's episcopal authority.
20. Nm 16.1.

lashed at us with your hands just as your forbears did with their tongues against God's great servant? Did you not take fright? Did you not have any qualms? Did not the very thought of these actions make your flesh collapse in a heap? And after all that, do you lift up these hands of yours to God? And after all that will you bring him gifts? And after all that pray for your people? My fear is that the sword of God may perhaps become rusty from such long disuse. Not only did you fail to win any great favor with your pastor but you inflicted the greatest damage upon yourself: you alienated yourself from God's grace.

4. And now, best and most excellent of pastors,[21] come join us, even lead us in receiving your congregation, which the Holy Spirit has entrusted to your care, which the angels convey, which your upright life has commended to you. And if you are succeeding to the throne at a time of trial and opposition, be not surprised. No worthwhile undertaking comes untested and untried. It is a law of nature that the ordinary is achieved with ease; the exceptional, with difficulty. You have heard Paul say *that through many tribulations, we must enter the kingdom of heaven.*[22] Say yourself also, *We went through fire and water; but thou broughtest us out into a place of refreshment.*[23] What a miracle! *Weeping tarried for the night, but joy comes with the morning.*[24] Let those who trouble the peace go ahead and rave and gape like dogs barking to no purpose, but let us not ourselves be drawn in. Help us learn to worship God the Father, God the Son, and God the Holy Spirit as three in their individual realities, one in glory and splendor. Be a seeker of the lost; a strengthener of the weak; a preserver of the strong.[25] We ask you to become distinguished in affairs of the Spirit to the same degree that we already know you to be in affairs of the world. May you be given a more perfect armor by your greater commanders[26] wherewith you will be able *to quench all the flaming darts of the evil one*[27] and deliver up to the Lord his *own possession, a holy nation, a royal priesthood,*[28] in Christ Jesus our Lord, to whom be the glory forever. Amen.

21. I.e., Eulalius, the homonym of Gregory's cousin. See n. 1.
22. Acts 14.22.
23. Ps 66.12 (LXX 65.12) LXX.
24. Ps 30.5 (LXX 29.6).
25. Ezek 34.4, 16.
26. Angels are frequently referred to in patristic literature as a military host.
27. Eph 6.16.
28. Ex 19.5–6; 1 Pt 2.9.

ORATION 14

*On Love for the Poor.*¹

Y BROTHERS and fellow paupers—for we are all poor and needy where divine grace is concerned, even though, measured by our paltry standards one man may seem to have more than another—give ear to my sermon on loving the poor. Do so not grudgingly but generously, that you may become rich in the kingdom, and join us in praying that this our gift to you shall be rich in turn as we nourish your souls with our words and break spiritual bread for the hungry, whether by causing food to rain down from heaven and providing the *bread of the angels*,² as Moses did of old,³ or by actually feeding thousands to the full with a few loaves in the desert, as Jesus later did,⁴ the true bread and source of the true life. It is not at all an easy task to discover the one virtue that surpasses all others and to give it the scepter and palm, just as it is not easy in a meadow fragrant with many blossoms to find the most fragrant and beautiful. One after the other they all beckon our sight and smell and plead to be picked first. At any rate, to the best of my ability, I propose to examine these matters as follows.

2. *Faith, hope, love,* are a fine thing, *these three;*⁵ Abram bears witness to faith, because he was justified for his faith;⁶ Enos, to hope, because he first *hoped to call upon* the name of the Lord,⁷ and also all just men who suffered because of their hope; the divine Apostle, to love, because he had the courage to call down a curse even upon himself for the sake of Israel;⁸ and *God* himself,

---

1. PG 35.857A–910D. Written in connection with the construction of a hospital complex in Caesarea in 368–72.
2. Ps 78.25 (LXX 77.25).
3. Ex 16.13–35.
4. Mt 14.15–21.
5. 1 Cor 13.13.
6. Gn 15.6.
7. Gn 4.26 LXX.
8. Rom 9.3.

whose name *is love*.⁹ Hospitality is a fine thing; among the just, the witness is Lot the Sodomite, no sodomite in character;¹⁰ among sinners, the harlot Rahab, no harlot by choice, who for her hospitality won praise and salvation.¹¹ Brotherly love is a fine thing; the witness is Jesus, who willed not only to be called our brother but also to suffer on our behalf. Love of mankind is a fine thing; the witness is again Jesus, who not only created mankind *for good works*¹² and joined his image to clay in order to guide us to the blessings of heaven in all their beauty and help us attain them, but also became man for our sake. Long-suffering is a fine thing; once again the witness is Jesus, who not only forbore to summon the *legions of angels* against those who rose in rebellion against him and to rebuke Peter for raising his sword, but even restored the ear of the man who had been struck.¹³ Stephen, too, the disciple of Christ, later acted in the same way when he prayed for those who were stoning him.¹⁴ Meekness is a fine thing, as Moses¹⁵ and David¹⁶ attest—this is the quality that Scripture ascribes to them above all—and their teacher, who neither wrangles, nor cries aloud, nor lifts up his voice in the street, nor offers resistance to those who lead him off.¹⁷

3. Zeal is a fine thing, as Phinehas attests, who by piercing the Midianite woman and the man of Israel with one blow that he might remove reproach from the people of Israel won a reputation for resolute action;¹⁸ and after him those who say, *I have been very jealous for the Lord,*¹⁹ and, For *I feel a divine jealousy for you*²⁰ and, *Zeal for thy house has consumed me;*²¹ and not only say these words, but also feel them. Mortification of the body is a fine thing; accept the evidence of Paul who continually disciplines himself and through Israel puts fear into those who in self-conceit indulge their bodies;²² and of Jesus himself who fast-

9. 1 Jn 4.8.
10. Gn 19.3.
11. Jos 2.1–24; Heb 11.31.
12. Eph 2.10.
13. Mt 26.53; Lk 22.50–51; Jn 18.10–11.
14. Acts 7.58–60.
15. Nm 12.3.
16. Ps 132.1 (LXX 131.1) LXX.
17. Is 42.2, 53.7; Mt 12.19.
18. Nm 25.6–8.
19. 1 Kgs 19.14.
20. 2 Cor 11.2.
21. Ps 69.9 (LXX 68.10); Jn 2.17.
22. Rom 11.17–25; 1 Cor 9.27.

ORATION 14

ed and was tempted and prevailed over the Tempter.[23] Prayer vigils are a fine thing; accept the evidence of God, who stayed sleepless praying before the Passion.[24] Purity and virginity are a fine thing; accept the evidence of Paul who prescribes rules for these matters and makes just provision for marriage and celibacy;[25] and of Jesus himself, who was born of a virgin in order to honor both birth-giving and especially virginity at the same time. Self-restraint is a fine thing; accept the evidence of David, who showed restraint in not drinking of the water from the well in Bethlehem but poured a libation instead, refusing to quench his own thirst with the blood of others.[26]

4. Solitude and quiet are a fine thing; this is the lesson I draw from Elijah's Carmel,[27] and John's wilderness,[28] and Jesus' mountain, to which he often retreated, as we know, and communed quietly with himself.[29] Simplicity is a fine thing; this is the lesson I draw from Elijah, who visits at the widow's house;[30] from John, who put on a garment of *camel's* hair;[31] from Peter, who fed on lupines bought for a farthing.[32] Humility is a fine thing; the examples are many and varied, but chief among them is the Savior and Lord of all who not only humbled himself to the point of taking the form *of a servant*[33] and submitted *his face* to the shame *of spitting*[34] and was numbered with the transgressors,[35] he who purges the world from sin,[36] but who also put on servant garb and washed his *disciples' feet*.[37] Poverty and contempt for worldly goods are a fine thing, as Zacchaeus attests and Christ himself, the one by offering almost everything he owned when Christ visited him,[38] Christ by defining a rich man's perfection as dependent on this very act.[39] And, to speak still more pointedly on these matters, contemplation is a fine

---

23. Mt 4.1–11.
24. Mt 26.36.
25. 1 Cor 7.25–39.
26. 2 Sm 23.15–17.
27. 1 Kgs 18.42.
28. Lk 1.80.
29. Mt 14.23; Jn 6.15; et al.
30. 1 Kgs 17.9–24.
31. Mt 3.4.
32. The allusion is not in Scripture, but cf. the Pseudo-Clementine *Homily* 12.6 (PG 2.305C). We thank Michael Slusser for this reference.
33. Phil 2.7.
34. Is 50.6.
35. Is 53.12.
36. Jn 1.29; 1 Jn 1.7.
37. Jn 13.5.
38. Lk 19.8.
39. Mt 19.21.

thing, as is action: the one because it rises above this world and advances towards the Holy of Holies and conducts our mind upward to what is akin to it, the other because it welcomes Christ and serves him and confirms the power of love through good works.

5. Each of these forms a single road to salvation, which has as its certain destination one of the blessed and everlasting abodes; for just as there is a wide variety of goals in life so in God's house also there are *many rooms*,[40] assigned and distributed on the basis of individual merit. One man may excel in one particular virtue, a second in another, a third in several, a fourth in all, if he can. Let him but attempt the journey and press forward, following in the steps of the one who with good guidance and direction leads us through *the narrow* way and *gate*[41] toward the wide spaces of heavenly bliss. Now if, following Paul and Christ himself, we must regard charity as the first and greatest of the commandments since it is the very sum of the Law and the Prophets,[42] its most vital part I find is the love of the poor along with compassion and sympathy for our fellow man. Of all things, nothing so serves God as mercy because no other thing is more proper to God, whose *mercy and truth go before*,[43] and to whom we must demonstrate our capacity for mercy rather than condemnation;[44] and by nothing else more than by showing compassion to our fellow man do we receive compassionate treatment in turn at the hands of him who weighs mercy in his scale and balance and gives just recompense.

6. We must, then, open our hearts to all the poor and to all those who are victims of disasters from whatever cause, for the commandment enjoins us to *rejoice with those who rejoice and weep with those who weep.*[45] Kindness is the gift we must, as human beings, proffer our fellow humans whatever the cause of their plight: widowhood, orphanhood, exile from homeland, savagery of tyrants, callousness of magistrates, ruthlessness of tax-

40. Jn 14.2.
41. Mt 7.13–14; Lk 13.24.
42. Mt 22.36–40.
43. Ps 89.14 (LXX 88.15) LXX: "steadfast love and faithfulness" RSV.
44. Lk 6.35–38.
45. Rom 12.15.

collectors, brutality of bandits, rapacity of thieves, confiscation or shipwreck. All alike deserve our pity and look to our hands just as we look to the hands of God whenever we are in need of something. And of these very victims those whose plight stands in contrast to their former state arouse greater sympathy than do those whose misfortune is chronic. I am referring particularly to those wasted with the sacred disease[46] that devours their flesh and bones and marrow clear through—the visitation that Scripture threatens against certain individuals[47]—and betrayed by this wretched, vile, and faithless body. How I came to be joined to it, I do not know; nor how I am the image of God and concocted of clay at the same time, this body that both wars against me when it is healthy and when warred against, brings me pain, that I both cherish as my fellow-servant and evade as my enemy; that I both try to escape as my chain and respect as my fellow heir. If I struggle to suppress it, I lose the helper I need to achieve my noble aims, knowing as I do why I was created and that it is through my actions that I am to ascend to God.

7. I show it consideration as a co-worker but I do not know how to suppress its insurgency nor how I can help falling away from God when the weight of its shackles drags me down and keeps me pinioned to the ground. It is an affable enemy and a scheming friend. What an incompatible alliance! I take good care of the object of my fear and feel dread before the object of my love. Before making war, I come to terms with it; before making peace, I am at odds with it. What is this wisdom that I embody? What is this great mystery? Or, is it his will that we, who are a portion of God and have our source in heaven above, should always look to him as we wrestle and fight against the flesh and that the weakness to which we are harnessed should serve to impress upon us our true worth, lest we disdain our Creator out of pride and an inflated sense of our own impor-

---

46. Although the term "sacred disease" normally refers to epilepsy, here it means leprosy. See LSJ, s.v., ἱερός IV.8, *PGL*, s.v., νόσος 1, and section 10, below. Cf. also *Or.* 43.63 (PG 36.577C–80C) where Gregory uses similar language in describing the leprosarium founded by his friend Basil as part of a larger hospital complex in Caesarea.

47. Ps 38.3 (LXX 37.4), 102.3–5 (LXX 101.4–6); cf. Jb 33.19–22.

tance? that we may know that we are at once most exalted and most humble, earthly and celestial, ephemeral and immortal, heirs of light and fire—or of darkness—depending on which way we turn? Such is our hybrid nature which, in my view at least, takes this form so that whenever we feel exalted because of our likeness to God's image, we may be brought down because of our clay. Let who will ruminate on these matters; we shall join him ourselves at a more appropriate time.

8. But now, though confronted with the suffering of others, I have been dwelling on the infirmity of my own flesh. We must, my brothers, as I started to say, look after it as being our kinsman and fellow-servant. For, even if I have denounced it as my enemy for the distress it causes, still, I also embrace it as a friend because of him who joined us together. And we must look after the physical needs of our neighbors, both the healthy and those consumed by the same ailment, no less than we do our individual persons. For we are all one in the Lord, rich or poor, slave or free, healthy or sick in body; and there is one head of all, Christ, who is the source of all things; and the same relationship that exists between the members of the body exists between ourselves, both as individuals and collectively.[48] This is why we must not overlook or neglect those who have fallen victim to our common infirmity before us; nor should our contentment, because we enjoy physical well-being, exceed our distress that our brethren fare ill. It is incumbent upon us to believe that the welfare of our own bodies and souls lies in this one thing, loving regard for our fellow man. Let us consider the matter as follows.

9. The pitiful plight of other people is due to one thing alone, a lack of material resources, a condition that might perhaps be corrected by time, or hard work, or a friend, or a relative, or a change in circumstances. But for these people, what is no less pitiful, indeed, even more so, is that, in addition, they are deprived of the opportunity to work and help themselves acquire the necessaries of life; and the fear of their illness ever outweighs any hope in their minds for well-being. As a result, hope, the only antidote for victims of misfortune, can be of little help to them. Besides poverty, they are afflicted with a sec-

48. Rom 12.5.

ond evil, disease, indeed, the most abhorrent and oppressive evil of all and the one that the majority of people are especially ready to label a curse. And third, there is the fact that most people cannot stand to be near them, or even look at them, but avoid them, are nauseated by them, and regard them as abominations, so to speak. It is this that preys on them even more than their ailment: they sense that they are actually hated for their misfortune. I cannot bear to think of their suffering without weeping; I am overcome by the mention of it; and I hope that you will feel as I do, and, through tears, dry their tears. Everyone present who loves Christ as well as the poor and who has a capacity for pity, which both defines God and derives from him, I am sure feels the same. But you have witnessed their distress even yourselves.

10. There lies before our eyes a dreadful and pathetic sight, one that no one would believe who has not seen it: human beings alive yet dead, disfigured in almost every part of their bodies, barely recognizable for who they once were or where they came from; or rather, the pitiful wreckage of what had once been human beings. By way of identification they keep calling out the names of their mothers and fathers, brothers, and places of origin: "I am the son of so-and-so. So-and-so is my mother. This is my name. You used to be a close friend of mine." And this they do because they cannot be identified from the way they used to look: mutilated, stripped of their possessions, their families, their friends, their very bodies; the only people in the world who hate and feel pity for themselves at the same time; who know not whether they should grieve more for the limbs they have lost or for those they have left; for those that disease has already eaten away or those it has not touched. The first have been eaten away in misery, the rest in greater misery preserved; the first have perished before burial, the others can rely on no one who will commit them to the grave, since even the most kind and considerate person shows no feeling at all for them. And on this account alone we have lost sight of the fact that we are flesh[49] and compassed in a lowly body, and we are so

---

49. Gn 6.3.

derelict in our obligation to look after our fellow man that we actually believe that avoiding these people assures the well-being of our own persons. There are those, of course, who handle ripe and, it may be, fetid corpses and haul the stinking carcasses of dumb animals and have no objections to being covered with muck. These unfortunates, on the other hand, we avoid at all costs—the inhumanity of it!—hardly abiding the thought that in fact we breathe the same air as they.

11. What could be more loyal than a father? What more devoted than a mother? Yet even their natural instincts have been denied to them. A father spontaneously grieves over his own son, the one he fathered and brought up, whom he regarded as the only light of his life, the object of so many fervent prayers to God; yet he drives him away in spite of himself. His mother relives the pain of giving birth and her heart is wrenched; and with piteous cries she keeps calling out his name and lays him out and makes lament over him living as though he were dead. "Hapless child of a heart-broken mother!" she sobs. "The disease has taken its bitter toll of us both. My poor child! My child that I do not recognize! My child that I raised in crags and *mountains and deserts*,[50] with wild beasts you will dwell and a rock will be your shelter and none but the most pious of men will look upon you." And then she cries out those piteous words of Job, *Why* were you formed in your mother's *belly* and *not* come forth *from the womb* and expire *immediately* so that your birth and death might be simultaneous? *Why* did you not die untimely, before tasting the sorrows of life? *Why* did *your knees* receive you? Why did you suck *the breasts*[51] when you were doomed to a life of misery, a life worse than death? As she says these words she unleashes a flood of tears; the poor woman wants to embrace her child's flesh but shrinks from it in hostile fear. Outcries and persecutions become their public lot, directed not against criminals but hapless victims. A man thinks nothing of taking up residence with a murderer and invites an adulterer to share not only his home but his board as well and chooses a temple-

---

50. Cf. Ezek 33.28, 35.15; Heb 11.38.
51. Jb 3.11–12.

robber as his boon companion and becomes friends with those who have mistreated him. Yet from the suffering of one who has done him no wrong he turns away as though it were a crime. And so malice wins out over disease and we embrace viciousness as the mark of the gentleman and reject sympathy as degradation.

12. They are driven away from cities, they are driven away from homes, from the market-place, from public gatherings, from the streets, from festivities, from drinking parties, even—how they suffer!—from water itself. They neither share the flowing springs with everyone else nor are they permitted the use of rivers to rinse away their contamination; and the strangest thing of all is that we drive them away from our midst as pariahs on one hand, and on the other bring them back to us claiming that they are really harmless, but all the while denying them shelter and failing to provide them with basic sustenance, treatment for their wounds, and dressing for their sores as best as we can. And so they wander about night and day, helpless, naked, homeless, exposing their sores for all to see, dwelling on their former state, invoking the Creator, leaning on each other's limbs in place of those they have lost, devising songs that tug at the heartstrings, begging for a crust of bread or a bit of food or some tattered rag to hide their shame or provide relief for their wounds. To them a kind benefactor is not someone who has supplied their need but anyone who has not cruelly sent them away. With most of them not even discomfiture is a deterrent from attending celebrations; quite the contrary, their destitution compels their attendance. I am referring, of course, to those religious festivals that we have organized for the public as a way of ministering to souls, when we meet either for some sacramental occasion or to celebrate the martyrs of truth with the aim of both honoring their trials and emulating their piety. Still, being human, they are both ashamed in the presence of their fellows on account of their misfortune, and they would rather be hidden in the mountains or crags or forests or, as a last resort, in the darkness of the night. Yet they throw themselves in our midst, miserable chattels, enough to make one weep (in fact there is perhaps a reason for this: they can serve as

reminders to us of our own weakness and dissuade us from attaching ourselves to any single circumstance in our present visible world as though it were permanent); yes, throw themselves, some from a desire to hear a human voice, others to look upon a human face, others to collect scraps of food from the well-to-do, but all to enjoy a measure of relief by baring their private woes.

13. Who is not overcome as their plaintive cries rise in a symphony of lament? What ear can bear the sound? What eye take in the sight? They lie beside one another, a wretched union born of disease, each contributing his own misfortune to the common fund of misery, thus heightening each other's distress; pitiful in their affliction, more so in the sharing of it. Some bystanders gather round them like spectators at a drama, deeply affected, but only for a moment. In the hot sun and the dust they writhe at men's feet; and sometimes, too, they are tormented by biting cold and rain and blasts of wind and narrowly escape being trampled on only because we find it repugnant to come into contact with them. Their mournful pleas stand in jarring contrast to the sacred chanting within and their piteous lament forms a counterpoint to the mystic voices. Why lay out the full measure of their tragedy to those in the midst of celebration? Perhaps I might raise a dirge even among yourselves, if I were to evoke in tragic detail all their sorrows; then their suffering will overwhelm your festal spirit. I speak this way because I am not yet able to persuade you that sometimes anguish is of more value than pleasure, sadness than celebration, meritorious tears than unseemly laughter.[52]

14. This is how they suffer, and in fact far more wretchedly than I have indicated, these, our brothers in God, whether you like it or not; whose share in nature is the same as ours; who are formed of the same clay from the time of our first creation, knit together *with bones and sinews* just as we are, clothed *with skin and flesh*[53] like everyone else (the divine Job says as much when in the course of his suffering he comes to understand how in-

---

52. Eccl 7.3.
53. Jb 10.11.

significant is our outward appearance); or rather, more importantly, who have the same portion as the image of God just as we do and who keep it perhaps better, wasted though their bodies may be; whose inner nature has put on the same *Christ*[54] and who have been entrusted with the same *guarantee of the Spirit*[55] as we; who have been given to share with us the same laws, prophecies, testaments, liturgies, sacraments, hopes; for whom Christ, *who takes away the sin of all the world*,[56] died just as he did for us; who are *fellow heirs*[57] of the life in heaven, even if they have met with so much misfortune here on earth; who are buried with Christ and raised with him,[58] *provided* they *suffer with him in order that* they *may also be glorified with him.*[59]

15. But what of ourselves? We have received as our inheritance the great and new designation derived from Christ's name, we, *the holy nation; the royal priesthood;* the *peculiar* and chosen *people;*[60] the one zealous *for good* and salutary *deeds;*[61] the disciples of Christ, the gentle[62] and loving[63] who has borne *our* infirmities,[64] who humbled himself so as to assume the lump of which we consist,[65] who *for* our *sakes* became poor in this flesh and earthly tabernacle of ours, who experienced pain and was bruised for us that we might become rich in divinity?[66] Yes, what of ourselves, who have been given so great a model of sympathy and compassion? What will our attitude towards these people be? What shall we do? Shall we neglect them? Walk on by? Dismiss them as corpses, execrable, the vilest of beasts and creatures that crawl? Most certainly not, my brothers! These actions become neither ourselves, the flock of Christ, the good shepherd[67] who brings back *the one that went astray* and seeks *the one which is lost* and strengthens the weak one;[68] nor do they become our human nature, which, learning piety and kindness from

---

54. Gal 3.27; 2 Cor 4.16.
55. 2 Cor 1.22, 5.5.
56. Jn 1.29.
57. Rom 8.17.
58. Col 2.12; Rom 6.4.
59. Rom 8.17.
60. Ex 19.5–6, 23.22; 1 Pt 2.9.
61. Ti 2.14.
62. Mt 11.29.
63. Cf. *Or.* 42.13 (PG 36.473A) for similar language.
64. Mt 8.17.
65. Phil 2.8; cf. 1 Cor 5.6–7; Gal 5.9.
66. Is 53.5; 2 Cor 8.9.
67. Jn 10.11.
68. Ezek 34.4–16; Mt 18.12; Lk 15.4.

our common weakness, has given compassion the force of law.

16. Will they, then, continue to suffer in the open while we lounge within luxurious homes bedecked with stone of every description, resplendent with gold and silver and the inlay of delicate mosaic and varied fresco that charm and beguile the eyes? Some we shall occupy ourselves, others we shall build, but for whom? Possibly not even for our own heirs, but for strangers and others not our kinsmen, and of these not even for the ones who are fond of us, I imagine, but—worst of all—our bitterest and most resentful enemies. They, in the meantime, will be shivering in their worn and tattered rags, if, that is, they are fortunate to have even those, while we pamper our own selves with soft, flowing gowns and filmy garments of linen and silk, costumes that will detract from rather than enhance our appearance—for this is how I regard anything that exceeds the bounds of need or practicality—while others we shall store away in vain and futile provision to be consumed by moths and all-devouring time. They, on the other hand, will lack even food enough to live—shame on my self-indulgence! woe for their misfortune!—but, fainting and famished, will lie in front of our doorways, without even the bodily wherewithal to beg—no voice to cry out in pain, no hands to stretch forth in supplication, no feet to carry them to the prosperous, no breath to swell their lamentation, deeming the heaviest of their ills the easiest to bear in that they actually feel gratitude to their eyes alone that they are spared the sight of their own ravaging.[69]

17. Such is their condition. As for us, we shall magnificently ensconce our magnificent selves on a high and lofty bed amid exquisite and delicate coverlets and be put out of temper if we so much as hear the sound of their begging. Our floors must be scented with flowers—oftentimes out of season at that—and our table drizzled with perfumes—naturally the most fragrant

---

69. Blindness is not a symptom of leprosy, at least in its modern form, although severe inflammation of the tissues surrounding the eye may produce the same practical result. Λώβη, "ravaging," is also Galen's term for the effect on the extremities of the limbs. See Pseudo-Galen, *Introductio seu medicus,* ed. C. G. Kühn, *Claudii Galeni opera omnia* (Leipzig, 1827; rpt. Hildesheim: Georg Olms, 1965), vol. 14, p. 757.

ORATION 14

and costly perfumes—that we may coddle ourselves all the more; and we must have slave boys to dance attendance on us, some lined up in order, their tresses loose and effeminate, their beards betraying too much care, their eyes made up to lascivious excess, others balancing wine cups on their finger tips with consummate at once poise[70] and care and others artificially stirring the air over our heads with fans or generating a breeze with their palms to cool our mass of flesh; and beside this, a table lavish with meats that all the elements of nature, air, earth, water, contribute in profusion to our meal, and crammed with the creations of cooks and caterers, all engaged in a contest to see who will have the most success in pandering to our indecent and ungrateful belly, that oppressive burden and author of evils, that most insatiable and treacherous beast, doomed to elimination along with its eliminated food.[71] While *they* would be quite satisfied with plain water, *we* keep demanding bowls of wine until we are drunk—or I should say even more than drunk, at least the more excessive among us. One vintage we shall send back, another will receive our seal of approval for its fragrant bouquet, we shall wax eloquent about the virtues of a third and we shall feel cheated if some imported name brand is not included along with the domestic variety to dominate the occasion like some foreign potentate. We feel obliged either to be, or to have the reputation of being, extravagant voluptuaries, as if it were shameful not to be considered depraved, slaves to the belly and what is below it.

18. Why is this so, my friends and brothers? Why are we ourselves sick in our very souls, with a sickness far worse than any that affect the body? For it is clear to me that bodily sickness is involuntary, but the other the result of deliberate choice; that the one comes to an end with the present life, but the other accompanies us when we leave this world; that the one is the object of pity, the other of hatred, at least on the part of those with any intelligence. Why do we not lend nature a helping hand while we have the chance? Why do we creatures of flesh make

---
70. I.e., without slipping.
71. Cf. 1 Cor 6.13 and *Or.* 6.6.

no attempt to succor our poor fleshly existence? Why do we revel amid the misfortunes of our brothers? God preserve me either from being prosperous when these are in want, or healthy if I do not try to assuage their wounds; from having enough food and clothing and a comfortable home if I do not offer them bread and give them as much to wear as I can and open my home to them. No; either we must set everything aside unto Christ that we may become his true followers, taking up the cross, and, unencumbered by anything that would drag us down, buoyantly soar to the world on high and gain Christ at the cost of everything else, ennobled through our humility and through our poverty enriched; or we must share what we have with Christ so that owning possessions may somehow be sanctified in itself by our putting them to good use and sharing them with those who have none. But even if I should sow for myself alone, then let me sow—but let others eat as well. To quote once again the words of Job, *Let thorns grow instead of wheat and foul weeds instead of barley*,[72] and a searing wind steal upon me, and a whirlwind wipe out my efforts so that my hard work go for naught. And even if I should build barns and store up wealth upon wealth, may my *soul this night*[73] be required to justify the treasures I have wickedly hoarded.

19. Will we never learn restraint, however late? Will we not repudiate our want of feeling, not to say petty selfishness? Will we not take note of our human condition? Will we not dedicate our own resources to the misfortunes of others? Nothing in human life is naturally secure or smooth or self-sustaining or permanent. Our fortunes run in a cyclical pattern that brings changes one after another, frequently within the space of a single day and sometimes even an hour, and one may rather count on the shifting winds, or the wake of a sea-faring ship, or the illusory dreams of night with their brief respite, or the lines that children at play trace in the sand, than on human prosperity. The wise are those who because of their distrust of the present save for themselves the world to come[74] and because of the un-

72. Jb 31.40.
74. Cf. Mt 6.20.

73. Lk 12.20.

certain and fickle nature of human success embrace the kindness that does not fail. Their aim is to gain in any case one at least of three things: never to become the victims of misfortune, since the Deity who elicits our compassion by his own kindness frequently honors the pious in kind here on earth; or to have a deep-seated confidence in God and believe that their misfortunes result not from sinfulness but somehow because of his plan; or, finally, to demand as their right from the prosperous the generosity that they showed to the needy when they enjoyed good fortune themselves.

20. *Let not the wise man glory in his wisdom,* says Scripture, nor *the rich man in his riches,* nor the *mighty man in his might,*[75] even if they have reached the pinnacle, respectively, of wisdom or wealth or power; and, I shall add also the corollaries, nor the celebrity in his fame, nor the robust in his health, nor the handsome in his good looks, nor the young man in his youth; in short, let no one be puffed up in anything else that is valued here on earth, *but let him who glories glory in this* alone, in the *understanding*[76] and seeking out of God, in sympathy for the afflicted, and in the laying by of something that will benefit him in the life to come. The other advantages are transitory and ephemeral and, like the pieces in a children's game, move this way and that and pass back and forth to different persons at different times, and nothing is so particularly one's own that it does not come to an end in time or change hands as a result of malice. These, on the other hand, are permanent and abiding; they never withdraw or fail or cheat the faithful of their hopes. But I think there is a further reason why no earthly good is trustworthy or durable for man (and, like everything else, the creative Word and the Wisdom that exceeds every intelligence has well contrived this too, that we be pawns amid the objects of sight, which change and are changed now one way now another, are borne up and down and all around, and slip away before we can lay hold of them): that when we contemplate the changeableness and caprice of this world we may seek out the

75. Jer 9.23.
76. Jer 9.24; cf. 1 Cor 4.6.

secure haven of the one to come. For what should we have done if our prosperity were permanent, given that now, though it is not, we are so firmly attached to it and held in such thrall by its deceptive pleasure that we cannot imagine anything better or higher than our present circumstances; and this despite the fact that we are taught and believe that we are created in the image of God which exists on high and draws us to itself?

21. *Who is wise, and will understand these things?*[77] Who will leave behind what is fleeting? Who will throw in his lot with what abides? Who will think of the present as passing away? Who what is hoped for as here and now? Who will distinguish between appearance and reality, ignore the one and court the other? Who between fact and fiction? Who between the tabernacle below and the city above? Who between temporary and permanent home? Who darkness from light? Who between the slime of the abyss and holy ground? Who between flesh and spirit? Who between God and world-ruler? Who between the shadow of death and the life eternal? Who will barter the things of the present for the future? Who the wealth that slips away from the kind that is not lost? Who things visible for things unseen? Yes, blessed is the man who distinguishes between these things, dividing them in accordance with the separation of the Word that divides the better from the worse,[78] and purposes *in his heart to go up,* as the divine David says at one point, and, fleeing this *valley of weeping,*[79] seeks with all his might *the things that are above,*[80] and takes his place at Christ's side, crucified to the world along with Christ,[81] and together with Christ ascends, heir to the life that no longer fails or deceives, where there is found no more *a biting viper by the path,*[82] watching against our *heel,* even as his own *head* is watched against.[83] The same David, just like a herald most loud of voice booming an important public proclamation, calling the rest of us slow of heart and lovers of *lies,*[84] rightly cries out to us not to cling so tightly to the visible world or to regard the sum of earthly happiness as nothing

---

77. Hos 14.10 LXX.
79. Ps 84.5–6 (LXX 83.6–7).
81. Gal 6.14.
83. Gn 3.15.

78. Cf. Heb 4.12.
80. Col 3.1.
82. Gn 49.17.
84. Ps 4.2.

more than a full supply of food and drink, perishable things. And I expect the blessed Micah too has something like this in mind when he says, confronting those who make a show of virtue as they creep along the ground, *Draw ye near to the everlasting mountains. Arise; for this is not thy rest.*[85] These are almost the very words that our Lord and Savior uses to admonish us. What does he say? *Rise, let us go hence.*[86] He is not merely conducting his disciples of the moment from that specific place, as one might think, but he is drawing all his disciples as well away for all time from the earth and the things of earth to the heavens and the blessings of heaven.

22. So let us now follow the Word; let us seek the repose on high; let us cast aside the opulence of this world; let us have recourse to only that portion of it that serves a good end; let us gain our lives by acts of charity;[87] let us share what we have with the poor that we may be rich in the bounty of heaven. Give a portion of your soul too, not just your body; give a portion to God too, not just the world; take something from the belly, dedicate it to the Spirit; pluck something from the fire, place it far from the devouring flame below; rob from the tyrant, commit to the Lord. *Give a portion to seven,* that is, to this life, *and even to eight,*[88] the life that will receive us after this one; give a little to him from whom you have so much; give even the whole to him who has bestowed all. You will never surpass God's generosity even if you hand over your entire substance and yourself in the bargain. Indeed, to receive in the truest sense is to give oneself to God. No matter how much you offer, what remains is always more; and you will be giving nothing that is your own because all things come from God. And just as a man cannot overtake his own shadow, which recedes with every forward step and always stays the same distance ahead; nor his bulk surmount the head that always lies above it, in the same way also we cannot outdo God in our gifts, for we do not give anything that is not his or that surpasses his own bounty.

23. Recognize the source of your existence, of your breath of

---

85. Mi 2.9–10 LXX.
87. Lk 21.19.
86. Jn 14.31.
88. Eccl 11.2.

life, your understanding, your knowledge of God (itself the greatest of all gifts), your hope of gaining the heavenly kingdom, equality of honor with the angels, the contemplation of glory that now appears in a mirror, dimly, but then will be more perfect and clear;[89] recognize that you have become a son of God,[90] fellow heir with Christ,[91] if I may be so bold, even very God. Where did you obtain all these things? From whom? Or, to speak of lesser matters, that is, the visible world around us, who gave you to see the beauty of heaven, the sun in its course, the orb of the moon, the countless stars and the harmony and order, just as in a lyre, that prevails among all these, the turning hours, the changing seasons, the cycle of years, the equal portioning of night and day, the burgeoning earth, the flowing air, the expanse of ocean at once fixed and free, the river depths, the streaming winds? Who gave you rain, husbandry, food, the arts, dwellings, laws, governments, a civilized mode of life, friendly converse with your fellow man? How is it that some animals have been domesticated and pull a plow while others supply you with meat? Who made you lord and king of everything on earth? Who, without listing them individually, endowed you with all the things that lift man above the rest of creation? Is it not he who now in return and exchange for all asks that you show kindness to your fellow man? Can we then not be ashamed if we, after all we have received from him and hope yet to receive, will not grant him even this one thing, kindness? He set us apart from the brute beasts and alone of the creatures on earth honored us with reason. Shall we now brutalize our own selves? Have we been so corrupted by our life of ease, or deranged, or I know not what, that along with the bran and barley cakes that we have procured for ourselves, possibly by foul means, we shall imagine that we are naturally superior to our fellows?[92] And just as there was once, at least so legend tells us, a race of giants set apart from the rest of mankind, shall we too tower over these people like supermen, like the famous Nim-

---

89. 1 Cor 13.12. 90. Rom 8.14; Gal 3.26.
91. Rom 8.17.
92. I.e., superior fare marks the superiority of those who eat it.

ORATION 14

rod[93] or the race of Anak that once oppressed Israel,[94] or those who provoked the flood that swept the earth clean?[95] He who is God and Lord does not shrink from being called our Father; shall we for our part deny our own kinsmen?

24. In no way, my friends and brothers! Let us not become bad *stewards* of the gifts we have received[96] lest we hear Peter say to us, Shame on you for clinging to what belongs to another; imitate God's equality, and no one will be poor.[97] Let us not struggle to amass and hoard fortunes while others struggle in poverty, lest from one direction the divine Amos reproach us with these harsh and ominous words, Come now, you who say, *When will the new moon be over,* that we may sell, *and the Sabbath,* that we may open our treasures? along with the words that follow, which hold the threat of God's wrath over the heads of those who possess a large and small weight;[98] and the blessed Micah, from another, who, convinced that excess breeds a wanton contempt towards others, rails, it would seem, even against all extravagance itself, the living delicately on beds of ivory and pampering oneself with the sleekest of ointments and waxing fat on the flesh of tender calves *from the midst of the stall* and lambs *from the flock* and clapping to *the sound of the harp* and, still more, believing that any of these things is abiding and permanent (but it may be he regards these activities as less shocking when compared with the fact that in their revelry they[99] were not grieved *over the ruin of Joseph,* for he adds this to his indictment of excess).[100] May we avoid the same fate in our day; may we not be so addicted to luxury as actually to scorn the compas-

---

93. Gn 10.8.
95. Gn 6.4–7.
94. Nm 13.32–33; Dt 9.2.
96. 1 Pt 4.10.
97. This citation of Petrine apocryphal material appears to be otherwise unattested except for a more extensive version preserved in the *Sacra Parallela,* an anthology attributed to John of Damascus (PG 95.1461D; K. Holl, *Fragmente vornicänischer Kirchenväter aus den Sacra Parallela* [Leipzig, 1899], p. 234, no. 503). See also E. von Dobschütz, *Das Kerygma Petri* (Leipzig, 1893), pp. 105–18, especially 110. Additional references in *Gregor von Nazianz, Reden: Über den Frieden. Über die Liebe zu den Armen,* trans. P. Haeuser, ed. M. Kertsch (Munich, 1983), p. 52, n. 3.
98. Am 8.5.
99. I.e., the sinners in Israel.
100. Am 6.4–7; Micah *lapsu memoriae,* or possibly conflated with Mi 6.10–16.

sion of a God who condemns this behavior, even though he does not turn his wrath upon sinners at the moment of their transgression or immediately after it.

25. Let us put into practice the supreme and first law of God, *who sends rain on the just and* on the sinners and makes his *sun rise* upon all alike.[101] To all the earth's creatures he has spread out land in spacious expanse and springs and rivers and forests; to the winged species he has given air, and to the creatures of the deep, water, and the basic requisites for life to all without stint, subject to no power, restricted by no law, isolated by no boundaries. On the contrary, he has set out the same necessities amply for all to share yet, for all that, in no way in short supply, thus both bestowing honor by the impartiality of his gift upon the equality of honor within the natural world and displaying the abundance of his own goodness. Yet men squirrel away gold and silver and quantities of soft and superfluous clothes and glittering jewels and similar items that bear the stamp of war and dissension and of the first act of rebellion, and then in their folly arch their brows and refuse to show compassion towards the unfortunate among their kinsmen. They are neither willing to help them with basic necessities out of their superfluity—what perversity! what stupidity!—nor do they reflect, if on nothing else, at least on the fact that poverty, wealth, what we call freedom, slavery, and such kinds of terms were introduced into human history at a later stage and stormed upon the scene like so many epidemics, as the companions of evil, whose brain-children they in fact are. But, as Scripture says, *from the beginning it was not so.*[102] He who created man from the beginning left him free and with free will, subject only to the law of his commandment and rich in the delights of Paradise. This was the gift he chose to bestow upon the subsequent generations of mankind also, through the one first seed. Freedom and wealth meant simply keeping the commandment; true poverty and slavery are its transgression.

26. But ever since, there have been jealousies and dissen-

---

101. Mt 5.45.
102. Mt 19.8.

sions and the deceitful tyranny of the serpent, which constantly seduces us with lewd pleasures and incites the more audacious against the weaker; and our human family has been so fragmented that we are now alienated from one another with a variety of labels, and greed has hacked away at the nobility of our nature to the point of arrogating even the legal process, the right arm of the power of government. But as for you, I ask you to look to that original egalitarian status, not the latter-day discrimination; not the law of the tyrant, but that of the Creator. Help nature as much as you can; honor your ancient freedom; cultivate your self-worth; draw a veil over the ignominy of our race; treat sickness; alleviate need: the healthy man, the need of the sick; the rich man, the need of the poor; the man who has not stumbled, that of him who lies fallen and crushed; the man full of spirit, that of the one discouraged; the one who enjoys prosperity, that of him who toils in adversity. Offer a gift of thanks to God that you are among those who are able to benefit others instead of those who require assistance; that you do not look to others' hands for help, but they to yours. Grow rich not in property alone but also in piety; not in gold alone, but also in virtue, or rather in this alone. Come to be held in higher esteem than your neighbor by proving yourself more kind. Come to be a god to the unfortunate by imitating God's mercy.

27. In nothing does man's affinity with God lie so much as in his capacity to do good. Even though God performs good works in greater and we in lesser number, each, I think we may say, does so in accordance with his power. God created us; and, when he frees us, he gathers us to him again. Do not you, in turn, neglect the one who has fallen. God has been merciful in the greatest ways, giving us in addition to everything else law and the prophets and, before these, the unwritten law of nature, the watchdog of our actions, by way of pricking our consciences and advising and directing us; ultimately surrendering himself to redeem the life of the world; blessing us with *apostles, evangelists, teachers, pastors,*[103] healings, miracles, restoration to life, abolition of death, triumph over him who prevailed over

---

103. Eph 4.11.

us, covenants, one in figure, one in realization, gifts *of the Holy Spirit*,[104] the mystery of the new salvation. As for you, if you are in fact capable of even higher things, things that have a salutary effect on the soul—for here too God has made you rich, if you should so choose—do not withhold also these benefactions from the one in need; or rather, as your first and foremost concern, try to give to him who begs from you even before his petition,[105] being merciful and ever lending your words[106] and solicitously seeking repayment of the loan with interest in the form of the spiritual increment of the one you have benefitted. In this way the beneficiary adds steadily to the deposit of your words and little by little makes grow in his own right the seeds of piety.[107] If you cannot, do at least the secondary, less important things and all that you can: extend a helping hand; offer food; give old clothes; provide medicine; bandage wounds; ask after them; counsel fortitude; offer encouragement; keep them company. You will not demean yourself in the process; you will not catch their malady even if the squeamish deceive themselves into believing such nonsense; or rather, this is how they justify their, call it over-cautious or sacrilegious, behavior; in point of fact, they are taking refuge in cowardice as though it were a truly worthwhile and wise course of action. On this score accept the evidence of science as well as of the doctors and nurses who look after these people. Not one of them has ever yet endangered his health through contact with these patients. You, then, servant of Christ, who are devoted to God and your fellow man, granted we are dealing with a terrible affliction, one that should make us careful, do not give in to small-mindedness; draw strength from your faith; let compassion overcome your misgivings, the fear of God your fastidiousness; let piety come before considerations of the flesh; do not disregard, do not walk past your brother; do not turn away from him as though he were an abomination, a blight, or anything else that one should avoid and repudiate. He is part of you, even if he is bent down with misfortune. *The hapless commits himself to thee*,[108] as to God, even if

104. Heb 2.4.
106. Ps 37.26 (LXX 36.26).
108. Ps 10.14 (LXX 9.35).

105. Mt 5.42.
107. Cf. 1 Cor 3.6–7.

you arrogantly hurry past him (perhaps my choice of words will make you feel ashamed). The opportunity to show compassion lies open to you even if the Alien One alienates you from the satisfaction.

28. For everyone who puts out to sea shipwreck is an ever-present possibility, and all the more so the more intrepid the sailor. Likewise, bodily ills are ever-present to everyone invested with a body, and all the more so if he walks with his head held high and pays no heed to those lying at his feet. As long as you sail with the wind at your back, give a hand to the castaway. As long as you are prosperous and whole, help the one in distress. Do not wait to learn first-hand what a terrible thing inhumanity is and what a blessing a heart open to those in need. Do not invite God to raise his hand against those too proud to take notice of the poor. Here is how you should respond to the misfortunes of others: give something to the needy even if it is a little; it is not to the one who is utterly destitute, nor to God either, if it is the best in your power. Offer your hearty goodwill in lieu of a large donation; if you own nothing, shed a tear; compassion that issues from the heart is a great balm for the afflicted, and sincere sympathy goes a long way in lightening the burden of misfortune. A human being, my good fellow,[109] is not less important to you than a farm animal that has fallen into a ditch or wandered off and that the Law obligates you to extricate and return.[110] (Whatever other meaning, deeper and more hidden, the Law masks in the profundity it so often employs, this is not for me to know but the Spirit who searches and understands *everything*.[111] My limited understanding of the passage, at any rate, is that it is exercising us in the kindness that applies to little matters and guiding us toward the greater and more perfect form of it.) If we are expected to show kindness even to brute beasts, how much do we owe our own kind, our equals in worth?

29. This, then, is what reason and the Law demand, as well as the most sensible among us, who agree that it is more honor-

---

109. Gregory uses the generic term for human being, ἄνθρωπος, in this phrase, which might be literally rendered as "Man, O man."
110. Dt 22.1–4.
111. 1 Cor 2.10.

able to be a benefactor than a beneficiary and that compassion should be more keenly cultivated than profit. What would you say of the sages in our midst? I am excluding the heathens: they dream up gods to cater to their baser instincts, particularly the Bringer of Gain,[112] on whom they bestow highest honors. In fact—and this is worse—there are a number of tribes that practice even human sacrifice by way of honoring some of their deities. Barbarity for them is a form of piety. They derive great pleasure themselves from sacrifices of this sort, and, becoming in the process vicious priests and devotees of vicious rites, think that their gods share their sentiments. Yet there are certain people in our own midst—it is enough to make one weep—who, so far from commiserating with those in distress and helping them, actually subject them to cruel verbal and physical abuse. Mouthing vain and empty platitudes and truly speaking *from the earth*[113] and talking to the air instead of to discriminating ears familiar with God's precepts they even have the impudence to say, "Their affliction comes from God, as does our prosperity. Who am I to overturn God's ruling and appear more merciful than God? Let them struggle, let them suffer, let them be unfortunate; it is God's will." This, in truth, is the only time they display any love for God, that is, when they feel obliged to watch their pennies and bully the helpless. Their words make it quite plain that they do not believe that their good fortune comes from God. After all, who could entertain such notions regarding the needy if he were convinced that it is God who gave him his possessions? For those who possess a gift from God and those who use their possessions in his service are by definition one and the same.

30. But whether their affliction actually comes from God will remain obscure so long as matter stays true to its nature, unsteady as in a stream. Who really knows whether one man is punished for his misdeeds while another is exalted for praiseworthy behavior, or whether the opposite holds true: one man is placed on a pedestal because of his wickedness while another

---

112. I.e., Hermes. Cf. *Or.* 4.121 (PG 35.661A) and 5.32 (PG 35.705B).
113. Is 29.4.

is tested because of his goodness, the one raised higher that he may fall the harder, allowed to let his evil erupt like an abscess beforehand in order that his punishment may be all the more justified, the other persecuted for no discernible reason in order that any impurity he has, even if scant, may be smelted out, like gold refined in a furnace? For no one is completely free from corruption, certainly if born in nature, as we are told,[114] even though he may appear worthy. I find a similar sense of mystery in Scripture although it would take long to enumerate all the expressions of the Spirit that lead me to this conclusion. Nay, *who* could measure the grains of sand *of the sea, and the drops of rain,* and the fathoms of the deep? *Who* could find out the depths of God's wisdom[115] in all things whereby he has both created the universe and directs it in the way he himself both wishes and knows? It is enough, as the divine Apostle says, merely to express wonderment at the inscrutability and incomprehensibility of it and pass on. *O the depth of the riches and wisdom and knowledge of God! How unsearchable are his judgments, and how inscrutable his ways!* and, *Who has known the mind of the Lord?*[116] Job says, Who has come *to the limit* of his wisdom?[117] *Who is wise and will understand these things*[118] and will not measure by a standard beyond his reach what is beyond measurement?

31. So let someone else flaunt a cavalier attitude toward these matters, or, rather, let no one do so. As for me, I am reluctant to attribute every instance of hardship here below to moral turpitude or the reprieve therefrom to piety. The fact is that, sometimes, for some utilitarian end, either evil is held at bay through the misfortune of malefactors or the cause of virtue advanced by the prosperity of the righteous; on the other hand, not always, of course, or fully, because this, I say, is the function only of the age to come, when one group will receive the rewards of their virtue and the other the wages of their sinfulness. The one will arise *to the resurrection of life* and the other *to the resurrection of judgment,*[119] says Scripture, whereas the things of this earth are of a different kind and a different mode of existence:

---

114. Jb 25.4.
115. Sir 1.2–3.
116. Rom 11.33–34.
117. Jb 11.7.
118. Hos 14.9 LXX.
119. Jn 5.29.

they tend all toward the other life where the very treatment that appears to us inequable possesses, we may be sure, a kind of equity in God's eyes, just as in the body beauty is to be found and appreciated in the interrelation between its prominences and its recesses, large and small, and, in a landscape, between its heights and its valleys. The same holds true with a craftsman: material that is uneven and asymmetric at the start becomes an artistic whole if it is shaped with a particular composition in mind. When we see the creation in finished form, that is when we too realize and concede its beauty. So, unlike ourselves, neither does God lack artistry nor does he manage our affairs indiscriminately just because we are not privy to the reasons behind them.

32. If we may adopt an image to describe our condition, there is not much difference between ourselves and those who are seasick and dizzy. They think that everything is spinning round when it is they who are doing the spinning. The persons of whom we are speaking are in a similar predicament. They refuse to accept that God is wiser than they if some incident throws them off balance. They should direct their efforts to learning the reason in the hope that their labor will be rewarded with the truth; or they should have a serious discussion with those who are wiser in these matters than themselves and more spiritual (since this, too, is a special gift;[120] knowledge is not a universal attainment); or they should pursue this knowledge through a purity of life and seek wisdom from the true Wisdom. Instead—what stupidity!—they take the easier way and condemn the universe as irrational when the irrationality arises from their own ignorance. And so they are wise in their stupidity, or rather, unwise and unknowing in a wisdom I can only describe as bizarre.[121] As a result, one school of thought has for-

---

120. Cf. 1 Cor 12.8.
121. The unifying theme of the following passage is the attack on those who from one perspective or another denied or in some way compromised the operation of Providence or Πρόνοια. The views put forward here thus do not represent the positions of any particular contemporary sect but rather reflect the rich eclecticism of late antiquity, an age when the educated elite, Christian as well as pagan, were conversant with the concepts and vocabulary of a philosophical tradition that extended from classical antiquity and the ancient near east to their

ORATION 14   65

mulated the doctrine of fate and a mechanical universe, themselves truly mechanical and fortuitously contrived concepts;[122] another postulates some kind of irrational and indissoluble dominion of stars that orchestrate our existence to suit themselves, or, I should say, are themselves moved to do so by some external necessity; and, further, conjunctions and oppositions on the part of certain planets and fixed stars as well as a universal motion that controls all things.[123] Others have resorted to inflicting their private fantasies upon the poor human race and have broken down every aspect of Providence that eludes their perception and understanding into diverse systems of jargon and belief. There are others still who charge that Providence actually has very limited resources at its disposal; while holding to the view that the realm above us is governed by it, they shrink from bringing it down to our human level where it is really needed,[124] as though afraid that they will make our benefactor too benevolent if too many people profit from his benefactions, or that they will be neglected if God becomes exhausted from benefiting too many.[125]

---

own day. For further discussion and references, see F. Trisoglio, "Reminiscenze e consonanze classiche nella XIV orazione di San Gregorio Nazianzeno," *Atti della Accademia delle Scienze di Torino* 99 (1964–65): 129–204, especially 189–93, and Haeuser and Kertsch, *Reden,* cited above in section 24.

122. On the terms τύχη and τὸ αὐτόματον, here translated as "fate and a mechanical universe," see especially Aristotle, *Physics* 2.4–6 (196b31–98a12) and the collection of sources assembled by the fifth century A.D. anthologist Stobaeus 1.6, ed. Wachsmuth-Hense, vol. 1, pp. 83–90. These concepts reflect the views not only of the original Atomists, such as Democritus, and of course their latter-day representatives, the Epicureans, but also those Stoics who from an opposing standpoint found such terminology useful for describing the unknown modes of operation of a basically providential universe.

123. On the conjunctions of planets and stars, cf. Aristotle, *Meteorology* 1.6 (343b30), where such lore is attributed to the Egptians; on the "universal motion that controls all things," cf. Aristotle, *Physics* 2.4 (196a27).

124. Gregory is arguing here against the largely Peripatetic notion that limited the operation of Providence to the upper realm or steadily reduced its influence the closer it came to human affairs and the more distant from the heavens. Our author is basically on the side of the Stoics with their view of an all-pervading Πρόνοια *(Pronoia).* Cf. also *Or.* 27.10 (PG 36.24C), where Gregory is similarly critical of "Aristotle's trifling providence."

125. For this satirical approach, cf. Gregory's *Poemata Dogmatica* 1.6, lines 8–9 (PG 37.430A): "Away with those who deny *Pronoia,* as if fearing salvation

33. But, as I have said, let us have nothing at all to do with these people. Scripture has in fact already dealt with them effectively. *Their senseless minds became vain*, the Bible says; *claiming to be wise, they became fools, and exchanged the glory of the immortal God*[126] by insulting universal Providence with fairy stories and shadowy figments. As for us, let us neither invent these monstrous fantasies ourselves if indeed we, who use reason and are devotees of reason, have any regard for reason, nor let us endorse those who entertain such ideas, even if their ridiculous theories and beliefs roll glibly off their tongues and they enjoy the novelty in them. No; let us rather both believe that God is the Maker and Creator of all things—for how could the whole have come into existence if someone did not give it substance and form?—and also include Providence, whose role it is to bind and keep this whole together, since one who creates necessarily also makes provision for his creation. The alternative is to assume that the whole proceeds under its own power and will, like a ship in the storm, founder and break up amid the turmoil of matter and revert to its original chaos and disorder. And let us have faith that our—call him what you will, Maker or Shaper—gives especial attention to our affairs even if our lives take an adverse turn quite unintelligible to us, perhaps for the purpose of having us admire, through our difficulty of comprehension, the reason that transcends all things. For everything that is easily grasped is easily despised, but what is beyond us increases our admiration in proportion to our difficulty in apprehending it; and everything that exceeds our reach whets our desire.

34. This is why we should neither admire health nor loathe disease indiscriminately; nor embrace ephemeral prosperity more warmly than behooves us and become caught up in its flux and in the process bankrupt, as it were, a portion of our soul on account of it; nor attack poverty as though it were thoroughly damned and despicable and in the class of hateful

---

from God." The technique adopted in this section as a whole owes much to the habits of Cynic-Stoic diatribe. Cf. also the Academic attack on the Stoic position in Cicero, *De natura deorum* 3.92–93.
126. Rom 1.21–23.

things. Instead, let us cultivate both contempt for that benighted health whose fruit is sin and respect for that disease that bears the badge of saintliness by showing reverence toward those who have triumphed through suffering, lest perchance there lie buried among the sick a second Job, one far more worthy of our reverence than the healthy, even if he is scraping away *the discharge*, even if he is suffering night and day *in the open air*, assailed by his wounds and his wife and his friends.[127] Our aim must be both to turn away from ill-gotten gains—the reason why the rich man is justly tormented in the flame and pleads for a sip of refreshment—and to applaud the poverty that shows patience and gratitude, the one by which Lazarus secures salvation and is rich in repose in *Abraham's* bosom.[128]

35. There is, however, in my opinion, an additional reason for regarding love of one's fellow man and compassion towards those in need as necessary: we are thus enabled to put a curb on those who feel as they do about these unfortunates, and we do not succumb to vacuous arguments and in the process lay the groundwork for cruelty against our own selves. There is one commandment and model that we should honor before any other. Which is it? Notice how timeless its truth is. Men of the Spirit have not been content with making a pronouncement about the poor once or twice, and be done with it; nor have only some done so and not others, or some to a greater, and others to a lesser extent, as though one were dealing with a matter of no great importance or one not on the list of very pressing concerns. Quite the opposite: this is the first cause, or among the first, that everyone to a man urges with great feeling, sometimes with exhortations, sometimes with threats, sometimes with reproaches, and sometimes also with words of approbation for those who do good deeds in this way, in order that by their persistent reminders they might make the commandment a living force. Scripture says, *Because the poor are despoiled, because the needy groan, I will now arise, says the Lord.*[129] Who does not fear the Lord aroused? It says, *Arise, O Lord my God; lift up thy hand; forget not the afflicted.*[130] Let us pray that there be no such lifting

127. Jb 2.8–9 LXX.
129. Ps 12.5 (LXX 11.6).
128. Lk 16.22–25.
130. Ps 10.12 (LXX 9.33).

up; let us be determined not to see his hand raised against those who reject him, or still more, raining blows on the pitiless. It says, *He does not forget the cry of the afflicted;*[131] it says, *The needy shall not always be forgotten;*[132] it says, *His eyes* (better and stronger than "eyelid") behold *the poor.* It says, *His eyelids test the children of men*[133]—the lesser, so to speak, and secondary form of oversight.

36. Someone might interject, "These remarks are by way of support for the destitute and impoverished who are the victims of injustice." I do not disagree. Let this, however, be an added incentive to philanthropic effort on your part. So many words expended on their unjust treatment! If we gave them some actual help, their gratitude—do not doubt it—would be greater. For if he who mocks the poor insults his maker,[134] then he honors the Creator, who looks after his creature. Again, when you read, *The rich and the poor meet together; the Lord is the maker of them both,*[135] do not suppose that his making one poor and the other rich justifies harsh treatment of the poor on your part. There is no evidence that such a distinction originates with God. Both alike are God's creation, according to Scripture, despite their superficial disparities. Let this fact shame you into showing sympathy and brotherhood, so that when your pride is puffed up by those externals, this realization may chasten you and make you grow more humble. What else? *He who is kind to the poor lends to the Lord,*[136] says Scripture. Who does not welcome such a debtor, who in time will repay the loan with interest? And again, *By alms and faithfulness iniquity is atoned for.*[137]

37. Let us therefore purify ourselves through acts of mercy; let us take the fine soap and wash away the marks of filth and defilement from our souls; and let us become white, some *like wool* and others like snow[138] according to the measure of our compassion. Let me mention something even more frightening: if you do not have a fracture, or a *bruise* or a *bleeding*

131. Ps 9.12.
132. Ps 9.18.
133. Ps 11.4 (LXX 10.4).
134. Prv 17.5.
135. Prv 22.2.
136. Prv 19.17.
137. Prv 16.6 (15.27 LXX); "alms," LXX; "loyalty," RSV.
138. Ps 51.7 (LXX 50.9); Is 1.18.

ORATION 14

wound,[139] or any leprosy of the soul, either *an eruption* or *a spot*,[140] conditions that require the healing power of Christ, since the old dispensation did little to clear them away, still, you should revere him who endured wounds and frailty for our sakes; and you will show your reverence if you are kind and compassionate to one who is a member of Christ.[141] If, on the other hand, the thief and usurper of our souls by chance so crippled you either as you came down from Jerusalem to Jericho,[142] or overtaking you in some other place, helpless and unarmed, so that you might with good reason utter those words of Scripture, *My wounds grow foul and fester because of my foolishness*,[143] if your attitude is such that you neither seek treatment nor are aware how you might be cured, woe indeed for your wound and the depth of your affliction! If, on the other hand, your condition is not yet completely and hopelessly incurable, approach the Healer, pray to him, heal your wounds through his, acquire like through like, or, rather, be cured of things greater by things lesser. He will say *to* your *soul, I am your deliverance*,[144] and *Your faith has made you well*,[145] and *See, you are well*,[146] and all his words of compassion, provided he sees you compassionate towards those in pain.

38. *Blessed are the merciful*, says Scripture, *for they shall obtain mercy*[147] (Mercy is not low on the list of the beatitudes); it says, *Blessed is the man who thinks on the poor and needy*;[148] it says, *It is well with the man who deals generously and lends*;[149] it says, *The just man is ever giving liberally and lending*.[150] Let us appropriate the beatitude; let us earn a name for thoughtfulness; let us become good. Not even night should interrupt your mission of mercy. *Do not say, go and come again, tomorrow I will give* it to you.[151] Do not let anything come between your impulse to do good and its execution: compassion, this alone, cannot be put off. *Share your bread with the hungry, and bring the homeless poor into your house*,[152]

139. Is 1.6.
140. Lv 13.2.
141. 1 Cor 6.15.
142. Lk 10.30.
143. Ps 38.5 (LXX 37.5).
144. Ps 35.3 (LXX 34.3).
145. Mt 9.22.
146. Jn 5.14.
147. Mt 5.7.
148. Ps 41.1 (LXX 40.2) LXX.
149. Ps 112.5 (LXX 111.5).
150. Ps 37.26 (LXX 36.26).
151. Prv 3.28.
152. Is 58.7.

and do so gladly. *He who does acts of mercy,* says Scripture, let him do so *with cheerfulness.*[153] The good you do has twice the value when done promptly. What is done in bad grace or under duress is both distasteful and repellent. Doing good is cause for celebration, not complaint. *If you take away the yoke,* says Scripture, *the pointing of the finger* (I take this to mean hypercritical or suspicious scrutiny), *and speaking wickedness,* what will be the result? What a great and wonderful thing! What a magnificent reward for your actions! *Your light shall break forth like the dawn, and your healing shall spring up speedily.*[154] Is there anyone who does not wish for light and healing?

39. I am moved also by Christ's *money box,*[155] which urges us to feed the poor; and Peter and Paul's pact to include the poor in their evangelical mission;[156] and by the young man whose perfection is defined by the precept of giving one's goods to the poor.[157] Do you think that compassion is not an obligation upon you but a matter of choice? Not rule but recommendation? This is what I myself also should very much like to think, but I stand in terror of his left hand, and the goats,[158] and the rebukes leveled against them by the one who has summoned them. They are condemned to take their places on the left not because they stole, or committed sacrilege, or fornicated, or violated any other taboo, but because they did not serve Christ through the poor.

40. If, then, you place any credence in what I say, servants of Christ and brothers and follow heirs,[159] while we may, let us visit Christ, let us heal Christ, let us feed Christ, let us clothe Christ, let us welcome Christ,[160] let us honor Christ, not with food alone, like some;[161] nor with ointments, like Mary;[162] nor with tomb alone, like Joseph of Arimathea; nor with obsequies, like Nicodemus,[163] who loved Christ in half measure; nor with gold and frankincense and myrrh as the Magi[164] did before these oth-

---

153. Rom 12.8.
155. Jn 12.6.
157. Mt 19.21.
159. Rom 8.17; Eph 3.6; et. al.
161. Lk 7.36.
163. Jn 19.38–39.

154. Is 58.8–9.
156. Gal 2.10.
158. Mt 25.32–33.
160. Mt 25.35.
162. Jn 12.3.
164. Mt 2.11.

ers. Rather, since the Lord of all will have *mercy, and not sacrifice*[165] and since a kind heart is worth more than myriads *of fat sheep*,[166] this let us offer to him through the poor who are today downtrodden, so that when we depart this world they may receive us into the eternal habitations[167] in Christ himself, our Lord, to whom be the glory forever. Amen.

165. Mt 9.13.
166. Dn 3.39 LXX.
167. Lk 16.9.

ORATION 15

In praise of the Maccabees.[1]

THE MACCABEES: the festival today is indeed in their honor, though not many recognize them because their martyrdom antedates Christ.[2] Yet they deserve universal recognition for their unswerving devotion to the ways of their fathers. Consider what they, whose martyrdom preceded Christ's passion, would have achieved if they had been persecuted after the time of Christ and were able to emulate his death on our behalf. If they were able to display valor of this magnitude without the benefit of such a model, how could they not have gained in heroic stature had they undertaken their trial with the example before them? Not one of those who attained perfection before the coming of Christ accomplished his goal without faith in Christ. While this statement is both arcane and even to a certain extent mystic, I for one consider it very persuasive, as do all who love Christ. For although the Logos was later openly proclaimed in his own era, he was made known even before to the pure of mind, as is evident from the large number of persons who achieved honor before his day.

2. Such noble figures, then, are not to be overlooked because they lived before the time of the cross, but should rather be acclaimed for having lived in accordance with the cross, and are entitled to the honor that words bestow, not with the object of enhancing their reputation—how could it be? Their exploits have secured them renown—but to glorify those who sing their praises and inspire those in the audience to emulate their valor,

---

1. PG 35.912A–33A. Delivered December 362 in Nazianzus.
2. Although the Maccabean martyrs were known and cited by early Christian writers along with other Old Testament figures such as Daniel, they do not appear to have been singled out for special veneration prior to this sermon.

goading them, as it were, by commemoration into matching it. Who were these people? Where did they come from? What kind of culture and education did they have so as to rise to such a peak of valor and renown that they are both honored annually with these festal processions and every heart treasures their glory in greater measure than these visible expressions indicate? The studious and diligent will find the answers to these questions in the book[3] about them that advances the view that reason is dominant over the emotions and has the power to incline us in both directions, virtue or vice. The author focuses on the struggles of the Maccabees but employs a number of other examples as well to corroborate his thesis.[4] I, however, shall confine my remarks to what follows.

3. On the one side we have Eleazar,[5] who was the first of the pre-Christian martyrs, just as Stephen was the first in the Christian era,[6] a priest and an elder, hoary of hair, hoary in wisdom. In an earlier day he had prayed and sacrificed on behalf of his people, but now, in an auspicious prelude to martyrdom, he offered himself up to God as a perfect sacrifice, a cleansing of all his people, and an exhortation to them both by his words and by his silent example; and he offered up also the seven young men, the fruit of his own guidance, as *a living sacrifice, holy and acceptable to God*,[7] one more splendid and more pure than any ritual observance of the law. It is among both the most right and the most just of sentiments to ascribe children's qualities to their father.[8]

On the other side there are the children,[9] high-souled and high-minded, noble scions of a noble mother, zealous champions of the truth, more princely than the age of Antiochus,[10]

---

3. Gregory is referring to 4 Maccabees, a Stoic diatribe formerly known under the title *On the Supremacy of Reason* and ascribed to Josephus, which elaborates on the story told in 2 Mc 6.18–7.42.
4. 4 Mc 1.7–8. These examples include Joseph, Moses, Jacob, David, Daniel, and the Three Children.
5. 2 Mc 6.18–31; 4 Mc 5–7.   6. Acts 7.59.
7. Rom 12.1.
8. Here, "father" should be understood in the spiritual rather than biological sense as at 4 Mc 7.1; cf. 4 Mc 18.9.
9. 2 Mc 7; 4 Mc 8–12.
10. Antiochus IV Epiphanes, Seleucid king of Syria (175–164 B.C.).

true disciples of the Mosaic Law, scrupulous observers of ancestral custom, their number [i.e., seven] held in high regard by the Hebrews, who celebrated it as a symbol of the rest on the seventh day,[11] breathing one spirit, having one goal, knowing one way of life, namely, to die in God's service, brothers in soul no less than in body, vying with one another over death, rushing forth—how miraculous!—to accept their torments as if they were pieces of gold, eager to lay down their lives in defense of the law that was their guide, not so much afraid of the tortures that were being inflicted as they were desirous of the ones still kept in reserve, their only fear being that the tyrant would tire of his cruelties and let some of them depart uncrowned, separated from their brothers against their will by a possible reprieve and thus an ignoble victory.

4. There was their mother,[12] noble and of high mettle, devoted alike to her children and to God, her mother's heart brutally[13] wrenched because, instead of pitying her children's suffering, she was racked by the fear that they would not suffer at all; nor did she miss the ones who had passed away so much as she hoped that the survivors would be united with them; and it was these last that concerned her more, not the departed, because their contest was still undecided while the others had already secured the outcome. These she had already commended to God; the rest she was anxious for God to take. The heart of a man in a woman's body![14] What an incredibly magnanimous act, a sacrifice the equal of Abraham's, unless we dare call it even greater! For Abraham willingly offered one son, though it was his only child and the one of promise, indeed, the one to whom the promise referred and, more important, who formed the root and origin not only of his race but also of sacrifices of this kind;[15] while she, on the other hand, consecrated her whole brood to God, showing herself without peer among mothers

---

11. Cf. 4 Mc 14.7–8.
12. 2 Mc 7.20–41; 4 Mc 14.11–20.
13. Literally, "contrary to the likelihood of nature."
14. Cf. 2 Mc 7.21. Gregory refers to his mother Nonna in similar language at *De vita sua* 60.
15. Cf. 4 Mc 16.20.

and priests because of the willingness for slaughter that the victims, these eager sacrifices and spiritual holocausts, displayed. She bared her breasts and reminded them of the nurture they had given[16] and pointed to her grizzled head and, instead of pleading with them, cited her advanced years. She sought not to save them but to hasten their martyrdom. In her mind the danger lay not in death but in delay. Nothing made her bend or flinch or lose courage, not the joint-dislocators dangled before them, not the torture-wheels being brought up, not the racks, not the catapults,[17] not the sharp iron claws, not the honing of swords, not the seething cauldrons, not the fanning of the flames, not the tyrant's threats, not the crowd, not the impatience of the guard, not the sight of her family, not the dismembering of limbs, not the shredding of flesh, not the gushing torrents of blood, not the ravaging of young life, not the horrors at hand, not the pains to come; and the drawn out ordeal, which others in similar straits find hardest to bear, was for her the easiest thing of all: she gloried in the sight. For their agonies were somehow prolonged not only by the variety of the torments, the whole of which they treated with a contempt that a single person could not muster for even one, but also by the verbal wiles of the persecutor who alternately railed, threatened, wheedled. Was there anything he did not do to accomplish his goal?

5. What is more, the children's replies to the tyrant were marked by such a combination of wisdom and dignity that the collective virtues of the rest of mankind pale in comparison with their endurance; but even their endurance pales before the shrewdness of their words. For they alone had the capacity, amid their grievous suffering, to retain their composure in facing the persecutor's threats and the dire punishments that confronted them. The brave children did not flinch before a single one, nor did their even braver mother. Instead, she rose high above it all and, commingling courage and love, gave herself as a glorious funeral offering for her children by following after those who had already passed on. In what way? Of her own accord she took

---

16. Homer, *Iliad* 22.79–89.
17. An instrument of torture here and at 4 Mc 8.13.

up their trials and delivered—what kind of eulogy? Fine were the words that those fine children spoke to the tyrant, very fine indeed. How could they not be, since it was with them that they took their stand and assailed the despot? Yet finer still were the words their mother addressed to them both when she was encouraging them and later when she buried them. What was it, then, that the children said? It is good for you to be aware of these assertions so that you might have an example not only of the struggle for martyrdom but also of the words proper to martyrs in such circumstances. They were different in each case according to the way each brother found reinforcement in the persecutor's remarks or the sequence of the tortures or his own spiritual ardor. In sum, however, they were as follows:[18]

"For us, Antiochus and all of you here present, there is but one king, God, from whom we have our being and to whom we shall return; and but one lawgiver, Moses, whom we will not betray or offend—we swear this by the perils that the great man faced for virtue's sake and by his many miracles—not even if a second Antiochus more brutal than yourself should threaten us. Our only security is the keeping of the commandment and desisting from any breach of the law, which is our bulwark; our only glory the contempt with which we reject all glory in favor of aims so great; our only riches the expectation of things to come; and we fear nothing save that anything should supplant our fear of God. These are the beliefs on which we take our stand; these are the weapons with which we are armed; such are the young men you address. A sweet thing is this world and our ancestral homeland and our friends and kinsmen and comrades and this temple with its great and celebrated name and our time-honored festivals and rites and all the things that in men's eyes set us apart from other people; but in no way are they sweeter than God and the dangers we encounter on behalf of goodness. Do not imagine so. We belong to a different world far more sublime and abiding than what you see around you. Our homeland is *the Jerusalem above*,[19] the mighty and invincible one that no Antiochus shall besiege or hope to subdue; our kin-

---

18. Cf. 4 Mc 9–12.
19. Gal 4.26.

ship is with the inspiration that we draw from the sons of virtue; our friends are prophets and patriarchs, on whom we peg our piety; our comrades, those who share our trials today, our peers in courage. As for a temple, heaven holds greater splendor; and for a festival, we have a choir of angels; and a single rite, magnificent—indeed, the most magnificent, and not for the mass of people—God, to whom also the rites of this world are directed.

6. So stop promising us trivial and worthless things. What is dishonorable will bring us no honor; nor will a liability redound to our credit: we shall never agree to such a miserable bargain. Stop threatening us, too, or we shall in turn threaten to expose your weakness and add our own forms of correction: we too have fire with which to punish our persecutors. Do you think that your opponents are nations or cities or pusillanimous kings, some of whom will prevail while others presumably will be defeated? The risks they take are after all for goals not so great as these. No; it is against the law of God that you are marshaling your ranks, against tablets engraved by God, against ancestral customs honored by time and reason, against seven brothers bound together by a single heart, who will immortalize your shameful conduct with seven trophies. To prevail over them is not a great thing; but to be defeated would in fact bring utter disgrace. We are both sons and disciples of men who were shown the way by a pillar of *fire* and *cloud*,[20] for whom the sea parted[21] and the river stood still[22] and the sun was stayed[23] and the bread rained down[24] and who stretched forth their hands and, with prayers as their missiles, put thousands to flight;[25] who overcame wild beasts and whom fire did not singe and before whom kings, awed by their courage, gave way.[26] Let us also mention something of which you are personally aware: we are the initiates of Eleazar, whose bravery you know.[27] The father spearheaded the fight; the sons will rank close behind. The priest has departed; the victims will follow. You use many tactics to scare us; we are ready for more. Just what can you do to us with your

20. Ex 13.21.
21. Ex 14.21.
22. Jos 3.16.
23. Jos 10.13.
24. Ex 16.4.
25. Ex 17.11.
26. Dn 3–4.6.
27. 2 Mc 6.18–31; 4 Mc 5–7.

threats, presumptuous one? What can we suffer? Nothing can match the power of those prepared to suffer all. Executioners, *why do you delay?*[28] What holds you back? Where is that worthy order you have been waiting for? Where are the swords? Where are the chains? I demand action. Let the fire be kindled higher; let the beasts be more fierce, the instruments more refined; let everything be lavish, fit for a king. I am the first-born; consecrate me first. I am the youngest; let the order be reversed. Let also one from the middle be put among the first so that we might share the honor equally. You hesitate? Perhaps you expect us to change our minds? We shall say the same thing again and again: we will not eat polluted meat; we will not give in. You will pay homage to our ways sooner than we shall yield to yours. In short, either devise more novel tortures or know that your present ones are beneath contempt."

7. This is what they said to the tyrant. As for their words of encouragement to one another and the sight that they presented to view, how beautiful and full of sanctity they were for those who love God, how sweeter than any sight or sound! I myself am transported with ecstasy in recalling them; my thoughts become theirs at their martyrdom, and I am enhanced in the telling. They threw their arms around one another and embraced; their air was festive, as at the completion of athletic events. "Onward, my brothers, to our trials!" they kept shouting; "Onward! Let us hurry while the tyrant is seething against us. If he softens we shall forfeit our salvation. A banquet lies full before us; let us not decline. It is a fine thing for brothers to live and drink together as comrades in arms; it is finer to brave danger together for virtue's sake. If it had been possible we would have used our bodies to engage in open warfare on behalf of our ancestral rites. This too is a commendable way to die. But since we do not have this opportunity, let us simply contribute our bodies alone. Consider: even if we do not die right now, shall we not eventually? Shall we not keep faith with our mortality? Let us turn necessity into glorious opportunity; let us give meaning to our death; let us make what is common to all something specially ours; let

---

28. 4 Mc 6.23.

us purchase life with death. Therefore let none of us show cowardice or too great a fondness for life. Let his encounter with us make the despot abandon his designs on everyone else as well. It is he who will impose the sequence of tortures, but it is we who shall impose an end to his persecution of victims. On this issue let our zealous fervor be the same for us all: the first will lead the way for the rest and the last will be the seal of our martyrdom, both alike. Let us all show the same firm resolve to win the crown together as one family and keep the persecutor from drawing any of us to his side and in a burst of wickedness exulting over one as if he had triumphed over all. Let us show ourselves true brothers, in death as well as in birth; and let us face the danger all as one and each for all. Eleazar, welcome us; mother, follow after us; Jerusalem, give your dead a magnificent burial, if there are any remains to be buried. Recite, if you will, our deeds and point out to posterity and to those who love you the sacred common sepulcher of men born of one womb."

8. When they had said and done these things and whetted one another's zeal to a point as sharp as a boar's tusk, in the order of their years and all with equal enthusiasm they proceeded bravely to meet their fate. Their countrymen were thrilled and awed; their persecutors paralyzed with fear: they had launched a campaign against the entire nation, but in their attack against seven brothers fighting with one heart on behalf of their religious beliefs, they were defeated so soundly that now not even against the rest did they entertain any real expectations. In turn, their brave mother, true genetrix of heroes so distinguished for the magnitude and purity of their goodness, the mighty and high-souled nursling of the law, was pulled throughout by two concurrent emotions, joy and fear: she was joyous over their show of courage, she feared for the future and the excruciating punishments it would bring; and just as a bird chirps shrilly and flutters about her brood when a snake or some other predator is slithering to attack,[29] she entreated and flinched at every blow. Was there anything she did not say, anything she did not do to spur them to victory? She collected the jets of their blood; she

---

29. Homer, *Iliad* 2.308–19; cf. 4 Mc 14.15–17.

scooped up the battered remnants of their limbs; she kissed what was left of her children; she rallied one as she surrendered another and readied yet a third, all the while keeping up the cry to them all, "Bravo, children! Bravo, my heroes! Bravo, you who in body are almost incorporeal; bravo, champions of the Law and my white head and the city that nurtured you and raises you to this pinnacle of virtue! Just a little longer and the victory is ours. The torturers are worn out: this alone I fear. Just a little longer, and I shall be blessed among mothers and you among children. Do you yearn for your mother? I shall not abandon you: this I promise you. I could not hate my children so."

9. And as soon as she saw that they had achieved their goal and their success had set her mind at ease, she raised her chin and smiled broadly just like an Olympic champion high of heart, and, lifting up her hands, exclaimed in a loud and radiant voice, "I thank thee, holy Father, and you, the Law, our mentor, and you, Eleazar, our father, who preceded your children in the struggle, because you have received the fruit of my womb and I have become a mother hallowed above all mothers. I have left nothing for the world; I have given my all to God, my fortune, the hopes that comforted my old age. How royally I have been honored! How superlatively I have been comforted in my old age! Children, I have been amply repaid for your upbringing. I have witnessed your battles in the name of virtue; I have beheld the spectacle that placed the crown of martyrdom on every head. I look upon the torturers as benefactors; I almost even confess gratitude to the despot for seeing to it that I was saved to be tormented last, in order that I might first set the stage for my children and participate in the drama of martyrdom of each of my sons and thus with perfect serenity follow those perfect victims in death. I will not pull out my hair; I will not tear my clothes; I will not slash my flesh with my nails; I will not raise lament; I will not invite other women to lament with me; I will not shut myself in the dark to have the surrounding gloom share my lament; I will not wait for anyone to offer condolences; I will not put out mourning bread.[30] These things or-

---

30. Cf. Jer 16.7.

dinary mothers do, mothers in flesh alone, whose children die without any record of achievement. Dearest children, in my eyes you are not dead but vowed in full flower to God; have not vanished, but changed abode; not been torn apart but joined firmly together; no wild beast has carried you off; no wave overwhelmed you; no robber done away with you; no disease ravaged you; no war made you a casualty; no, nor any other human tragedy, great or small. I should have been consumed with grief if any of these misfortunes had overtaken you. Then my tears would have proved my love for you, as my dry eyes do now. Even these things are yet of no consequence. I should really have grieved over you had you purchased your safety at the cost of your good name, had you been vanquished by your tortures, had your persecutors got the better of anyone of you as they have now been vanquished. Instead, those who survive you now have occasion for rejoicing, for gladness, for glory, for choirs singing your praises, for transports of rapture. Indeed, I pour out my own life in the sacrifice and follow you. We shall take our place alongside Phinehas[31] and be glorified together with Hannah[32] except that he was one person compared to so many zealous slayers of harlots as you, who impale the harlotry not of the body but of the soul. Hannah, too, consecrated a single son, a gift from God, and him an infant, while I have devoted to God seven grown men, and these acting of their own will. Let me bring my eulogy to a close with the aid of Jeremiah, not in lamentation but with a benediction for a holy death: You sparkled brighter *than snow;* you swelled more richly *than milk;* you are a band more precious than *sapphire* stone who have been both born and delivered unto God.[33] What more? If even enemies can bestow a favor, unite me too with my children: our common martyrdom will glorify you the more. Would that I had run the gauntlet with them and mingled the ooze of my aged flesh with theirs. Because of my children I feel affection even for your instruments of torture. But, if this is not to be, at least let me mingle my ashes with theirs and the same tomb receive

31. Nm 25.7–13.   32. 1 Sm 1.22–2.11.
33. Lam 4.7.

us. Do not begrudge a death of equal honor to those equal in honor through their virtue. Farewell, mothers! Farewell, children! This is the behavior you should nurture in your offspring; this the behavior you should nurture in yourselves. We have given a noble example; go forth and enter the lists."

10. After she finished speaking, she advanced to join her children. How? By moving with eager anticipation to the pyre—this was the punishment decreed—as though to a bridal chamber, without even waiting for the guards to take her, lest any impure hand so much as touch her pure and noble body.[34] Observe how Eleazar turned his priesthood to account: an initiate himself, he initiated others into the mysteries of heaven and sanctified Israel not with sprinklings from some external source but with the drops of his own blood, thus transforming his death into a last sacramental act; in like fashion the young men turned their youth to account: no slaves to pleasure they but masters of impulsive desire, they purified their flesh and were translated to the life that knows no suffering. The same is true of their prolific mother: she gloried in her children while they were alive and in death shared with them the repose of the grave; the sons she had born to the world she made over to God; she tallied the pains she endured in giving birth against the agonies of their martyrdom; and as they died relived their successive births. For the throes of martyrdom engaged all her children from the youngest to the oldest; like rising waves one after another each performed heroically and, galvanized by the punishment inflicted on the brother ahead of him, was all the more impatient to suffer. Hence the despot was glad that their mother had not borne more children, for he would have skulked away in even more humiliating defeat. And then for the first time he realized that his weapons were not all-powerful; he had attacked defenseless children armed only with their piety and more eager to undergo the ultimate in suffering than he was prepared to inflict it.

11. Here is a sacrifice that was both less reckless and more noble than Jephthah's.[35] It was not, as in that case, a promise made in the heat of the moment and a desperate craving for

---

34. 4 Mc 17.1.
35. Jgs 11.30–40.

victory that forced them into self-sacrifice, but a voluntary holy act, its only reward the hope of things to come. Here is an act to be held in no less esteem than the trials of Daniel, who was consigned as prey to lions and who vanquished the beasts by spreading his hands.[36] Here is an act in no way second to that of the young men in Assyria whom an angel refreshed in the midst of the fire when they refused to violate the law of their fathers by eating profane and desecrated food.[37] Here is an act not less generous than that of those who later sacrificed themselves for Christ. They, as I observed at the beginning of my sermon, imitated Christ's shedding of his blood, and it was God who blazed the trail for such prizes with his own so great and so marvelous offering on our behalf. The Maccabees, on the other hand, could not point to many, or such, demonstrations of virtue. In their case, all of Judea was lost in wonder at their determination and exulted and rejoiced as if she herself had been crowned. For the challenge was this, the greatest of the challenges that had ever yet affected the city: whether on that day the Law would be overturned or glorified. It was a time when the fate of the whole Hebrew nation in the form of the trials of those young men was poised, as it were, on the razor's edge.[38] Antiochus himself stood dumbstruck as his threats gave way to awe. Even enemies are capable of marveling at the valor of brave men once their fury subsides and they judge their exploits on the merits.[39] And so he departed in frustration, with high praise for his father Seleucus for the honor he had conferred on the nation and his munificence toward its temple,[40] and with deep reproach for Simon, who had led him astray and whom he held responsible for his own cruelty and disgrace.

---

36. Dn 6.16–24, where, however, Daniel's deliverance is attributed to an angel rather than the spreading of hands.
37. Dn 3.49–50 LXX (= S of 3 Y 26–27). Note that Gregory has confused the young men's rejection of Nebuchadnezzar's food (Dn 1.8–16) with their refusal to worship the golden idol, the offense for which they were consigned to the fiery furnace (Dn 3.13–25).
38. Homer, *Iliad* 10.173.
39. Cf. 4 Mc 17.23–24.
40. 2 Mc 3.1–3. Antiochus IV succeeded his brother, Seleucus IV Philopator (187–175 B.C.), not his father, Antiochus the Great (223–187 B.C.).

12. Priests, mothers, children, these let us have as our model: priests, in honor of the spiritual father, Eleazar, who epitomized excellence by his actions as well as his words; mothers, in honor of that noble mother, by showing true devotion to your children and commending them to Christ: such a sacrifice will bring sanctity to the married state as well; children, by revering the holy children and spending your youth not in the gratification of shameful desires but in resistance to the passions and by struggling heroically against the daily Antiochus who assaults us in every limb and subjects us to torments of every description. I long to have champions ready to fight on any occasion and with every means at their disposal, champions of both sexes and of every age, whether engaged in open warfare or the object of covert plots; and to have the inspiration of tales both old and new and, like the bees, to collect from every source all that will be of the greatest service in fashioning a single honeycomb filled with sweetness, that God may be honored among us through the Old Testament and the New, God who is glorified in the Son and the Holy Spirit, who knows and is known by his own,[41] who acknowledges those who acknowledge him,[42] who honors those who honor him,[43] in Christ himself, to whom be the glory forever and ever. Amen.

41. Jn 10.14.
42. Mt 10.32.
43. 1 Sm 2.30; cf. Jn 17.22.

ORATION 17

To the frightened citizens of Nazianzus and the irate prefect.[1]

AM PAINED *in my bowels, my bowels, and the sensitive powers of my heart are in great commotion.*[2] So says Jeremiah, the most compassionate of the prophets, in one of his heartfelt protests against Israel's disobedience and estrangement from God's tender mercy. He is using the word "bowels" in a figurative sense to indicate his soul. This is an image that I find in numerous passages of Scripture, either with reference to what is hidden and invisible (concealment applies equally to both soul and belly) or to the capacity to retain and digest the nourishment of reason: reason is to the soul what food is to the body. "Sensitive powers" presumably refers to the thoughts and stirrings of the soul, especially those that result from sense perception and tear into the just man, firing him up and rousing in him impulses that thanks to the ardor of the Spirit he cannot at all control; for the expression "to be in great commotion" suggests a kind of urgency streaked with anger. If, however, one understands these sensitive powers in a physical sense as well, he will not be off the mark. Our eyes and ears are not limited to registering distress upon seeing or hearing something bad; thanks to our sense of compassion they also desire to hear and to see good things as well. But, whatever the interpretation, the just man is pained and in great commotion and does not accept Israel's misfortunes with resignation, whether one takes these to

---

1. PG 35.964B–81A. The reference to Gregory's father in section 12 provides the *terminus ante quem* of this sermon, which has traditionally been assigned to late 373 or early 374 at the latest. Although *Or.* 17 has been linked to the natural disasters that afflicted Nazianzus in 372 and form the subject of *Or.* 16 (PG 35.963B–81A), the internal evidence does not allow the precise identification of the circumstances that prompted this sermon.

2. Jer 4.19 LXX.

86   ST. GREGORY OF NAZIANZUS

mean material misfortunes, what is physically visible, or spiritual ones, that is, what is spiritually sensed. For the same prophet asks for *a fountain of tears* and yearns for *a wayfarers' lodging place*[3] and embraces the wilderness to pour out his massive grief and somehow ease his inner wound by lamenting for Israel in solitude.

2. Some time earlier the divine David himself expresses the same sentiment in his distress over his personal troubles: *O that I had wings like a dove! I would fly away and be at rest.*[4] He asks for the wings of a dove either because they are lighter and swifter, qualities that every just man has, or else because they foreshadow the Spirit, by which alone we escape disaster, in order to flee as far as he can from the troubles that beset him. Then he gives himself hope, the balm for human difficulties. *I waited,* he declares, for God *that should deliver me from distress of spirit and* from *tempest.*[5] We see him doing the same thing on another occasion too: he administers the remedy for his affliction at once and by his actions as well as his words provides us with a fine example of fortitude in the face of adversity. *My soul,* he says, *refused to be comforted.*[6] Do you detect here words of frustration and despair? You are not afraid, are you, that David is past curing? What is that you say? You have yet to hear a kind word? You despair of receiving any consolation? There is no one to heal you? No word, no friend, no relative, no one to give advice and share your misery, no one to tell you his life story, no one to talk about calamities from long ago, no one to compare your present circumstances with those of so many others who survived even worse? Is everything in ruins? vanished? razed to the ground? all hope lost? Are we simply to lie down and wait for the end? This is the predicament of the great David, David, for whom in tribulation God makes room[7] and who with his help resists *the shadow of death*[8] that envelops him. What, then, is to become of me, the small, the weak, the lowly, his spiritual inferior? If David does not know which way to turn, who then can be saved? What help can I find in my affliction? What comfort? To whom can I ap-

3. Jer 9.1–2.
5. Ps 55.8 (LXX 54.9) LXX.
7. Ps 4.1.
4. Ps 55.6 (LXX 54.7).
6. Ps 77.2 (LXX 76.3).
8. Ps 23.4 (LXX 22.4).

peal in my trouble? David the great healer, who charms away even evil spirits through the Spirit in him,[9] has the answer for you. Is it from me that you propose to learn in whom you can find asylum when you do not know yourself? Who is it that strengthens withered *hands* and raises *feeble knees*[10] and leads through fire and saves through water? You require no battle line, Scripture tells us, no weapons, no archers, no horsemen, no friends, no counselors, no outside assistance.[11] You have your ally within yourself, just as I do and everyone who so desires. Merely will it so; just take the first step. Comfort is *near, on your lips and in your heart.*[12] *I remembered God,* says the Psalmist, *and rejoiced.*[13] What could be easier than remembering? You too remember and rejoice. The remedy is so simple! The cure so fast! The gift so magnificent! The remembrance of God not only lulls the sense of desolation and anguish but also gives rise to joy.

3. Do you require further proof of God's compassion? When thou shalt turn to the Lord and *mourn,* says Scripture, *then thou shalt be saved.*[14] Do you notice that salvation is bound up with mourning? *You shall cry, and he will say, Here I am,*[15] and he will say *to* your *soul, I am your deliverance.*[16] Nothing comes between the petition and its fulfillment, not gold, not silver, not crystalline jewels, not any of the things that move human beings to clemency. When Zephaniah says, assigning the words as if to an angry and wrathful God, *I have laid waste their streets so that none walks in them; their cities have been made desolate, without* a man, *without an inhabitant;* when he makes the most frightful threats, when he overwhelms us with discouragement, when he casts a menacing pall over us, he directly holds out also the light of a better hope and restores me with these words, *I said, surely* you will *fear me,* you will *accept correction;* you will *not lose sight of it;*[17] and, a little further on, in a still more heartening and more compassionate vein, *on that day the Lord shall say, do not fear,* O

---

9. 1 Sm 16.23.
10. Is 35.3.
11. Hos 1.7.
12. Rom 10.8.
13. Ps 77.3 (LXX 76.4) LXX.
14. Is 30.15 LXX.
15. Is 58.9.
16. Ps 35.3 (LXX 34.3).
17. Zep 3.6–7.

Zion; let not your hands grow weak. The Lord your God is in your midst, who can save you and *he will rejoice over you with gladness and he will renew you in his love* and will gather the afflicted ones and will save the oppressed and receive those cast out.[18] This is what the saints as well as reason require and what my own sermon demands. So receive words of understanding, as the divine Solomon says,[19] so that, when you fall into a sea of troubles, you are not filled with resentment and dragged under by your own ignorance rather than by the crisis that weighs upon you.

4. Human affairs, my brothers, run in a circle, and God teaches us by means of opposites. His inscrutable and incomprehensible judgments guide and direct the universe, including our affairs, with the same wisdom by which he fashioned and secured all things. For in a manner of speaking the universe moves and oscillates around the unmoved one, not, to be sure, by virtue of its law of being, which in fact remains stable throughout and unmoved even if we are unable to perceive it, but as a result of everyday happenings and occurrences. It is an old and fixed ordinance of God that he lies hidden in the darkness poured over our eyes and that the indications of his stewardship largely escape our ken except for obscure signs and images. Thereby he either quashes our delusions so that we may realize that in comparison with the first and true wisdom we are nothing and incline to him alone and always seek our illumination in the rays issuing from him; or else through the vicissitude of our visible world of change he leads us instead to the one that is stable and enduring. But, as I say, nothing remains unmoved or uniform or independent or the same from the beginning to end, neither joy nor sorrow, not wealth, not poverty, not strength, not infirmity, not high station, not low, not the present, not the future, not our possessions, not anyone else's, not the large, not the small, not anything one can imagine. Indeed, the one constant is inconstancy itself: everything is subject to change. All things effortlessly slip into a circular pattern: when one moves on another takes its place, so that we may rather put

18. Zep 3.16–19.
19. Prv 1.3.

ORATION 17 89

our faith in the breezes of the air or in words written on water than in human happiness. Too, envy puts an end to prosperity as mercy does to misfortune, and that is a wise and wondrous thing in my estimation, in order that there may neither be adversity without consolation nor prosperity without restraint.

5. Prudent men, those who are schooled in misfortune and purified in the fire like gold, declare, *It is good for me that thou hast afflicted me, that I might learn thine ordinances,*[20] for they realize that abasement generates understanding of his ordinances. Indeed, they act like Peter, who cried out for help when he was about to go under,[21] and their pain somehow draws them closer to God and through their distress they make him their friend, since a troubled soul is next to God and their need turns them to the one who can provide, him who is even perchance despised for his unstinted generosity. This is why, my brothers, we should look up to heaven; at all times and before every adversity let us exude good hope; let us relinquish neither anxiety in time of happiness nor confidence in time of sorrow. Even in fair weather let us not forget the gale, nor in the storm the pilot; yes, let us not lose heart in the midst of afflictions or become wicked servants who acknowledge their master only when he treats them well and repudiate him when he tries to correct them. Yet there are times when pain is preferable to health, patience to relief, visitation to neglect, punishment to forgiveness. In a word, we must neither let our troubles lay us low nor a glut of good fortune give us airs.

6. Let us submit ourselves to God, to one another, and to our earthly rulers: to God on all counts, to one another out of brotherly love, to our rulers for the sake of public order, and all the more so to the degree they are of a kindly and gentle disposition. It is dangerous to exhaust lenience by incessant demands for indulgence lest we become ourselves responsible for calling their severity down upon us if we disturb calm by a gust of wind, cast a dark shadow over the light, and add a dose of wormwood to the honey. Included in our laws there is this one in particu-

20. Ps 119.71 (LXX 118.71) LXX.
21. Mt 14.30.

lar—and it is one of those which we hold in esteem and that originate most finely in the Spirit, who has sanctioned and ordained what is feasible together with what is good—that, just as servants owe obedience to masters,[22] wives to husbands,[23] the Church to the Lord,[24] disciples to their teachers and pastors,[25] so too, inasmuch as we are payers of tribute, we must be *subject to all the governing authorities not only to avoid God's wrath but also for the sake of conscience.*[26] We must not direct our hatred toward the law when we transgress nor wait for the axe to fall, but rather, chasten our behavior and seek to win their approval out of respect for their authority.

7. There is one standard, the same for all, but it leaves what is upright untouched while the rampant it prunes back. There is one sun, yet to the healthy eye it brings light while the one that is weak it makes dim. May I take the liberty of using an example also from our own beliefs? There is one Christ, yet *he is set for the fall and rising;*[27] fall for the unbelievers, rising for the faithful. For the unbelievers, that is, all those who *have neither knowledge nor understanding* but *walk about in darkness,*[28] either worshipping idols or fixing their eyes on the letter and neither willing nor able to discern the splendor beyond it, he is a rock *that will make men stumble and a rock that will make them fall;*[29] but for the others, namely, all who abide fixed and secure in the bond of the Word, he is a chief cornerstone[30] and a rock of praise; or, if you will, the famous pearl that the good merchant buys with all he possesses.[31] But we, my brothers, when we grumble at authority instead of trying to correct our shortcomings, are in a sense like the wrestler who accuses the referee of incompetence when it is he himself who has broken the rules, or the patient who calls his doctor rash and ignorant for resorting to surgery and cautery when he is in fact seriously ill and drastic measures are indicated. This then is what I have to say to the governed by way at once of both encouragement and advice, the words, these, of

22. Eph 6.5; Col 3.22.
23. Eph 5.22; Col 3.18.
24. Eph 5.23–24.
25. Eph 4.11.
26. Rom 13.1, 5–6.
27. Lk 2.34.
28. Ps 82.5 (LXX 81.5).
29. Rom 9.33; 1 Pt 2.8.
30. Eph 2.20.
31. Mt 13.46.

a poor shepherd who guides a small flock and by the law of my ministry shares their joys and sorrows alike.

8. And what of you, the representatives of power and authority? My remarks are directed now to you. We do not wish to appear in any way partial by lecturing the others on proper behavior while giving you a wide berth because of your powerful station, as though we were so obsequious—or terrified—that we waive our Christian right to speak out; or to seem more concerned with the others while remaining oblivious to yourselves, who have an even greater claim on our attention insofar as your decisions, whichever way they tend, are of greater moment and your achievements of broader scope. May we never think or suggest to the contrary! What, then, do you have to say? What common ground is there between us? Will you listen to my remarks with an open mind? Mark what I have to say: the law of Christ puts you under my jurisdiction and authority, for we too are rulers ourselves; and, I might add, our rule is of a more important and perfect nature; else the Spirit must yield to the flesh and the things of heaven to the things of earth. You will, I know, accept the candor of my observations because you are[32] a sheep in my flock, a holy sheep in a holy flock, a nursling of the great shepherd, guided aright from above by the Spirit, and basking in the same light of the holy and blessed Trinity that we do. Hence my remarks to you will be brief and to the point.

9. You rule with Christ and you govern with Christ; it is from him that you receive your sword, not to use, but to brandish. May you preserve it as an unstained offering to him who conferred it upon you! You are an image of God, but you also control that image, which is governed on this earth by divine dispensation and migrates to another life to which we shall all repair once we have played out our small role in this—what shall I call it? prison-house? arena? phantom? figment?—of existence. Honor the nature you have in common; respect your archetype; ally yourself with God, not the ruler of this world;[33]

---

32. At this point, Gregory switches from the second person plural to the singular. The identity of this official remains uncertain, but he is probably not the same man as the addressee of *Or.* 19, the *peraequator* Julian.

33. The term κοσμοκράτωρ may refer either to Satan or the Emperor.

with the good Lord, not the harsh tyrant. *He was a murderer from the beginning;*[34] it was he who struck the blow against the first man through his disobedience and introduced the life of toil[35] and made the inflicting and suffering of punishment for transgression part of the order of things. As for you, man of God, remember whose creature you are and the task to which you are called; how many things you have received and the extent of your obligation; from whom come your reason, your law, your prophets, your very knowledge of God, your absence of despair for the future. For these reasons imitate God's philanthropy. It is in this, in doing good, that man is preeminently divine. You can become God without hardship; do not forgo the opportunity for deification.

10. Some men exhaust their coffers, others their bodies for the Spirit and are mortified in Christ and withdraw completely from the world; others consecrate what they hold most dear to God. Indeed, you have no doubt heard of the sacrifice of Abraham, who, more eagerly than when he first received the child from God, gave God his only son, the one who had been promised to him and who bore in himself the promise.[36] None of these things do we ask of you. In their stead offer compassion alone. God takes more pleasure in this than in all the other things put together, a special gift, a faultless gift, a gift that invites God to lavish his favor upon us. Mingle severity with clemency; temper threat with promise. I know that kindness accomplishes a great deal by winning us over into responding in kind; when we reject coercion in favor of forgiveness, our good will wins over the beneficiary of our mercy. Let nothing induce you to be unworthy of your office; let nothing block your pity and leniency, not circumstance, not a superior, not fear, not the hope of higher office, not rashness and its attendant excess. Win good will in times of distress: it is the good will of heaven. Loan God your pity. No one has ever regretted making an advance to God. He is generous in repayment, singling out for the blessings of heaven those who have made a down payment or

---

34. Jn 8.44.
35. Gn 3.1–20.
36. Gn 22.2–19.

advanced a loan; and sometimes he even rewards them with worldly blessings as collateral against future returns.

11. A little while longer and the world is a thing of the past and the stage dismantled. Let us take advantage of the time we have. Let us buy what abides with what does not. Each of us is subject to judgment; we creatures of clay carry many obligations. Let us pardon that we may be pardoned; forgive, that we may seek forgiveness. In the Gospel, you recall, a certain debtor is prosecuted for owing many talents and is forgiven the debt because he is brought before a kind master.[37] And, although he receives pardon, he does not give it for he is a slave in character as well. The lenient treatment he receives in a transaction involving a large sum he fails to show towards a fellow slave in a smaller one: he is not even affected by the example of generosity that touches him personally, not to speak of any other; and his master is much displeased. Well, I shall not give you the rest of the story except to say that it is better in every respect to advance a kindness on this earth as a credit against the account you will give in the other.

12. What do you say? Have our words given you pause? You have often confessed a fondness for them, most excellent of rulers, and, may I add, most gentle. Or should I, instead of a plea, proffer to you this hoary head and quantity of years and this long and untarnished ministry which perhaps even the angels, the pure servants of the most pure God, hold in regard because of its likeness to their own service? Do these things convince you? Or shall I take a greater liberty? My distress gives me the courage to do so. I give you Christ, and Christ's abasement for our sake, and the suffering of the one impervious to suffering, and the cross, and the nails that freed me from sin; I give you the blood and the burial and the resurrection and the ascent, or even this table that we approach in common, and the visible symbols of my salvation, this holy liturgy that lifts us up to heaven, which I perform with the same voice that makes this plea to you.

13. For all these reasons—if in fact one does not suffice—

---

37. Mt 18.23–35.

grant the favor to us as well as to yourself, to the church in your own house as well as to this good Christian congregation. Think of them as our fellow petitioners even though they cede the responsibility for the petition to us because of the higher standing that we enjoy thanks to him who has conferred it upon us, and because imperial regulation prevents them from joining me. Graciously accept defeat on this one issue; conquer us with kindness. Behold, I bring to you my suppliants before God and angels and heavenly kingdom and the rewards of the other life. Honor my faith, which has been entrusted to me and which I have entrusted to others so that yours too may find a place of honor in the realm that is greater and more perfect. In a word, you yourself also have a Lord, in heaven; may the judge you will face treat you as you treat your subjects. And may we all meet with acts both of kindness on this earth and of greater indulgence in the other, in Jesus Christ our Lord, to whom be the power and the glory, the honor and the kingdom, as he is and has been and will be forever and ever, together with the Father and the Holy Spirit. Amen.

ORATION 19

On his sermons and to the tax adjuster Julian.[1]

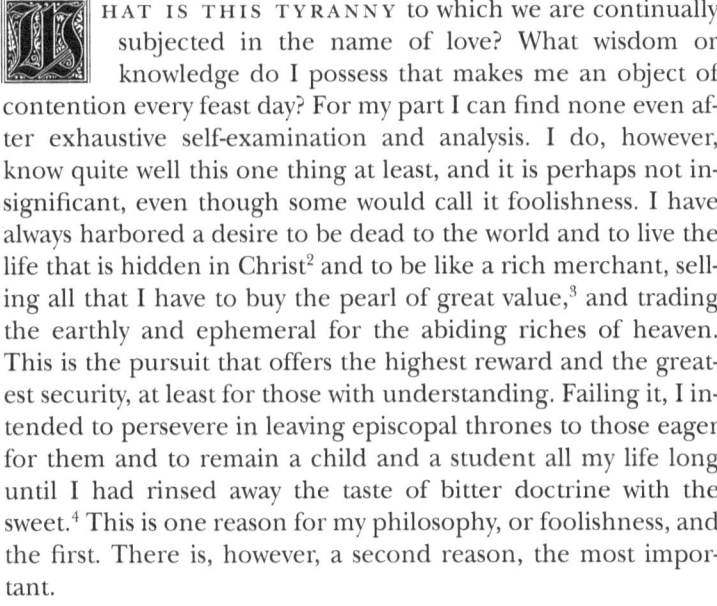HAT IS THIS TYRANNY to which we are continually subjected in the name of love? What wisdom or knowledge do I possess that makes me an object of contention every feast day? For my part I can find none even after exhaustive self-examination and analysis. I do, however, know quite well this one thing at least, and it is perhaps not insignificant, even though some would call it foolishness. I have always harbored a desire to be dead to the world and to live the life that is hidden in Christ[2] and to be like a rich merchant, selling all that I have to buy the pearl of great value,[3] and trading the earthly and ephemeral for the abiding riches of heaven. This is the pursuit that offers the highest reward and the greatest security, at least for those with understanding. Failing it, I intended to persevere in leaving episcopal thrones to those eager for them and to remain a child and a student all my life long until I had rinsed away the taste of bitter doctrine with the sweet.[4] This is one reason for my philosophy, or foolishness, and the first. There is, however, a second reason, the most important.

2. When I realized that nothing I said was able to curb popular talk or the current, all-pervasive passion to speak and lecture on the things of the Spirit without the inspiration of the Spirit, I

---

1. PG 35.1044A–64B. In addition to this sermon, Gregory also addressed three letters and a poem to his fellow Christian and former classmate, Julian, on the subject of the tax reassessment in Nazianzus during the period 374–75; see note 45 below. See also M.-M. Hauser-Meury, *Prosopographie zu den Schriften Gregors von Nazianz* (Bonn, 1960), pp. 110–11 and p. 97, n. 196 on the title and duties of the *peraequator*/ ἐξισωτής.

2. Col 3.3.
3. Mt 13.45–46.
4. Plato, *Phaedrus* 243D.

embarked on another course—a better one, I am convinced, and less agonizing—that of training everyone to be still by setting an example with my own silence. If they held me at all in high regard, they would follow my example out of respect for my prominent position; if their opinion of me was low, and only what I deserved, they should do so by adopting the more moderate claim of their peer. This is the reason for our silence; this the secret of our perseverance.

3. What am I to do? They yank and jerk us from one side to the other; they sue for my efforts, extorting sermons from me as they would payment for any other debt; and they show more love for me than I do for my very self; and all of them are wiser than I, for they know better than I when to speak and when to keep silent; and they claim they will keep on striking us with their reproaches, like steel against flint, until they succeed in kindling the full torch of words from a tiny spark. Yes, and now some of them are even promising choicer benefits and are dangling great rewards for my sermons, which, they say, will benefit themselves first of all, by enabling them to bear fruit for God and ourselves to their credit;[5] and second, through the assessment they will benefit all those here as well, my flock, my inheritance (if in fact I have inherited my father's calling), to whom I should do a very great injustice if I did not readily do all I could to help them. But the most gratifying thing of all is that, in order to elicit a speech from me, they are putting forth the tremendous amount of effort necessary to ensure that their own words are persuasive. How engaging their eagerness to win me over! What a marvelous bonus! Do you see how much my silence has accomplished? It has made you all the more desirous of the words themselves. Do you see the fruit of my indifference to fame? I only hope that my speech will be as productive as my silence.

4. Well, then, since this is your decision and you have conquered the unconquerable and triumphed over my life of quiet contemplation, come, let me say a few words to you; they will represent an improvement over my silence. Hence I shall not

---

5. Cf. Rom 7.4; Phil 4.17.

mince or ramble, or speak in the dulcet tones that the mass finds so appealing—I should ill reward my admirers if I did so. Instead, I shall be quite bold and to the point, speaking in such a way that you will, we hope, be morally improved, transported from the flesh toward the spirit and sufficiently edified of mind. *O men, how long shall my honor suffer shame?*—I shall take my opening remarks to you from the most grandiloquent David— *How long will you love vain words, and seek after lies?*[6] Do you imagine that this life with its luxury and empty glory and its petty dominion and deceptive good fortune is of any consequence? Such goals preoccupy not those who already enjoy them so much as those who have made them their hope; or rather not even these but those who have not even marked them as a possibility; goals blown and scattered about like dust *by a storm* from one person to the next, or vanishing like smoke and making sport of us like a dream and eluding us like a shadow;[7] neither, when absent, beyond the hopes of those who lack them; nor, when present, true to those who possess them.

5. Shall we not look to the heavens above? Shall we not mend our ways? Shall we not wipe the film from our eyes? Shall we not learn what true riches are, what genuine splendor is, and where to find the honor that does not fade away? What is happiness without end and where the good that is unshaken and abiding, or impervious to evil design? Shall we not labor with much sweat and toil, if need be, to acquire these things? Shall we not luxuriate in our hopes if luxuriate we must in the things of this earth? Shall we not recognize the holy martyrs and all the others who have wreathed our entire world like so many links in a chain and whom we honor with today's festival? Why did they endure wounds and shackles and tortures and menacing flames and sharp swords and wild beasts and darkness and hunger and dungeons and confiscations of their property and amputations of their limbs and finally death, and all with such eagerness as though the bodies with which they contended were not their own? To become what? To gain what? Or are not the answers

6. Ps 4.2.
7. Wis 5.14.

obvious to everyone without our stating them expressly? Shall we not make their hope our own and align ourselves with the same umpire and judge to fight against the same tyrant, the bitter persecutor of souls both then and now, the invisible enemy and foe? Shall we not try to act as heroes in this world of ours just as though it were a public theater, even if not to the point of utmost peril and the swift release it brings, still at least by daily efforts and struggles, so that we may earn the same crowns or as close to them as we can?

6. I urge each one of you, man and woman, old and young, townsman and rustic, private citizen and public leader, rich and poor—for the same contest, you see, extends a bid to us all—to strip for it with eagerness; do not cower or hesitate or put off the opportunity that can never be regained. The present is the time for action; the future, for remuneration. *Rise, let us go hence:*[8] You know the words of the Savior, who just as he led his then disciples from the land of Judaea, so also he raised all his subsequent followers from this world and drew them to himself on high, as he promised.[9] Let us follow our good master; let us shun worldly desires; let us shun the world of deceit and its temporal ruler; let us give ourselves in purity to our Maker; let us honor our image; let us respect our call[10] and change our lives. Why do we debase ourselves when our origins are lofty? Why do we cling to the visible realm?

7. Let each one of us, no matter what his walk of life or circumstances, offer to God[11] all that he can on every occasion according to the measure of his capacity, according to the gift bestowed upon him, in order that by displaying virtue in all its forms we may secure all the heavenly abodes, reaping all that we have sown,[12] or rather, storing up in God's silos all that we have garnered. Let one contribute his riches, another his abject poverty; one his zeal, another his appreciation of the zeal of another; one a commendable deed, another a perceptive thought; one a timely remark, another eloquent silence; one unimpeachable instruction and a way of life to match; another, an open

8. Jn 14.31.
10. Cf. 1 Cor 1.26.
12. Cf. Gal 6.7.

9. Jn 12.32.
11. Cf. Rom 7.4.

and receptive ear; one virginity that is pure and severs all contact with the world; another, a marriage that is devout and in no way divorced from God; one fasting that is not tainted with pride; another, feast tempered by restraint; one unbroken prayers and spiritual hymns, another, the care of the poor; all of us our tears, all of us our purification, all of us our upliftment and a straining forward *to what lies ahead.*[13]

8. Simplicity of heart, too, is a lovely gift, as are stifled laughter, wrath suppressed, a disciplined eye, a mind not permitted to wander. Nothing that we offer God, though it be the least, though far less than he deserves, is so insignificant that he does not heartily welcome and accept it, even though he knows how to balance compassion with just judgment.[14] He accepts Paul's planting because it is Paul's, as well as Apollos's watering[15] and the widow's *two copper coins*[16] and the tax collector's humility[17] and Manasseh's confession.[18] Moses pitched the tabernacle as an earthly representation of the heavenly realm[19] and all contributed what they had been called upon to give; and there were those who made additional offerings on their own, some gold, others silver, others precious *stones* for *the ephod*. Some of the women brought fine-spun *linen;* others, *scarlet* fabric; some of the men offered *purple* and others *tanned rams' skins;* still other women gave the most simple of gifts, *goats' hair* for the service of the tabernacle.[20] Everyone, man and woman, gave whatever each happened to have; all contributed; and no one, not even the poorest, came empty-handed. In the same way, let all of us alike make our contribution too, some a greater, others a lesser one, to the venerable tabernacle of God, that is, of this church, *which is set up not by man but by the Lord,*[21] constructed with virtue's manifold ornaments, and thus be joined and fitly framed *into* a perfect work, *a dwelling place* of Christ, *a holy temple*[22] according to the master plan of the Spirit. Yet, even if we give our all, it will still be less than we have received, since God

---

13. Phil 3.13.
15. 1 Cor 3.5–6.
17. Lk 18.13.
19. Cf. Heb 8.5.
21. Heb 8.2.

14. Cf. Is 28.17 LXX.
16. Lk 21.2.
18. 2 Chr 33.12–13.
20. Ex 25.4–5; 28.
22. Eph 2.21–22.

is the very source of our being and of our understanding of him and of our very possession of what we offer up. And herein lies the fairest expression of loving-kindness: God measures our donation not by the value of the gift but by the ability and motivation of the giver.

9. Do not, then, put off moral improvement but act now. Do not abandon your gift altogether because it is small in value. Just make your offering and at the same time wish in your heart that it could be more and ask indulgence for your slender means. *None shall appear before me empty-handed*,[23] Scripture says. Let no one be empty or barren, no soul sterile and unproductive. Let each person offer God the gift that is appropriate and in accordance with his means: the sinner repentance, the upright strength of character, the young self-discipline, the old wisdom, the rich man generosity, the pauper gratitude, the magistrate humility, the tax collector lenience. Priests, clothe yourselves in righteousness, or, more accurately, let us so clothe ourselves.[24] Let us not scatter and destroy *the sheep* of our flock[25] *for* whom *the good shepherd* laid down his life, he who knows his own and is known by them,[26] who calls them *by name* and leads them away[27] from unbelief into faith and away from this life towards heavenly repose. Let us fear that *judgment* will begin *with* us, as Scripture threatens,[28] let us not receive *from the Lord's hand double for all* our sins[29] because we not only fail to enter ourselves but also bar those who can.[30]

10. Members of the flock, do not seek to assume the role of pastor towards your pastors or try to exalt yourselves above your station. It suffices for you to receive good pastoral care. Seek not to judge your judges or give laws to the lawgivers, *for God is not a God of confusion* and disorder, *but of peace* and order.[31] So let no one seek to be a head when he is in fact scarcely a hand or a foot or some other less important part of the body,[32] but, my brothers, *everyone should remain in the* rank to *which he was*

---

23. Ex 23.15.
25. Ezek 34.5–6.
27. Jn 10.3.
29. Is 40.27.
31. 1 Cor 14.33.

24. Ps 132.9 (LXX 131.9).
26. Jn 10.14–15.
28. 1 Pt 4.17.
30. Mt 23.13.
32. Cf. 1 Cor 12.21–22.

called,³³ even if he deserves a better one. A man is more highly regarded if he acquiesces in his present status than if he aspires to a position that he has not been given. Let no one be eager to assume the risk of being a leader when he can without risk be a follower; and let the law of submission be kept intact, a principle that is binding both on earth and in heaven; and let us not turn the rule of many into a rule of none. You wordsmiths, do not presume to place too much confidence in the power of your words; do not act like sophists, clever beyond reason; do not insist on winning at everything at the cost of honor, but honorably accept the occasions of defeat. Dedicate your words to the Word; make your education a weapon *of righteousness*,³⁴ not of death.

11. Soldiers, *be content with* your *wages; do not seek more than is appointed you*.³⁵ These orders, which I confirm, come to you from John, the great herald of truth, the voice that was precursor of the Word. What do I mean by wages? The imperial allowance, clearly, and the legally sanctioned perquisites of rank. And as for whatever is more, to whom does that belong?³⁶ I am reluctant to use ill-omened language, but I am sure that you understand my meaning even if I hold back. *Render to Caesar the things that are Caesar's, and to God the things that are God's.*³⁷ You who bear the name of the realm, pay your taxes to the one, but your fear to the other. And when I speak of fear, I do so to inhibit covetousness. What great profit shall we realize, you may well ask? The greatest of all, both gainful expectations (through my mediation if you wish), and superior standing in the heavenly city, not this poor and least among cities, even to have dominion over which, if I may speak so slightingly of the city that nurtured me, is not a very exalted and glorious thing. It is in heaven that we should want to be the elite; to the glory there let us aspire; in *Abraham's* bosom³⁸ let us find rest as our reward for the compassion that we show on this earth; let us render *true judgment;* let us relieve the poor and needy; let us extend a help-

33. 1 Cor 7.20.
35. Lk 3.13–14.
37. Mt 22.21.
34. 2 Cor 6.7.
36. Mt 5.37.
38. Lk 16.22.

ing hand to the widow and the fatherless;[39] let us rescue *those who are being taken away to death*[40] or at the very least not ourselves be the executioners; let us not scorn him who asks of us, even if it is only the crumbs *from* our *table;* and let us not ignore the outcast full of sores at our gates; let us not wallow in luxury while others are in distress; let us not feel revulsion toward our fellow servant; let us avoid, my friends and brothers, the rich man's fate and be not in anguish *in the flame,* or let a gulf separate us from the sainted, or ask the beggar Lazarus to cool our burning *tongue* with the end of his finger[41] and fail to obtain even that little. Let us be kind, compassionate, sensitive to others; let us imitate the goodness of the Lord, who *makes* his *sun rise on the evil and on the good* and nourishes all alike with his rain.[42] Let us refuse wealth if it means poverty for others; let us not stray so far from our equality under God, or stain our wealth with others' tears, which will devour it like rust or moths,[43] or, to use the Scriptural term, cause it to be vomited up.[44] But are we more acquisitive than we should be? Good can come even from undue gain: let us give a little from our earthly store that we may enjoy the riches of heaven.

12. Now these injunctions apply to everyone, not just to those in authority. Moral disease is common to all and its treatment the same for all. And so, you who assess our taxes, assess us justly. Apply yourself not to an assessment of my sermon—there is little or nothing to be gained here other than the pleasure and gratification of the ear—but rather to a benevolent and righteous assessment of my people, out of regard for the occasion itself if for nothing else, for even our Savior is born during a period of assessment.[45] As Scripture says, *A decree went out from Caesar Augustus that all the world should be enrolled,* and it was en-

39. Zec 7.9–10. 40. Prv 24.11.
41. Lk 16.19–31. 42. Mt 5.45.
43. Cf. Mt 6.19–20. 44. Jb 20.15.
45. If Gallay is right in dating this homily to Christmas, 374, then the martyrs referred to in section 5 will be the Maccabees, whose cult Gregory introduced into the Christian calendar in December, 362. See P. Gallay, *La vie de Saint Grégoire de Nazianze* (Lyon, 1943), p. 128 and M. Vinson, "Gregory Nazianzen's Homily 15 and the Genesis of the Christian Cult of the Maccabean Martyrs," *Byzantion* 64 (1994): 166–92.

rolled. *And Joseph also went up to Bethlehem to be enrolled with Mary his betrothed wife because he was of the house and lineage of David.*[46] And it is in this setting that the wondrous event takes place, the birth of our Savior, the Maker and Lord of all, in a humble little inn. Let us tremble before the mystery; let us stand in awe before his incarnation and make a contribution ourselves in honor of the occasion. Now angels rejoice, now shepherds are dazzled by the gleam,[47] now a star from the east races to the greatest and *unapproachable light*;[48] now Magi fall down and present gifts and recognize the King of all and adjudge him king of heaven thanks to the glorious testimony of the star; and now Herod rages and slaughters the young children and because of the Deliverer destroys those entitled to deliverance.[49] Come then, let us join them in adoration; and to him who for our sake impoverished himself even to the point of assuming bodily form, let us offer not incense or gold or myrrh, the first to him as our God, the second as our King, and the third as one who tasted death for our sake, but gifts that are mystical and intangible: appropriating nothing, giving no advantage to wealth at the expense of poverty, and, as God's creatures, doing no wrong to one another.

13. It is with Christ that you compile your accounts, with Christ that you form your appraisals; it is with him as your head that you make your scrutiny, with him as the Logos that you reconcile your logbook. Now Christ is born to you and is God and becomes man and sojourns among mankind. What do the words mean? They give notice, in my view, to those entrusted with such matters that God ever accompanies administrative affairs at their most important. And, that he might instill a sense of humility among assessors it is in this setting that he takes on flesh and becomes part of the human race; and, that he might make it easier for us to bear our subordinate status and to give obligation (for this too we must not neglect) the force of law, himself pays the tribute money and not just for himself but also for Peter, the most honored of the disciples.[50] It was, after all,

46. Lk 2.1–7.
48. 1 Tm 6.16.
50. Mt 17.24–27.

47. Lk 2.9.
49. Mt 2.

for our sakes that he became man and assumed *the form of a servant*[51] and for our transgressions that he was led off to die.[52] This is the way the Savior brought salvation even though as the God who created the entire universe at a word he could have done so also by the mere expression of his will. What he did give us was greater and more compelling: he embraced human feelings and the human condition. Where then does duty lie for us, the disciples of Christ, the mild and merciful, who did so much for us? Shall we not emulate the Lord's compassion? Shall we not be kind to our fellow servants so that the Lord may in equal spirit repay us to the measure of our own kindness?[53] Shall we not gain our own lives though gentleness?[54] It is enough that free men find themselves in bondage and that we creatures of the same clay are so disparate that some are rulers and others subjects; and that some impose taxes while others are put on the rolls to pay them; and that some can be criminals and commit injustice while others struggle and plead not to suffer it; and that these are the facts of life for us, creatures made in one image and with one importance, heirs to the same life, for all of whom alike Christ died. These are burdens enough for free men. Do not make the yoke heavier nor the penalty we suffer for our original transgression.

14. How I wish that evil might be destroyed and its first seed along with the devil who sowed weeds among us while we were sleeping[55] so that evil might arise from our failure to do good just as the failing sun marks the onset of darkness! This is the harvest of the tree and its bitter fruit and the treacherous serpent and the disobedience that condemned us to live *in the sweat of* our *face*. As a direct result, I, naked and ugly, came to know my nakedness and clothed myself in a garment of skin and fell from the garden and returned *to the ground* from which I was taken[56] with nothing to show from that perfect existence except an awareness of my own misery; and for my brief moment of pleasure I was condemned to sorrow without end and to war against the false friend who through the tasting of the

51. Phil 2.7.
53. Lk 6.38.
55. Mt 13.25.
52. Is 53.5–7.
54. Cf. Lk 21.19.
56. Gn 3.19–20.

fruit deceived and swayed me to his side. Such are for me the wages of evil; this is why I am born and live and die in travail. Evil is the mother of want, want the mother of greed, greed the mother of wars, and wars the sires of taxation, the most oppressive burden to which we have been condemned. So let us not ourselves add to the penalty. We are all under the same judgment and must not be harsh to others. God asks us to show compassion to one another even though we are punished by him.

15. There will be both another assessment and another assessor, if you have heard of the book of the living and of the dead.[57] In it all of us, every single person, once his life on earth is completed, shall be entered, or rather is already entered, according to his merit. Wealth carries no advantage there nor poverty impediment; or favoritism or animosity or any of all the other faults that rob us of justice here on earth. The finger of God has written us all down and our book shall be opened on the day of revelation. *The small and the great are there, and the slave* along with his master, in the words of Solomon,[58] and the king with his subject and assessor with assessee and glory close to hand. I shall pass over what it would be ill-omened to describe except to say that as we record so shall we be recorded. Ensure a record for yourself in the heavenly roster that will be better if you are good and kind to us in this life.

16. How do you respond to this? What are you writing down, my dearest friend and companion,[59] who shared teachers and studies with us, though God has now given us the more important—I hesitate to say more demanding—role of instructing you, the authorities, about these matters? Son of a God-fearing nation and people, holy scion of holy parents, propagator of children still more holy, I wonder, what is your reaction to my sermon? Have we been able to reach you at all or should we keep trying to spellbind you? My sermons have carried weight with you for some time: there need be no uncertainty on this

---

57. Cf. Rv 20.12, 15. The literal meaning of the last phrase is "of those not saved."
58. Jb 3.19. *Lapsus memoriae.*
59. I.e., Julian.

score; I know it well. In fact, if we could not rely on anything else, we could count on the words themselves, which never fail to guide you effortlessly toward the good whether on your own or following the initiative of others. This is what sets the wise apart from the mass. I shall make one brief addition to my remarks. You have already provided my sermon with its reward, but it has a further inducement for you: the poor, the whole choir of priests, the choir of monks who are held down by no bonds, whose only possession is their body and not even that completely, who reserve nothing for Caesar and everything for God, their hymns, prayers, vigils, tears, possessions that cannot be commandeered, dying unto the world, living in Christ, mortifying the flesh, drawing forth the soul from the body. If you spare or even cede wholly to God these the servants of God and mystic followers, the full initiates of heaven, the choicest offering of our race, our bulwark, the crowning glories of our faith, the precious pearls, the building blocks of our temple, that is, the splendid membership of the Church whose foundation and chief cornerstone is Christ,[60] you would perform a noble service indeed not only for them, but also for yourself and all of us as well. These, then, are the riches I would have you take from us instead of vaults brimming with gold and silver that exist for the present but will shortly be no more.

17. Herewith my sermon, which I offer as my gift to you; if it falls short of your expectations, it is in any case the best I can do. I hope that you in turn will reward my contribution with a greater gift, your ready compliance, so that on other occasions too you will be less dependent on my sermons as you consider how *to stir up one another to love and good works*,[61] so that by obtaining a kind and charitable entry in the book of heaven and dancing about the King of all, which alone is vouchsafed to those enrolled therein, we may offer our praise to God, both contemplating and exalting the single glory and splendor of Godhead in Father, Son, and Holy Spirit, to whom be the glory and the honor and the worship forever and ever. Amen.

60. Eph 2.20.
61. Heb 10.24.

ORATION 20

On theology and the office of bishops.[1]

HEN I AM CONFRONTED with the longwindedness so prevalent today among the instant experts and ordained theologians, who think that they have only to wish it and they are wise, I yearn for the supreme wisdom and, like Jeremiah, I seek out *a wayfarers' lodging place*[2] and feel the need to withdraw by myself. Nothing appeals to me more than, by blocking out my senses, severing all ties with the flesh and the world, placing myself beyond the reach of human concerns except for the unavoidable, and communing with myself and with God, to live the life that transcends visible nature, ever containing within myself the reflections of the divine, their purity unclouded by the false images here below, and be and ever come to be a spotless mirror, as it were, of God and the divine, capturing light with light and the brighter through the more dim until we reach the fount of those rays that penetrate hu-

1. PG 35.1065A–80C. Because of its content, this homily has been closely linked to *Or.* 2, 6, 23, and the *Theological Orations* 27–31. Although it is generally agreed that *Or.* 20 was delivered at Constantinople in 380, the precise date and occasion of its delivery, as well as its chronological relationship with the *Theological Orations* (Fall, 380), remain uncertain. One of the difficulties concerns the title and the phrase περὶ . . . καταστάσεως ἐπισκόπων ("on the office of bishops"), which has been seen as particularly problematic because *Or.* 20 does not involve the ordination or installation of bishops, the normal sense of κατάστασις in this context. Yet Gregory himself offers a way out of the difficulty at the very end of the first section, where he links the responsibilities of the theologian and bishop: ἢ ψυχῆς ἐπιστασίαν δέξασθαι ἢ θεολογίᾳ προσβαλεῖν οὐκ ἀσφαλές ("it is dangerous either to accept responsibility for other souls or to take up theology"). In *Or.* 20, Gregory thus develops the theme that one ought not to undertake theology or the episcopacy lightly, but because he does so in a general way, that is, without reference to a specific individual or situation, it is difficult to indentify the precise circumstances of its composition. For a full discussion with bibliography, see Mossay's introduction in SC 270, pp. 45–53.

2. Jer 9.2.

man existence and we finally attain the blessed goal, our mirrors shattered by the reality of truth. For whether one were to pursue the study of philosophy in depth and gradually dissociate the noble and luminous element of the soul from the slough of darkness to which it is tied, or were to meet with a propitious God, or were successful in both respects and were to devote himself wholeheartedly to the contemplation of reality on high, it would only be with difficulty that he could gain mastery over the world of matter that drags him down. But before we rise above it as far as possible and sufficiently purify our ears and minds, I think it is dangerous either to accept the responsibility for other souls or to take up theology.

2. And so that you will not think me an inveterate worrier but may actually commend me for my prudence, I shall explain how I come to be apprehensive on this score by citing the testimony of Moses himself when he heard the words of God.[3] A great number had been summoned to the mountain, including Aaron and his two sons who were priests. The rest were all bidden to worship from afar. Only Moses was to approach. The people were not to go up with him. Now shortly before this, *lightnings* and thunder and trumpets and *the mountain wrapped in smoke*[4] and dire warnings and similar terrors kept the others down below. It was truly a great thing for them simply to hear God's voice, and this only after they had been thoroughly purified. But Moses went up and entered the cloud and spoke with God and received the Law, for the multitude the Law of the letter, for those above the multitude the Law of the spirit.[5]

3. I am familiar, too, with the stories of Eli[6] the priest and, shortly after him, Uzzah.[7] The one paid the penalty for his children's outrageous behavior in desecrating the sacrifices, and this despite the fact that he had refused to endorse their impiety but had on the contrary administered to them many a rebuke on many occasions. Uzzah, on the other hand, dared merely to touch the ark, which had been jostled from its place

---

3. Ex 19.21–24. 4. Ex 19.16–18.
5. Ex 24.12–15; cf. Rom 2.29, 7.6; 2 Cor 3.6–8.
6. 1 Sm 2.12–4.18. 7. 2 Sm 6.6–7.

by the ox, and, though he managed to save it, he himself perished. In this way did God preserve the sanctity of his ark. I know, too, that the multitude could not touch even the walls of the sanctuary with impunity[8]—it was for this reason that other, exterior walls were required—and that the sacrifices themselves could only be consumed by deserving persons and at a sanctioned time and place. No one so much as dreamed of entering the Holy of Holies and looking upon or touching the curtain or the mercy seat or the ark.

4. So, knowing these things, and that no one can be worthy of our great God, who was both victim and high priest, unless he first presents himself to God as *a living sacrifice*,[9] or rather, becomes a living holy *temple of the living God*,[10] how could either I myself blithely launch into a discussion about God or countenance anyone who, without further ado, does the same? That is not a commendable ambition; the attempt is fraught with peril. In fact, this is why one must first purify oneself and then enter into converse with the pure if we are not to share the fate of Manoah and, when we have beheld a vision of God, declare, We are destroyed, dear wife; we have seen *God*;[11] or, like Peter, urge Jesus to leave the boat because we are unworthy of so great a presence;[12] or, like the centurion in the Bible, seek healing but decline to receive the healer. So long as anyone of us is a centurion, with more than his share of wickedness and still in the service of Caesar, the universal ruler of creatures that creep on the ground, let him likewise say, *I am not worthy to have you come under my roof*.[13] But when I see Jesus, though I am small in spiritual stature, like the famous Zacchaeus, and climb the *sycamore*,[14] putting to death *what is earthly* in me[15] and wasting my *lowly body*,[16] then I shall both receive Christ, who will say to me, *Today salvation has come to this house*,[17] and I shall obtain salvation and live a more perfect life, distributing in virtue what I have garnered in wickedness, be it coin or doctrine.

8. Nm 17.13 (17.28 LXX).
10. 2 Cor 6.16.
12. Lk 5.8.
14. Lk 19.2–4.
16. Phil 3.21.

9. Rom 12.1.
11. Jgs 13.22.
13. Mt 8.8.
15. Col 3.5.
17. Lk 19.9.

5. Now that we have cleansed our theologian with our sermon,[18] come, let us talk a little about God too, drawing our inspiration from the Father himself and the Son and the Holy Spirit who form the topic of our sermon. I pray that I may be like Solomon and avoid eccentricity in what I think and say about God. For when he says, *For I am the most simple of all men, and there is not in me the wisdom of men*,[19] he presumably does not mean that he is guilty of a lack of discernment. How could he? Did he not, after all, ask God for this understanding above everything else[20] and obtain wisdom and insight and *largeness of mind* in richer and greater abundance than the grains of sand?[21] How does one so wise and blessed with such a gift call himself the most simple of all men? Clearly, because his understanding is not his own but the fullness of God's understanding working in him. This is also why, when Paul said, *it is no longer I who live, but Christ who lives in me*,[22] he of course was not speaking of himself as dead, but meant rather that he had attained a life beyond the ordinary by partaking of the true life, the one bounded by no death. Hence we worship the Father and the Son and the Holy Spirit, distinguishing their individual characteristics while maintaining their divine unity; and we neither confound the three into one, thus avoiding the plague of Sabellius, nor adopt the insanity of Arius and divide them into three entities that are unnaturally estranged from one another. Why must we violently swing in the opposite direction, attempting to correct one distortion with another, much as one might try to straighten a plant that leans completely to one side, when we can, by moving directly to the center, stay within piety's pale?

6. Now when I speak of the center I am talking about truth, the only object worthy of our consideration as we reject both the evil of contraction and the greater absurdity of division. We ought not, on the assumption that Father, Son, and Holy Spirit

---

18. There is a play on words between theologian (θεολόγος) and sermon (λόγος).
19. Prv 30.2 LXX.
20. 1 Kgs 3.9–14.
21. 1 Kgs 4.29 (LXX 2.35a and 5.9).
22. Gal 2.20.

are the same, adopt language that from a fear of polytheism contracts its reference to a single individually existing entity, keeping the names but stripping them of any distinction; we may just as well call all three one as say that each by definition is nothing, for they would hardly be what they are if they were interchangeable with one another. Nor, on the other hand, ought we divide them into three substances that are either foreign, dissimilar, and unrelated (which is to follow what is well called the insanity of Arius), or lack order and authority and are, so to speak, rival gods. In the first instance we are locked into the narrow position of the Jews, who restrict deity only to the ungenerated; in the second, we plunge into the equal but opposite evil of positing three individual sources and three gods, something even more absurd than the first case. We must neither be so partial to the Father that we actually strip him of his fatherhood, for whose father would he in fact be if his son were different in nature and estranged from him along with the rest of creation? Nor, by the same token, should we be so partial to Christ that we fail to preserve this very distinction, his Sonhood, for whose son would he in fact be if there were no causal relationship between his Father and himself? Nor again should we diminish the Father's status as source, proper to him as Father and generator, since he would be the source of small and worthless things were he not the cause of deity contemplated in Son and Spirit. It is our duty then both to maintain the oneness of God and to confess three individual entities, or Persons, each with his distinctive property.

7. The oneness of God would, in my view, be maintained if both Son and Spirit are causally related to him alone without being merged or fused into him and if they all share one and the same divine movement and purpose, if I may so phrase it, and are identical in essence. And the three individually existing entities will be maintained if we do not think of them as fusing or dissolving or mingling, lest those with an excessive devotion to unity end up destroying the whole. And the individual properties will be maintained if, in the case of the Father, we think and speak of him as being both source and without source (I use the term in the sense of causal agent, fount, and eternal

light); and, in the case of the Son, we do not think of him as without source but the source of all things. But when I speak of "source," do not think of time or imagine something midway between Creator and created, or by a false interposition split the nature of beings that are coeternal and conjoined. For if time were older than the Son, it would clearly be the first product of the Father's causal activity, and how can one who is in time be the creator of all time? And in what sense is he in fact the *Lord of all*[23] if he is preceded by and subject to the lordship of time? The Father, then, is without source: his existence is derived neither from outside nor from within himself. In turn, the Son is not without source if you understand "Father" to mean causal agent, since the Father is the source of the Son as causal agent, but if you take source in the temporal sense, he too is without source because the Lord of all time does not owe his source to time.

8. If, however, you are going to claim that the Son is subject to time for the reason that bodies are too, you will in fact be attributing corporeality to the incorporeal, and if you insist that the Son too made the transition from nonexistence to existence on the grounds that whatever is generated in our world does not exist at one point but comes into being after a time, you are comparing the incomparable, God and man, corporeal and incorporeal; hence because our bodies both suffer and perish so will he too. Your claim, then, is that, because bodies are generated in this way, so too is God; while I say that because bodies are so generated, God is not. Things that have a different kind of existence also have a different mode of generation, unless he is a slave to material influences in all other respects too, as for example pain and suffering and hunger and thirst and all the other afflictions either corporeal or corporeal and incorporeal together. But these are the things your mind does not accept; we are in fact speaking about God. So stop supposing that his generation too is anything other than of a divine sort.

9. But, someone retorts, if he is generated, what form did this generation take? Answer me, unerring dialectician that you

---

23. Rom 10.12.

are. If he has been created, how has he been created? And go ahead and ask me this: how was he generated? Does generation involve passion? Then so does creation. Are not mental conception and thought and the analysis of a single idea into its discrete parts a kind of passion? Is there time involved in generation? The created world also exists in time. Does space apply to this world? It does in the other too. Can generation miscarry? So too can creation. These are the arguments I have heard you make: the hand often fails to execute what the mind calls up. But, you argue, he brought everything into existence by his word and will, for *he spoke, and they were made; he commanded, and they were created.*[24] When you say that everything was created by God's word, you are not positing creation in human terms. None of us makes things happen by word. Nothing would be more sublime or effortless than ourselves if statement sufficed to bring about fact; hence, although God creates what he creates by word, his creation is not of human sort. Either show me a human being who also brings something about by word, or else admit that God does not create in a human way. All you need do is picture to yourself a city and lo! have it come into being; will yourself a son, and lo! have a boy appear; wish for anything else that can possibly happen and have your will become accomplished fact. But as surely as none of these things comes to pass as a result of our willing it so, while with God the act of will and its fulfillment are identical, man creates in one way and God, the Creator of all, in another. So if God does not create like a human being, how does it follow that he must beget like one? Once upon a time you did not exist; then you did, and now you beget. Accordingly, you bring into existence someone who did not previously exist or, in a deeper sense, perhaps it is not you at all who are doing the bringing, since Levi also, Scripture says, *was still in the loins of his ancestor*[25] before he was born. And let no one sneer at my words. I am not suggesting that the Son derives his being from the Father in that he first existed in the Father and later made his way into being, nor that he was

24. Ps 148.5 LXX.
25. Heb 7.10.

first unformed and was then formed, as is the case with human generation.

10. These are the views of malcontents, the views of those who are quick to jump on every word. They are not our thoughts or beliefs. We think that the ungenerated existence of the Father—he has always existed, for the mind's reach does not extend to a time when he did not—is coextensive with the generated existence of the Son. Hence the existence of the Father is concurrent with the generation of his only-begotten Son, who takes his being both from the Father and not after him, except in the sense that the Father is the source, that is, causal agent. I am repeating myself because your crassly materialistic cast of mind frightens me. And if you are going to refrain from inquiring impertinently into the Son's—what should I call it? generation? person? or anything better one can think of (the notion and its expression confound my powers of speech)—do not be too inquisitive about the procession of the Spirit, either. I am satisfied with the declaration that he is Son and that he is from the Father, and that the one is Father and the other Son; and I refuse to engage in meaningless speculation beyond this point. I have no wish to be like the man who loses his voice from overuse or his eyesight from staring directly into the sun: the more fully and sharply one wants to see, the more he damages his eyes and is blinded altogether, for his vision is overwhelmed by the magnitude of the sight if he insists on taking in the whole instead of only that portion that is without risk.

11. Do you hear the word "generation"? Do not go searching after the how. Do you hear "the Spirit going forth from the Father"? Do not go idly inquiring after the means. If you are curious about the Son's generation and the procession of the Spirit, I too am curious about the union of body and soul that is you. How are you dust and an image of God? What is it that makes you move or what that is set in motion? How can the same thing both move and be moved? How do your senses draw in impressions from the outside without themselves changing location? How does your mind stay with you and yet generate words in another mind? How are thoughts transmitted through words? And I have yet to ask the large questions: What is the circuit of

the sky? What is the movement of the stars or their order or measurements or conjunction or distance? What the confines of the sea? Whence the streaming winds or the changing seasons or the pouring rains? If you have not comprehended any of these things—and perhaps, my dear fellow, one day you will, when you attain *the perfect*,[26] for the words of Scripture, *I will look at thy heavens, the work of thy fingers*,[27] serve to indicate that what we see now is not truth but semblances of truth—if you have not come to know yourself, who you are who engage in these discussions, if you have not come to understand those things of which even your senses are your witness, how can you claim an exact knowledge of God, his nature and magnitude? That is the height of folly.

12. So if you have been listening to me at all, wary theologian that I am, you have understood something; now ask to understand what remains. Be content with what abides within you; let the rest abide in the treasuries of heaven. Ascend by an upright life; through purification obtain the pure. Do you wish to be a theologian one day, worthy of divinity? Seek to keep the commandments; walk in his statutes.[28] Conduct is the stepping-stone to contemplation. Devote your body to the service of your soul. Is there any man who can equal Paul's lofty status? Yet, for all that, he says that he sees *in a mirror dimly*, but that there is a time when he will see *face to face*. Are you better at discourse than another? You are most assuredly inferior to God. More sagacious perhaps than another? Your grasp of the truth is as deficient as your existence in comparison to God's. We have the promise that one day we shall know to the degree that we are known.[29] If while on this earth I may not possess to perfection knowledge of all that exists, what remains to me? What may I hope for? The kingdom of heaven, you will surely say. And I believe this to be nothing other than the attainment of that which is most pure and perfect; and the most perfect of the things that are is the knowledge of God. So one part let us secure and

26. 1 Cor 13.10.
27. Ps 8.3.
28. Cf. 1 Kgs 6.12.
29. 1 Cor 13.12.

let us reach another while we are on the face of the earth; and the remainder let us reserve for the other life that we may receive, as the fruit of our labor, this, the illumination of the Holy Trinity in the fullness of its being and character and magnitude (if to speak so violates no law of God), in Christ himself, our Lord, to whom be the power and the glory forever and ever. Amen.

ORATION 22

Second Oration on Peace. Delivered in Constantinople on the occasion of the strife that arose among the people regarding a quarrel among certain bishops.[1]

ELOVED PEACE, sweet both in fact and in name, the gift that I and my people have exchanged with one another—I do not know whether it is in every case a sincere profession and worthy of the Spirit and not just the sort of conventional public gesture that God refuses to countenance and that brings down upon ourselves even greater condemnation! Beloved peace, my preoccupation and my glory—we hear that it both belongs to God and characterizes God, represents in fact the very essence of God, as the Scriptural expressions, *the peace of God*,[2] and *the God of peace*,[3] and *he is our peace*,[4] attest, though this is not the way that we honor him! Beloved peace, the blessing celebrated by all but preserved by few, how did you abandon us for so long now? When will you return to us? How very much I miss you and more than all other men bid you welcome! Both when you are with me I am your devoted servant and when you are absent I cry out for your return with more tears and lament than either the patriarch Jacob exhibited for the famous Joseph himself, whom he believed to have been ravaged by a wild beast when he had actually been sold by his brothers,[5] or David for his friend Jonathan, a casualty of war,[6] or

---

1. PG 35.1132A–52A. Delivered in Constantinople, probably in 379. The chronological sequence of *Or.* 22 and 23, as well as their relationship to the *First Oration on Peace, Or.* 6, is in dispute. The most recent editor, J. Mossay in SC 270, follows the manuscript tradition in identifying *Or.* 22 as the *Third Oration on Peace* and *Or.* 23 as the *Second Oration on Peace;* this order is inverted in the Maurist edition published in PG.

2. Phil 4.7.
3. 2 Cor 13.11.
4. Eph 2.14.
5. Gn 37.34–35.
6. Cf. 2 Sm 1.17–27.

subsequently for his son Absalom.⁷ Jacob, his father's heart wrenched with grief, cried, *Joseph is without doubt torn to pieces* by a savage wild beast;⁸ and, holding his son's bloodied cloak in his hands, he clutched it as though it were his child's body, inflaming and soothing his grief at the same time. David, on the other hand, reacts in the first instance by cursing the mountains where the battle was fought with the words, *Ye mountains of Gilboa, let there be no dew or rain upon you*, and, *How* are the bow *of Jonathan* and his might fallen;⁹ but in the second he defends the parricide as though he had done no wrong and makes his peace with the dead, the deep grief he felt for his child resulting perhaps from the very fact that he had raised his hand against his father. So his father's heart; the son he had fought in battle as an enemy after he was dead he misses like a beloved friend, and natural instinct, than which nothing is more powerful, overcomes hostility.

2. Sad it was too when the ark fell into foreign hands¹⁰ and Jerusalem was razed and trampled by the nations, and the sons of Zion, prized and precious as gold, were led off into captivity to remain scattered to this very day, a people strangers and sojourners in the world. But horrible are what we both see and hear in our own day too: regions depopulated, casualties in the thousands, an earth groaning under the weight of blood and corpses, a race speaking a foreign tongue overrunning a country not their own as if it were their private preserve.¹¹ Let no one accuse our champions of cowardice: they are, after all, the ones who have conquered virtually the entire world. No, it is our own wickedness that is to blame and our current impiety towards the Trinity. Horrible things these, beyond horrible even! Can this be denied by anyone who knows the meaning of misfortune from personal experience or the suffering of others? There is

---

7. 2 Sm 18.33–19.4. 8. Gn 37.33.
9. 2 Sm 1.21–27. 10. 1 Sm 4.11.
11. Gothic tribes defeated and killed the emperor Valens at Adrianople in August 378 and continued to wreak havoc in the Balkan peninsula, overrunning Macedonia in 380, before they were brought to terms by Theodosius. Gregory likens the effect of their incursions to the Diaspora and characterizes them as barbarians both figuratively and in the literal sense of speaking a foreign (that is, non-Greek) language.

nothing worse than peace put to flight, the Church stripped of her beauty, her ancient dignity destroyed and her good order reversed to such a degree that we, who once became a people from a non-people[12] and a nation from a non-nation, now risk our disintegration as a matchless people and nation back into our former condition of a non-people and a non-nation, our original state when you did not rule us and we had not banded together under one name and one standard.

3. Indeed, it actually seems easier to endure adversity than to sustain prosperity: even we in time past, when we were beleaguered, drew strength from the persecutions and joined together; then, once we did, we fell apart. What thinking person could fail to deplore our present circumstances? Who can find words equal to the tragedy? Robbers enjoy peace united by their criminality, as do the henchmen of tyranny, or consorts in fraud, or conspirators in sedition, or partners in adultery, and one might add, bands of choruses and troops of soldiers and complements of ships; for I shall not mention the equitable distribution of legacies, political parties, the orderly succession of offices and public services according to law, and of course our much touted sophistic, or grammatic (not to say philosophy), a pursuit that is all the rage among our young people and rarely shows dissension but is for the most part a peaceful enterprise. We, on the other hand, are bound by no common bond or cause and can never reach agreement nor does there appear to be any way to cure our malady; we behave instead as though we were initiators and initiates not of virtue but of vice, fanning the flames of division while showing little or no interest at all in unity. Yet if those groups are at odds, their dissension is no serious matter. In some cases conflict is in fact better than concord, for what thinking person would approve of unions formed for evil purpose?

4. But if someone asked us, what is it that you worship and respect, we should readily reply, love, for in the Holy Spirit's own words our *God is Love*.[13] This is in fact the name God cherishes

---

12. 1 Pt 2.9–10.
13. 1 Jn 4.16.

above all others. What is the sum of the Law and the Prophets?[14] This is the only answer the Evangelist would accept. Why in the world, then, do we, the disciples of love, hate one another so? Why do we, the disciples of peace, engage in wars which do not admit of treaty or truce? Why are we, the disciples of the *chief corner stone*,[15] detached from one another? Why do we, the disciples of the rock, wobble this way and that?[16] Why are we, the disciples of light, blind?[17] Why are we, the disciples of the Word, so mute or foolish or crazed—I know not what term to use—that we glut ourselves with food and sleep and song and activities lewd in the highest degree, as they say; and our life is more than filled not only with all forms of pain but also of pleasure most sweet, all displacing and supplanting one another by turns. We exchange blows without limit not only against those who hold different views and stand apart from us on the definition of the faith—which would be less troubling since one could excuse the behavior on the grounds of religious zeal, a praiseworthy thing, provided it stays within bounds—but now even against those who profess the same faith and with whom we share a common enemy on common issues: this is what is most dreadful and deplorable.

5. And what is the reason? Love of power, perhaps, or of money, or envy or hate or arrogance or one of the vices to which we see not even the heathen succumb; and what is amusing is the way we alter our judgments. When we are caught we are God-fearing and orthodox and dishonestly take refuge in the truth as if our dispute were in defense of the faith; and the only decent thing we do (if vices can be decent)—were it not in fact the most disgraceful—is to feel uneasy about our immoral conduct and give it a respectable name by calling it piety. You madman! one might say. Devious rascal! Creature of the Devil, the master of evil, to behave this way, whoever you are! Or, more to the point, you mindless fool! Yesterday this man was pious as far as you were concerned. How then can he be impious today when he has not added or eliminated anything either in word

14. Mt 22.36–40.
16. Cf. Lk 6.48.
15. Eph 2.20.
17. Cf. Jn 12.35–36.

or deed but remains the same? Who breathes the same air, sees the same sun through the same eyes, and, if you will, when asked a question in arithmetic or geometry, for example, gives the selfsame answer? And the Joseph of yesterday is in your eyes today even a fornicator:[18] this is how far the controversy has actually gone, like flame racing through the brush and consuming what is around it; and today's Judas or Caiaphas was yesterday Elijah or John or someone else from among those who have taken up their post at Christ's side and wear the same belt and dress in the same gray or black habit to symbolize, in my view and estimation, their holy calling; and their pallor, the beautiful bloom of sublime beings, or their low, measured tone of voice, or calm and stately step we yesterday called philosophy but today vanity; and we have ascribed the same power over spirits and sicknesses to Jesus one day and to Beelzebul the next,[19] guided therein by the corrupt standard of contentiousness and passion.

6. And just as the same earth stands still for the strong and healthy but sways for those dizzy with vertigo, the condition of the observer being transferred to the object of observation; or, if you will, just as the same amount of space between columns appears greater to those close at hand and smaller to those farther away because distance creates a distorted impression of the spacing and the eye tends to run together things that have more bulk, in the same way we too, depending upon whether we are friends or not, are easily tricked by our enmity and fail to perceive the same things in the same ways. Indeed, circumstance easily, if contrary to all expectation, ordains many as saints in our eyes, but many, too, as atheists, or rather, all of us as miserable wretches not only because we follow a bad example (vice is so common a commodity that no one need drag us to it) but also because we readily grant everything to everybody so long as they join us in our madness. And formerly the mere utterance of an idle word was not without its peril,[20] while now we revile even the most pious; and at one time it was not permitted

---

18. Cf. Gn 39.7–20.   19. Cf. Mt 12.24–27; Lk 11.15.
20. Cf. Mt 12.36.

to read *the law without* and to call for *public professions,*[21] which I take to mean popular approval, while now we rely on the profane to judge our mysteries, casting what is holy *to the dogs* and throwing our *pearls before swine.*[22] And not only this, but we even regale their ears with our mutual insults and cannot grasp the simple fact that it is dangerous to entrust a weapon to an enemy or anti-Christian slogans to one who hates Christians. For the abusive language that we adopt today will be directed against us tomorrow, and the enemy laps up what we say, not because he approves, but because he is hoarding his bitter venom so that he may in due time spew it against the believer.

7. Why, my brothers, do we behave this way? And for how long? When shall we recover from our drunkenness or wipe the film from our eyes and gaze steadfastly at the light of truth? What sort of moral blindness is this? What is this twilight warfare? What this maelstrom that makes no distinction between friend and foe? Why have we become *a taunt to our neighbors, mocked and derided by those round about us?*[23] What is this zest for evil? Why this superhuman effort to the point of exhaustion? Did I say exhaustion? On the contrary, we are invigorated by evil, as the deranged commonly are, and we relish our own annihilation. And nowhere is there a word, no friend, no ally, no doctor to heal or excise the wound; no guardian angel, no God, but, along with everything else, we have shut our very selves off from God's tender mercy as well. *Why dost thou stand afar off, O Lord*[24] and how *wilt thou hide thyself for ever?*[25] When will you make your presence felt among us? Where will these things finally end? I fear that our present circumstances may be wisps from the fire to come, that the Antichrist may be keeping his eye on these events and seize upon our faults and frailties as an opportunity to assert his own supremacy. For there is every chance that he will not attack the strong or those who have closed ranks in love. No. First, the kingdom must be divided against itself; then the strong reason that is within us must be subjected to temptation and bound; then our goods must be

21. Am 4.5 LXX.
23. Ps 79.4 (LXX 78.4).
25. Ps 89.46 (LXX 88.47).

22. Mt 7.6.
24. Ps 10.1 (LXX 9.22).

plundered,[26] and we suffer what we now see the enemy suffering at Christ's hands.

8. This is why *I weep*, says Jeremiah in the Lamentations,[27] and I wish that *my eyes* were *a fountain of tears*[28] copious enough for our affliction; and I call on *the skillful women*[29] to make lament or to join us in ours; and *My anguish, my anguish! I writhe in pain!*[30] and there is nothing I can do or say to ease the pain. This is why past events are shrouded in silence while recent ones are given the color of comedy: my personal tragedy[31] is just that to my enemies, a comedy. This is why we have reduced the role of our churches to no small extent and transferred it to the stage, and have done so in a city such as this, which takes great relish in playing with matters divine as it does with anything else and would sooner ridicule something that demands respect than see no humor in the truly laughable. Hence I should be surprised if I too, the newly arrived preacher of piety, did not today become the butt of her ridicule for my remarks and for teaching that not everything is open to ridicule and that there are some things that must be treated seriously. And why do I say ridicule? It would be surprising if I were not asked to pay damages as well because of my willingness to help. For our affairs are such that I at least am not distressed, either by our occupied churches, as a mean spirit might be, or gold pouring into others' hands or by vicious tongues doing the only thing they know how, speaking evil because they have not learned how to speak good.

9. There is no danger that the Godhead will ever be circumscribed by space or become a piece of merchandise monopolized by the well-to-do. Neither my admirers nor my detractors will make me change—unlike those who mix perfume with mire or mire with perfume and in the process confuse their properties—so that, in consequence of my presumed transfor-

26. Mk 3.24–27.   27. Lam 1.15.
28. Jer 9.1.   29. Jer 9.17.
30. Jer 4.19.
31. It is unclear whether Gregory is referring to some specific event, such as the attempted assasination described in *De vita sua* 1445–65, or to his troubles in general.

mation, I take offense at disparaging remarks. I really should reward my admirers handsomely if their admiration made me a better person. But that is not now the case. How could it be? I remain just as I am, whether reviled or flattered. *But a mortal vainly buoys himself up with words,* says Job;[32] and just as foam swirls around a rock or breezes about a pine or a tall, bushy tree, to the same degree do tongues swirl around me and prompt me to reflect somewhat as follows: if my accuser is a liar, what he says is a mark against him more than me even though he attacks me by name; but if he is telling the truth, I shall blame myself more than I do him because, although I instigate his remarks, he is not responsible for my being the way I am; and so I shall ignore what he says as of no account and be my regular self, benefiting from his vicious slanders only to the extent of living my life with greater circumspection. Third, there is something quite grand and even noble about the verbal abuse to which we are subjected in that we are reviled in the same breath with God, for the same persons who deny Godhead also vilify the theologian. Consequently, none of these attacks is so terrible, even if most people think they are. What is terrible is that no longer is anyone considered trustworthy or guileless and good and free from sham even if he is most sound of soul and pure in his piety; rather one man is manifestly evil while another puts on a fair face as a cosmetic to seduce us with the appearance of probity.

10. The fact of the matter is that not all people are blackguards because some are; nor ill-bred, or homely, or cowardly, or dissolute because a great many are so, but each person is judged on his own merits and none of the things we consider praiseworthy or reprehensible is doled out indiscriminately to all alike. The poison of vice, however, with no difficulty inundates us all and its manifestation not just among many but even among few results in the universal indictment of us all, and the most frightening thing is that it does not limit itself to ourselves alone but reaches into our great and holy mystery. As almost always happens when people pass judgment on the affairs of an-

32. Jb 11.12 LXX.

other,[33] some of our critics are quite considerate and kind, while others are thoroughly harsh and insensitive. The one group holds us personally responsible for our depravity and absolves our dogma of any blame; the other finds the law itself[34] guilty of inculcating evil, especially when they meet up with the numerous rascals who have been entrusted with leadership.

11. Why these things, my friends, and for how long? Will we not show some restraint, late though it be? Will we not come to our senses? Will we not feel any shame? If nothing else, will we not defend ourselves against the tongues of the enemy with their glib and false vilifications? Will we not put an end to this wrangling? Will we not determine what issues admit investigation and to what degree, and which exceed our capacity? Which again are peculiar to our present situation and the confusion that clouds our judgment here below and which involve the life to come and our deliverance in it, so that we may in the meantime devote ourselves to these and purify ourselves for the others in the belief that one day we shall be made perfect and attain our desire? Will we not decide among ourselves which issues we should not look into at all, which should receive our attention, but with restrictions, and which we should concede and relinquish, whatever form they take, to those who like to argue, on the grounds that they are matters that do not adversely affect our doctrine in any way? Which, too, are the exclusive province of faith, and which are receptive to our powers of thought as well? Which again are also worth fighting for, not with weapons, but with reason ardently applied? For physical violence, even against those who hate us, has absolutely no place in the Christian community and should be repudiated.

12. Will we not hold to a single test of piety, the worship of Father, Son, and Holy Spirit, one Godhead and power in the three, without overworshipping or underworshipping one in particular (if I may permit myself for a moment to imitate those

---

33. Cf. Rom 14.4.
34. It does not seem necessary to make a clear-cut distinction between dogma and law; rather, the point is that some people blame the system when the leadership is corrupt while others are able to distinguish between individual and institutional failings.

who go in for these expressions; in point of fact, the one case is impossible, the other impious) and carving up their single majesty with novelties of language? Nothing is greater than itself, or less. Once this at least has been defined, we shall reach agreement on all the other points as well; after all, we worship the same Trinity, subscribe to virtually the same beliefs, and belong to the same body; and the futile and barren offshoots and excrescences of the issues currently under discussion we shall cut away like a public cancer and destroy. Or, I ask you—and here I shall confine myself to the more recent examples—was not Montanus's[35] evil spirit directed against the Holy Spirit enough; and Novatus's[36] arrogance, or rather, impure purity that tries to lure the multitude with fair-seeming words; and the ravings of the Phrygians,[37] continuing still today, who administer and receive sacraments in rites almost identical to those of old; and the folly of the Galatians[38] with their wealth of impious terminology; and the contraction of Sabellius and the division of Arius and the further subdivision by our own masters of sophistry,[39] who differ to the degree that a fast tongue differs from a slow one? And yet we too in effect differ among our very selves: while we are fundamentally sound, we are split for and against the same men.

13. I am referring of course to the internal conflict that recently arose between brothers and has brought dishonor to

---

35. Montanus founded a religious movement in Phrygia during the latter part of the second century. Montanism was characterized by ecstatic prophecy, which its adherents attributed to the inspiration of the Holy Spirit.

36. Novatus, or Novatian, was a Roman presbyter who, following the Decian persecution (249–51), formed a rigorist splinter group calling themselves the "pure ones."

37. Phrygia was home both to the Montanists, also known as Cataphrygians, and to the orgiastic cult of the mother goddess Cybele.

38. The Galatians were followers of Marcellus, bishop of Ancyra in Galatia, who died c. 374. He was the author of an anti-Arian treatise intended to refute arguments put forward by Asterius, a converted rhetorician. In the process, however, Marcellus fell into the error of monarchianism and was condemned by a succession of church councils, including that of Constantinople in 381.

39. The "masters of sophistry" have been identified as followers of Eunomius, a contemporary of Gregory and leader of an extremist Arian sect known as the anomoeans because of their view that Father and Son were dissimilar (ἀνόμοιος) in essence.

both God and man.[40] God is dishonored by the view that he was not even born for us at all nor nailed to the cross, and, obviously, was neither buried nor arose, as some perverse "lovers of Christ" have thought, but receives honor only here on earth, where honor is in reality dishonor. The result is that he is cut—or combined—into two sons. Man, on the other hand, is dishonored by the view that he was not fully assumed, or honored, but was rejected and estranged in his greatest attribute, the greatest attribute in man's nature being precisely his divine image and intellectual faculty. For the uniting of Christ's divinity would necessarily require the dividing of his humanity, and those who are in other respects wise would be mindless with regard to his mind and I should not be wholly saved, I who have wholly sinned and was condemned through the disobedience of the first-formed and the treachery of the Devil. Here the result is that God's grace and our salvation are diminished. And there is the further fact that we who have been made secure by salvation from God engage in war on behalf of men and have such a superabundance of contentiousness that we have supplied it even to the aspirations of others and adopt enmities of our own to advance thrones not our own,[41] thereby committing two most serious transgressions in one: we both inflame their rapacity and use it ourselves to bolster our own fanaticism, just as those who have slipped clutch at the more sturdy bushes or the rocks that are within reach.

14. We should in fact strive to make them weaker too by refusing to become involved. In this way we should be doing them a greater favor than by fighting for them. As it is, they make and receive allies—a most deplorable state of affairs, in my view at least—with the result that the world has now actually been divided into two opposing camps, and this after it had been

---

40. The conflict referred to here is Apollinarianism, which diminished the humanity of Christ and thus the promise of salvation by holding that Christ incarnate lacked reason and that this human faculty was replaced by the divine word.

41. The schism that originated in Antioch with the appointment of two rival bishops, Meletius and Paulinus, in 360 and 362 respectively, continued to embroil the sees of Alexandria, Constantinople, and Rome during Gregory's tenure in the capital.

brought together by arduous effort, little by little, and with much shedding of blood. And everything that makes for peace and moderation suffers badly at the hands of both whether through scorn or open attack. We who today make these accusations include ourselves in this number as well and this is why we have accepted this office that has been fought over and contested so bitterly. It is therefore not at all surprising that we are worn down by the friction of both parties and after much sweat and toil withdraw from our post of moderation in the middle and leave them to unleash the full force of their wrath against one another at close range with no wall or barrier between them. For it is God who first and foremost will decide and settle these issues, he who establishes a bond between all things; and second, those of mankind who work for the good and recognize the blessings of concord. These blessings originate with the Holy Trinity, whose unity of nature and internal peace are its most salient characteristic, are received by the angelic and divine powers who are peaceably disposed towards God as well as one another, extend to the whole of creation, whose glory is its absence of conflict, and regulate our own life: in our soul, on the one hand, through the reciprocal and cooperative allegiance of its virtues; in our body, on the other, through the happy marriage of form and function in its constituent members. Of these, the former both is and is called beauty; the latter, health.

15. For my part I applaud the words of Solomon who, just as he does *for every matter*, lays down a time for both war and peace.[42] I shall add only this: we must see to it that we observe the due season for both since, according to the precept expressed in his verse, it is actually possible in some cases to fight a good war; but, as long as we can, we should incline rather to peace as the more Godlike and sublime course. How absurd it is to hold that harmony constitutes the greatest good in private life but does not serve the public interest in like degree; and that the best managed household and city are those that display the least possible internal dissension or none at all, but if they

---

42. Eccl 3.1, 8.

do, very quickly return to normal, their wounds healed, while for the community of the Church, on the other hand, there is some other standard that is better and more seemly. It is also absurd that each and every person strives for inner peace (peace being our individual goal, along with the mastery of the passions) but does not show himself the same to others, believing instead that his neighbor's ruination is his own renown; and that God bids us forgive even those who trespass against us not just seven times but with a frequency based on the conviction that forgiving is the guarantor of our being forgiven,[43] while we, on the other hand, are more eager to maltreat even those who do us no harm than to receive kindness from others. It is equally absurd to know that the blessedness reserved for the peacemakers is so great that they alone of the ranks of the saved are called the sons *of God*,[44] while we, on the other hand, relish hostility and then imagine that we are actually doing things dear to God, him who suffered for our sake that he might reconcile us to himself and dissolve the war in our hearts!

16. No, my friends and brothers, let us banish such thoughts. Let us revere peace, the gift of the God of peace, which he left for us as his special parting legacy when he went from this world.[45] Let us know a single war, that against the power of the Adversary. Let us say "brother" even to those who hate us, if they will permit it. Let us forgive the small affront that we may espouse the greater good, concord. Let us give way that we may prevail. You observe the techniques in athletic contests: by taking the lower position wrestlers often prevail over those on top of them. These let us emulate, not the more voracious types of dinner-guest or merchant who, after stuffing themselves beyond limit with the food laid before them, or overloading their boat, burst or go under before they can enjoy their greediness and so pay a big price for a small return. This, then, is both my cry and my testimony, and I shall not cease to carry out the Biblical injunction, *For Zion's sake I will not keep silent and for Jerusalem's sake I will not rest*,[46] because *I am fainting before the* slain,[47] that is, our-

43. Mt 18.22.
45. Jn 14.27.
47. Jer 4.31.
44. Mt 5.9.
46. Is 62.1.

selves, who bear the wounds not of the sword or starvation, but of the lust for glory or power, so that those who fall do not even become the objects of pity so much as of hatred. As for you, if you take my words to heart, that will be an advantage to us both; but if you scorn and repudiate them because your fury has got the better of your reason, I have sufficiently discharged my duty to both God and man. No one, not even if he is among the most peaceable and God-loving of men, will ask for anything more. You yourselves will know the consequences. I shall not add anything in a harsher vein myself, since it is the custom of fathers to be lenient toward their children. May you find the great judge propitious and peaceable, now and in the day of retribution, in Christ himself our Lord, to whom be the glory and the power forever and ever. Amen.

ORATION 23

Third Oration on Peace. On the accord that we of common faith have reached following our quarrel.[1]

EAL IS FERVENT, the Spirit is gentle, love is something kind, or rather, the very essence of kindness, and hope something long-suffering. Zeal lights a fire, the Spirit soothes, hope abides, and love binds together the good that is within us and does not permit it to dissolve, even though our nature is subject to dissolution, and one of three things may happen to it: love either remains as it is, or, if it is disturbed, steadies itself, or, if it is deflected it returns, just like plants that have been forcibly bent back with our hands and then released.[2] They quickly revert to their true nature and in so doing show their basic proclivity: they can be made to bend by force but they do not right themselves by force. For vice is by nature something easily accessible and the road to corruption wide, a torrent tumbling straight down or a bit of brush that is easily kindled by wind and spark and, as it turns to flame, con-

---

1. PG 35.1152B–68A. The date of this homily as well as its relationship to *Or.* 6 and 22 is problematic because the internal evidence is so ambiguous as to preclude the positive identification of the quarrel referred to in the title and thus the time and place of its delivery. A related difficulty concerns the identity of the father and son mentioned in section 5. If, as many have assumed, Gregory is referring to himself and his own father, then *Or.* 23 must antedate 374, the year of the elder Gregory's death. On this basis, the most recent editor, J. Mossay, follows the ancient tradition and groups it with *Or.* 6, given at Nazianzus in 364, noting that intellectually *Or.* 23 is closer to Gregory's student days in Athens than to his episcopal career in Constantinople. However, the same observation could also be made of *Or.* 25, and other scholars such as J. Bernardi, *La prédication des pères cappadociens* (Paris: Presses Universitaires de France, 1968), pp. 177–81, place *Or.* 23 after *Or.* 22, assigning its delivery to Constantinople in 380. See SC 270, pp. 260–75, and, for the related problem of the title of this homily, *Or.* 22, n. 1.

2. This image also appears in *Or.* 6.8. and 20.5

sumes itself along with the product of its own creation. For fire is the product that matter produces, as well as the agent of its destruction, just as vice destroys the vicious and vanishes along with what feeds it. If one has nurtured some good quality that has molded his character, transgression becomes more difficult than becoming good in the first place, for every virtue that is firmly rooted by time and reason becomes second nature, as does the love within us too, with which we worship the true love and which we have folded to our hearts in love and adopted as the guiding principle for all our existence.

2. Where then are those who keep a close watch on our affairs, successes and failures alike, not to judge them, but to voice their disapproval; not to share in our happiness but to gloat over us and belittle our accomplishments and in melodramatic tones to magnify our faults and use the lapses of their neighbors as an excuse for their own miserable conduct? Would theirs were a fair evaluation! For there would be a certain benefit even in bile,[3] as the proverb has it, if fear of the enemy could keep us more secure; as it is, their judgment of us is tainted by hostility and a malevolence that beclouds their minds, so that even their invective lacks credibility. Where then are those who hate the Godhead as much as they hate us? This is the most magnificent thing to happen to us: we are put in the dock together with God. Just where, we ask you, are those judges who are lenient when their own personal affairs are concerned but ruthless in their scrutiny of matters affecting others so that here too they may misrepresent the truth? Just where, we ask you, are those who berate us for our bruises when they bear the marks of wounds themselves? who ridicule us for stumbling when they themselves fall down flat? who take delight in our flecks of dirt while they themselves wallow in the mud? who are blinded by the logs in their own eyes yet point the finger at the specks in ours which neither cause discomfort because they are not deeply embedded nor are difficult to blow away or remove?[4]

3. Come, partake of our mysteries! We invite you to meet

---

3. This proverb appears to be otherwise unattested.
4. Mt 7.4.

with us, even though we are the objects of your hatred. We submit to the arbitration of our enemies—what arrogance, or should I say confidence!—so that you may go off ashamed and defeated—and what is the greatest paradox of all—having learned our true strength from the signs of our weakness. For it was not about the Godhead that we disagreed. Our conflict instead was in defense of protocol; nor were we arguing over which of two impieties we should choose, the one that contracts God, or the one that severs from the divine essence either the Spirit alone or the Son as well as the Spirit; in other words, a single or a double dose of impiety. These, in short, are the issues that mark our present malaise. *In* their hearts they purpose *to go up*,[5] not to a profession but to a denial of faith, and not to theology but to blasphemy. One man is more lavish than the next with his rich store of impiety, as though out of fear, not of committing impiety, but of showing moderation in the process and more sensitivity than anyone else.

4. We, however, are a different sort. We concur and agree regarding the Godhead in no less a fashion than the Godhead is in internal agreement with itself, if it is not presumptuous to say this; and we have become *one lip and one language*,[6] but in an opposite way from those who once built the tower. They were unanimous in their pursuit of an evil end, whereas our efforts toward harmony have as their object every highest good, the exalting of Father, Son, and Holy Spirit, with one heart and one voice that it may be said of us, and not only said, but also believed, that *God is really among* us,[7] who unites those who unite him and exalts those who exalt him. There are, however, other points on which we have been in disagreement, and regrettably so here too, I shall not deny it (we ought not give the Devil any opening or opportunity, nor malicious tongues free rein). Still, these differences have not been so great as our detractors imagine. As humans, it was to be expected that we should commit some sin. Our transgression is simply that we have been too loyal to our pastors[8] and that we could not decide, agreeing as we

5. Ps 84.5 (LXX 83.6).   6. Gn 11.1 LXX.
7. 1 Cor 14.25.
8. The context does not permit the identification of these pastors, but those

did that both were equally admirable, which of two goods we should prefer. This is our crime. This is the evidence on which anyone who so wishes should condemn or acquit us. It is on this that the heretics base their case; nothing more, however much you may wish it. *Flies make the ointment give off an evil odor,* says the preacher, when they die and decay in it.[9] Envy aspires to contaminate morals but will not succeed. I range myself with Esdras: *Truth is the strongest thing of all.*[10]

5. And so, we have ourselves managed to resolve our own differences in the past, and we will continue to resolve them. It is not possible for children to judge their parents unfairly,[11] especially under the intercession of the common Trinity on whose behalf we are attacked and for whose sake we shall forbear to take up arms. I am the guarantor of peace, inadequate though I am to so great a task, because the Lord gives grace to the humble[12] and brings the lofty to the ground.[13] But how will this help you, our collective mediators? For mediators you are, even though you serve reluctantly. If we show our wickedness in some matter, trivial or important, you do not thereby become pious; if we commit some infraction, of course we do not merit commendation for our behavior; but the fact that it is we who sin does not make you less impious: you may perhaps be even more so insofar as you are more hardened sinners than the rest of us.[14] And so that you may know that we are of one mind on every issue, and may learn that accordingly we shall be of one mind on every occasion in the future as well, not only has the evidence before you already, I think, supplied the proof but let my own words also confirm it: a conscientious father and a dutiful son,[15] sitting side by side complementing one another and

---

who favor a later date for this homily, i.e., ca. 379–80, see here a possible allusion to Melitius and Paulinus, the bishops involved in the Antiochene schism.

9. Eccl 10.1.
10. 1 Esd 4.35.
11. Here, Gregory is speaking metaphorically.
12. Prv 3.34; Jas 4.6.
13. Ps 147.6 (LXX 146.6).
14. The point of this convoluted passage is that Gregory's failings, however great they may be, do not justify his opponents' behavior.
15. It is unclear whether Gregory is referring to himself and his own father or someone else. See n. 1, above.

helping to kindle that spark of harmony and good will that is within you. As for him, you have heard him speak, and your applause is still ringing in my ears; and, I am sure that what lies in your hearts is of greater moment than what is diffused in the air. As for us, you will hear us again, as often as you like. And, if anyone considers our frequent public statements insufficient proof, let the trials and the stonings[16] convince him, both those that we have already suffered and those that we are prepared to suffer, confident that it is not suffering that is the punishment but the lack of it, all the more so since we have tasted danger for Christ's sake and have come away with its noblest fruit, the increase of this people.

6. What, then, is your wish? Are you convinced? There is no need for any further effort on my part? You do not require a second discourse on the Deity and so spare my infirmity, thanks to which I can hardly address you even now? Or should the same message reverberate over and over again, as for the hard of hearing, so that the constant din may penetrate your ears and we be heard? Your silence seems to be an invitation to speak. As the saying goes, Silence is assent.[17] So listen to us both: we speak with one heart and one mouth. I am sorry that I cannot climb a high mountain, find a voice equal to the strength of my feeling and declaim before the world and all the wrongheaded people in it as though before a grand theater: *O ye sons of men, how long will ye be slow of heart? Wherefore do ye love vanity, and seek falsehood?*[18] You posit not a single nor an uncompounded nature of divinity but either three that are alienated and disjoined from one another and, not surprisingly, in conflict by virtue of their being proportionately superior or inferior; or you posit a single nature, but one that is constricted and mean, and which is not in a position to be the source of anything significant precisely because it cannot or will not, and this for two reasons, either

---

16. Gregory's autobiographical poem, *De vita sua* 665, contains a reference to stoning that took place in April 379. See further the discussion by J. Mossay in SC 270, p. 291, n. 3.

17. Alexander of Aphrodisias, *Commentaria in Aristotelem Graeca*, ed. M. Wallies (Berlin, 1898), vol. 2.3, p. 53.28: "Silence means yes"; cf. also p. 60.35; John Chrysostom, *In Transfigurationem*, PG 61.721.

18. Ps 4.2 LXX.

envy or fear: envy, because it wishes to avoid the introduction of something that is of equal importance; fear, lest it take on a hostile and belligerent element. In fact, God is the object of proportionately more honor than his creatures are to the degree that it is more in keeping with the greater majesty of the first cause to be the source of divinity rather than of creatures and to reach the creatures through the medium of divinity rather than the reverse, that is, for divinity to acquire substantive existence for their sakes, as our very subtle and high-flown thinkers imagine.

7. For if, while admitting the dignity of the Son and the Holy Spirit, we implied that they are either without source or from a different source, we should in fact face the terrible risk of dishonoring God or of setting up a rival deity. But if, no matter how highly you exalt the Son or the Spirit, you do not proceed to place them above the Father, or alienate them from him as their cause, but attribute their noble generation and marvelous procession to him, I shall simply ask you, my friend, you who are so fond of the expressions "unbegotten" and "without source," who dishonors God more, the one who regards him as the source of the kinds of beings you yourself introduce, or the one who regards him as the source not of such, but of those which are like him in nature and equal to him in honor, the kind that our doctrine professes? Your own son is to you a great, indeed, a very great, cause for honor, and all the more so if he takes after his father in all respects, and bears the true stamp of his sire, and you would prefer to be the parent of a single child rather than the master of countless slaves. Similarly, is there any greater cause for honor in God's case than being the Father of his Son? This adds to his glory, not detracts from it, as does the fact that the Holy Spirit also proceeds from him. Or are you unaware that in regarding God as the source of "creatures," by which I mean the Son and the Holy Spirit, you not only fail to honor the source but you also dishonor whatever issues from it? You dishonor the source by referring it to beings that are inconsequential and unworthy of divinity; you dishonor the issue, by making them inconsequential, and not merely creatures, but of all creatures the least honored. If in fact it was for the sake of

these creatures that the Son and the Spirit came into existence at some point in time, like a craftsman's tools that do not exist before the craftsman has made them, their only reason for being would be that God chose to use them to create something, on the grounds that his will was not enough; for everything that exists for the sake of something else is held in less esteem than the thing for which it was produced.

8. I, on the other hand, by positing a source of divinity that is independent of time, inseparable, and infinite, honor both the source as well as its issue: the source, because of the nature of the things of which it is the source; the issue, because of their own nature as well as of the nature of the source from which they are derived, because they are disparate neither in time, nor in nature, nor in holiness. They are one in their separation and separate in their conjunction, even if this is a paradoxical statement; revered no less for their mutual relationship than when they are thought of and taken individually; a perfect Trinity of three perfect entities; a monad taking its impetus from its superabundance, a dyad transcended (that is, it goes beyond the form and matter of which bodies consist), a triad defined by its perfection since it is the first to transcend the synthesis of duality in order that the Godhead might not be constricted or diffused without limit, for constriction bespeaks an absence of generosity; diffusion, an absence of order. The one is thoroughly Judaic; the other, Greek and polytheistic.

9. I also take into consideration the possibility, one that perhaps does not reflect ignorance and naivete on my part so much as careful thought, that you do not assume any risk at all when you posit the Son as begotten. For, you may be sure, the ingenerate does not experience generation in the way that bodies and material substances do since he is not a body. This even the popular conceptions about God concede. So why do we feel fear *where there is no fear*[19] and why do we engage in vain impiety, as Scripture says? I, on the other hand, believe I do run the risk of compromising the Deity if I admit the creature, for what is created is not God, and what shares the yoke of servitude cannot be

---

19. Ps 14.5 (LXX 13.5) LXX.

defined as master, even if it represents the very best that the world of servitude and creation has to offer and is the only thing in this vile station to display the quality of loving-kindness.[20] For whoever withholds the honor due bestows not honor through what he gives but rather dishonor through what he takes away, even though his act gives the semblance of honor.

10. And if you start to speculate on passions in connection with generation, I too shall do so in the matter of creation; I am, of course, aware that no created thing is created without passion. But if he was not begotten and if you were not created, admit the rest of your argument since your use of the term "creature" presumes the like for all practical purposes. There is nothing that you hesitate to venture or attempt, perverse judge and critic of the Deity that you are. The only way that you could gain any credibility at all is by relegating God to a position far removed from any real power, just as on earth those of a tyrannical or avaricious bent do to those weaker than they. As for myself, I shall say only one thing, succinctly and in a few words. The Trinity, my brothers, is truly a trinity. Trinity does not mean an itemized collection of disparate elements; if it did, what would prevent us from calling it a decad, or a centad,[21] or a myriad, if the number of components so justified? The arithmetical possibilities are many; indeed, more than these examples. Rather, Trinity is a comprehensive relationship between equals who are held in equal honor; the term unites in one word members that are one by nature and does not allow things that are indivisible to suffer fragmentation when their number is divided.

11. Our minds and our human condition are such that a knowledge of the relationship and disposition of these members with regard to one another is reserved for the Holy Trinity itself alone and those purified souls to whom the Trinity may make revelation either now or in the future. We, on the other

---

20. The divinity of Christ was compromised by the Arian view that he was a created being, albeit the first of creatures. The reference to Christ's mercy despite his sufferings on earth is a patristic commonplace.

21. Gregory's term, centad, that is, a hundred, has been retained for the sake of euphony.

hand, may know that the nature of divinity is one and the same, characterized by lack of source, generation, and procession (these correspond to mind, word, and spirit in humans, at least insofar as one can compare things spiritual with things perceptible and things that are very great with those that are small, for no comparison ever represents the true picture exactly); a nature that is in internal agreement with itself, is ever the same, ever perfect, without quality or quantity, independent of time, uncreated, incomprehensible, never self-deficient, nor ever so to be, lives and life, lights and light, goods and good, glories and glory, true and the truth, and *Spirit of truth*,[22] holies and holiness itself; each one God, if contemplated separately, because the mind can divide the indivisible; the three God, if contemplated collectively, because their activity and nature are the same; which neither rejected anything in the past as superfluous to itself nor asserted superiority over any other thing for there has been none; nor shall leave anything to survive it or will assert superiority over anything in the future, for there will be none such; nor admits to its presence anything of equal honor since no created or servile thing, nothing which participates or is circumscribed can attain to its nature, which is both uncreated and sovereign, participated in and infinite. For some things are remote from it in every respect; others come close to it with varying success and will continue to do so, and this not by nature, but as a result of participation, and precisely when, by serving the Trinity properly, they rise above servitude, unless in fact freedom and dominion consist of this very thing, attaining a proper knowledge of sovereignty and refusing to confound things that are distinct because of a poverty of intellect. If to serve is so great an office, how great must be the sovereignty of those whom one serves? And if knowledge is blessedness, how great must be that which is known?

12. This is the meaning of our great mystery, this, our faith and rebirth in the Father, Son, and Holy Spirit, and in our common name, our rejection of godlessness and our confession of the Godhead. This is the meaning of our common name. And

22. Jn 16.13.

so, to dishonor or separate any one of the three is to dishonor our confession of faith, that is, our rebirth, our Godhead, our deification, our hope. You see how gracious the Holy Spirit is to us when we confess him as God and how he punishes us when we deny him. I will not speak of the fear and the wrath that threatens, not those who do him honor, but those who dishonor him. This brief discussion has been offered in the interests of doctrine, not of controversy; as a fisherman would, not some precious Aristotelian; with spiritual, not mischievous intent; in a manner suited to the Church, not the market place; as a benefit to others, not as a rhetorical show. Our object is to inform those of you who agree only on the desirability of making pompous and defamatory speeches against us that we are united in our views and are of one inspiration and breathe one spirit; and to keep you from pecking like starvelings at our tiny scraps, call them faults or follies, and broadcasting them indiscriminately. It is the nadir of depravity to base one's security not on one's own sources of strength but on the weaknesses of others.

13. Look! We are joining right hands with one another before your very eyes. Behold the handiwork of the Trinity, which we glorify and worship alike! This is what will make you more charitable, as well as more orthodox. How I wish that our words may be heard and that it come to pass that this day become a day of convocation, holy, a day not of controversy, but of *room for all*,[23] not a monument to tribulation but a festival of victory, so that you too may find a source of salvation and renewal in the mutual concord that exists among us and in virtually the entire world, which has remained sound in some areas, and has recently been restored in others and is beginning to be so in the portions that remain! O Trinity, holy and adored and long-suffering—long-suffering you are indeed to have endured for so long those who divide you!—O Trinity, whose worshipper and undisguised herald I have long been privileged to be! O Trinity, who will in time come to be known by all, some through illumination and others through punishment! Be pleased to receive as your worshippers even these who now treat you with dis-

23. Cf. Gn 26.22 LXX.

dain and let us suffer no one to be lost, not even of the least, even if I myself should have to lose some measure of grace (I stop short of the sweeping declaration made by the Apostle).[24]

14. What? My words are not to your liking? Your tongue is convulsed and labors to produce a retort? This, too, we shall witness one day, or those who have more leisure than we. We shall come to know also your delightful offspring, or rather, their aborted remains, when we *hatch adders' eggs* or crush them with our reason, stern and unyielding, show them to be addled and full of air, and expose the *viper* of impiety that lurks in them, *a viper*,[25] to be sure, but one that is dead and undeveloped, motionless, stillborn, with no existence prior to generation—to pay you a slight compliment by using one of your own expressions—one as abominated for its conception as pitied for its abortion. This, I know, will be granted to us by him who has given us to *tread on the adder and viper*[26] and to *tread upon serpents and scorpions*[27] and who *will soon crush Satan under* our *feet*[28] whether he *falls like lightning from heaven*[29] because of his former brilliance or is slithering away like a snake as a result of his later deviousness and his transformation into a creature that crawls on the ground, so that we may enjoy a brief respite from our troubles, our pain completely gone, and our grief and anguish, both now and in the future, in Christ Jesus our Lord, to whom be the glory and the power forever and ever. Amen.

24. Rom 9.3: "For I could wish that I myself were accursed and cut off from Christ for the sake of my brethren, my kinsmen by race."
25. Is 59.5.
26. Ps 91.13 (LXX 90.13) LXX.
27. Lk 10.19.
28. Rom 16.20.
29. Lk 10.18.

ORATION 24

In praise of Cyprian, the holy martyr and saint, when Gregory had returned from the country the day after the celebration.[1]

E NEARLY FORGOT CYPRIAN![2] What an opportunity we missed! And you, his greatest admirers, who hold a festival in his honor every year, allowed it to pass: Cyprian, whom we should make a special effort to remember even if we are inclined to forget everything else. It is especially important to honor the memory of exemplary individuals because commemorating them is at once an act of piety and a step toward moral betterment. So let us repay our debt with the interest due if we truly have sufficient resources to do so and are not thoroughly impoverished and destitute. But even if we are very much so, I am sure that he will forgive us not only our late payment but also our destitution since he is a man who is in every respect generous as well as reasonable. We have but to give thanks that we have not forgotten him entirely. Let us then offer thanks. It is only fitting that we do so. And at the outset, let us express our gratitude that it is at such an opportune moment and according to God's good measures, who orders and regulates *all things by weight and measure,*[3] that we have returned to you, forsaking silence for speech, the friend of martyrs[4] for the

---

1. PG 35.1169D–94C. Delivered October 379 in Constantinople.
2. Gregory has confused Cyprian of Carthage, who was martyred under Valerian in 258, with a legendary figure of the same name, who was a professional sorcerer in Pisidian Antioch before his martyrdom at Nicomedia under Diocletian in 304. Both men were Christian converts who became bishops and were executed by decapitation.
3. Wis 11.20.
4. This sermon contains an unusually large number of references to women, beginning with this unnamed "friend of the martyrs," who may be one of Gregory's relatives.

martyrs themselves, and the recreation of the flesh for a feast of the spirit.

2. We missed you, my children, and I believe that we, too, were missed to an equal degree. You see a father's affection: I am attesting to your feelings as much as I am stating my own. After being separated from one another long enough for us to have brought out our mutual longing and confirmed it by the vantage point of distance, as painters do their paintings, we have been reunited once again. How brightly glows the memory of friends and how brief the time we have with them if we have a loving heart, one that reflects God's love of mankind! As the disciples of Christ, who for our sake emptied himself to the point of adopting a servant's form[5] and has gathered to himself those alienated from the blessings of heaven,[6] how could we not reach out and embrace one another and maintain *the unity of the Spirit in the bond of peace*,[7] which is the hidden meaning, the sum and substance, if you will, of the Law and the Prophets?

3. The one, and the first happy consequence is this, that we ran to one another's arms as fast as we could. Intense emotion does not tolerate delay; for those in the throes of love a single day is an entire lifetime. But the second and most important is that we have not rushed late to the feast and missed the joyous and spiritually invigorating experience that the rites by which we honor martyrs make us feel. As for myself, I admit that, where all other things are concerned, I am more indifferent than anyone else. Ever since I joined the ranks of Christ, I have divested myself of desire in all its forms. None of the pleasures that others pursue holds attraction for me, not wealth, grubby and fickle, not gastronomical pleasures and satiety, the father of insolence, not soft and flowing robes, not the charm of glittery jewels, not sounds enchanting to the ear, not effeminate perfumes, not the madding applause of crowds and theaters which we have long since abandoned to whoever wants it, not one of the things that have their genesis in that first taste that brought us death; but I also condemn as gross fools those who allow

5. Cf. Phil 2.7. 6. Cf. Eph 2.12.
7. Eph 4.3.

themselves to be slaves to such pleasures and to destroy the nobility of their soul by their petty preoccupation with these appetites and attach themselves, as if they were permanent, to things fleeting. What my insatiable desire craves, what I embrace, the passion to which I surrender is this: it is in the homage to the martyrs that I take my delight, in the blood of our Christian champions that I glory. The contests and the victory belong to others; the crowns are mine. Such is my own greed in appropriating their glory and claiming their achievements as my own!

4. We should hold festival for every martyr and readily make a place for them all in our mouths and ears and thoughts; we should be eager to talk about them and to hear about them and to believe that nothing surpasses their heroism. Truly, there are many things that serve to guide us towards perfection and many things to instruct us in virtue: reason, the Law, the Prophets, the apostles, the very passion of Christ, the first martyr, who gathered me to himself as he mounted the cross that he might crucify my sin[8] and triumph over the serpent and sanctify the tree and vanquish pleasure and redeem Adam and restore our fallen image: such and so great are our models; but no less edifying for us are the martyrs, spiritual sacrifices, perfect victims, acceptable offerings,[9] proclamations of the truth, denunciations of falsehood, fulfillment of the Law in its spiritual sense, abolition of error, persecution of evil, inundation of sin, purification of the world.

5. And you, my Cyprian, are my most precious treasure, both in name and in fact, more than the other martyrs (there is no jealousy among martyrs). Your virtue overwhelms me, the thought of you elates me, and I am, as it were, in transports of joy. I believe myself somehow present at your martyrdom and sharing in your struggle, and I am oblivious to everything but you, perhaps out of an affinity for your eloquence, in which you eclipsed the rest of mankind to the degree that rational creatures are superior to brute nature (deep affection comes to ex-

---

8. Cf. Col 2.14–15.
9. Rom 12.1–2.

ist, I know not how, between those who share a common bond, whether of blood or anything else); and perhaps in response to your sudden and wondrous conversion,[10] an unparalled event that exceeds my power to describe. Sweet is the sight of the sun emerging through the dark veil of clouds; sweeter the springtime that follows the winter's gloom; and more delightful the smiling calm and the smooth expanse of sea as it frolics with the shore after the turbulence of the winds and the thrashing waves.

6. Gentlemen, I give you Cyprian, so that for those of you who are already familiar with him, the reminder may prove an added source of pleasure, while those who are not may have the opportunity to learn of the finest chapter in our history, one in which all Christians can take pride; this is he, once the great name of the Carthaginians, now of the whole world, a man celebrated for his wealth, respected for his power, high-born (if the fact that he was a member and president of the senate best indicates his family's lineage), the flower of youthfulness, the monument of nature, a bastion of learning not only in philosophical studies but in the other disciplines and any of their divisions you will, so as to be admired more for the range of his learning than for his mastery of any one branch and more for his preeminence in each than for his encyclopedic knowledge of all; or, to make the distinction more clear, he was superior to some in the range of his learning, to others in his mastery of individual subjects, to still others in both, and to everyone in everything.

7. The many brilliant works that he authored for us stand as testament to his erudition,[11] for thanks to the loving-kindness of God, who makes *all things and* changes them,[12] he put his education to better use and made unreason bow to reason. This is why I am at a loss how to proceed with my sermon and what to do next. If I enumerate all of Cyprian's achievements, my talk

---

10. Cyprian of Antioch was converted to Christianity as a result of his failed attempt to seduce St. Justina by means of black magic.
11. Cyprian of Carthage was a rhetorician prior to his conversion; see further *Saint Cyprian. Treatises,* trans. and ed. R. J. Deferrari, FOTC 36 (1958) and *Saint Cyprian. Letters (1–81),* trans. R. B. Donna, FOTC 51 (1964).
12. Am 5.8 LXX.

will inevitably be drawn out to an inordinate degree and I shall most certainly run out of time. On the other hand, if I omit anything, I shall inevitably do a very great disservice to the present company. So, in order to steer a middle course between the limitations of time and the wishes of my audience, here is what I propose to do: leave everything else for those who are familiar with it, instruct those who are not, if indeed there are any—in this way, both teachers as well as pupils may profit equally from his exploits, since not only is the very mention of the man a sanctifying experience but words are the most effective means of exhorting others to virtue—and briefly recall one or two of his achievements in all essential details, that is, the facts one could not leave out even if one were inclined to do so.

8. I shall talk about his former life as well as his path to salvation, his calling, and his conversion to a higher existence. It betrays a very mean and niggardly spirit to imagine that we defame a martyr by mentioning the sorrier side of his life. If this were in fact the case, even the great Paul would lose his credit with us, and Matthew the tax collector would be included among the dregs of society, and Cyprian himself. The first informs us of his earlier acts of persecution and his new redirected zeal in order to heighten the glory of his benefactor by the comparison;[13] the second adds "the tax collector" after his name as a respectable mark of identification like any other when he gives the list of disciples;[14] and the third publicizes at length and in severe terms the depravity of his former life so that he might bring forth this very gift, his public confession, as fruit *for God*,[15] and offer an avenue of better hope for many of those who have begun to turn from their wicked ways. Just consider the nature and magnitude of his depravity. The man who later was a disciple of Christ was a worshipper of demons; the great champion of the truth was a persecutor of the most vicious sort; the man who once applied his formidable powers of both eloquence and action toward confusing our path,[16] later enlisted both to the utmost in the service of Christians. How

13. 1 Tm 1.13; 1 Cor 15.9.
15. Rom 7.4.
14. Mt 10.3.
16. Is 3.12.

ORATION 24 147

very wicked, too, was his use of sorcery (the unmistakable trademark of his misdeeds) in carrying out these nefarious activities! And what a still more terrible thing was his voracious appetite for carnal pleasure, which can drive mad even those otherwise sane and which cannot but affect their minds adversely by galloping off with their wits like some frisky colt!

9. We have now come to the heart of my sermon. Let no one observing Cyprian's early career abandon himself to pleasures. Rather, let subsequent events help to moderate his behavior. There was a young woman of good family and high morals. Hear this and join in rejoicing, young women and, more, all you matrons, too, who are chaste and love chastity. Our tale is a source of pride that both of you can share. And the young woman was very beautiful.[17] Let the divine David join us in singing of her: *The King's daughter is all glorious within,*[18] true bride of Christ, beauty without peer, a living work of art, an unsullied offering, an inaccessible shrine, *a garden locked, a fountain sealed*[19] (to let Solomon too join in our hymn), reserved for Christ alone. It was with this thoroughly irreproachable and virtuous maiden that the great Cyprian was somehow taken, I know not why or how. Of all the parts of the body, the eyes are the most difficult to control and appease; in their lust, they manage to touch even the untouchable. Well, Cyprian was not merely taken with her, but he actually made an attempt on her virtue. What idiocy to think that he could ravish her! Or rather, what shamelessness on the part of him who takes such liberties and encourages others to do the same! He is the very one who first crept into paradise itself to plot against the first creature;[20] who comes to stand in the company of angels to demand that Job be handed over to him;[21] who reaches the point of challenging the Lord himself, who will destroy and make an end of him; and who, because God made manifest was in his sight merely another Adam, parades temptation before the one who is beyond temptation[22] as if to wrestle even him to the ground. Little

17. 2 Sm 11.2.
19. Song 4.12.
21. Jb 1.6–12.
18. Ps 45.13 (LXX 44.14) KJV.
20. Gn 3.1–5.
22. Mt 4.1–11; Jas 1.13.

did he know that in attacking humanity he would come afoul of divinity. Why then should it surprise that Cyprian too was his chosen instrument in the attempt on her sainted soul and virginal body?

10. Anyway, make an attempt on her he did. For a go-between, he selects not an old hag from among those who practice the trade, but one of the demonic devotees of carnal delights, for the spiteful hosts of apostasy,[23] constantly on the lookout for large numbers of recruits to share in their fall, are quick to offer their services in such affairs. The price of procurement consisted of sacrifices and libations, and the kinship that is born of bloodshed and smoke: exactly the kinds of payment that those who bestow such benefits require. But when the young girl sensed the evil and realized what was afoot—souls that are pure and God-like very quickly ferret out the schemer, no matter how clever or varied his attack—what does she do? What strategy does she devise to counter the artificer of evil? In utter desperation she seeks refuge with God and takes as champion against the loathesome infatuation her bridegroom, the one who once rescued Susanna from cruel elders[24] and saved Thecla from a tyrant suitor and even more tyrannical mother.[25] Who might this be? Christ, who rebukes spirits[26] and buoys up those who are drowning[27] and walks on the sea[28] and consigns a legion of spirits to the deep;[29] who rescues from the lions' den a just man who, thrown to them for food, vanquishes the beasts by stretching out his hands,[30] rescues the fugitive prophet swallowed by a whale,[31] because he maintained his faith even in its belly, and preserves the Assyrian children in the fire by sending an angel to quench the flame and adding him as fourth to their three.[32]

---

23. Evil spirits are meant here rather than heretics.
24. Sus.
25. *Acts of Paul and Thecla* 20. PG 1181A corrects the reading "more tyrannical father" found in the manuscript tradition.
26. Mt 17.18. 27. Mt 14.30–31.
28. Mt 14.25. 29. Mk 5.13.
30. Dn 6.16–24. Note that the stretching out of hands is not in Scripture; the same error is found in *Or.* 15.11.
31. Jon 2.
32. Dn 3.49–50 LXX (= S of 3 Y 26–27).

11. Invoking these and still other models and beseeching the Virgin Mary to help a virgin in distress, she takes refuge in a regimen of fasting and sleeping on the ground. Since it was her beauty that placed her in this predicament, she tries by these means to ravage her looks and so pull the kindling from the flame and dissipate what fuels our passions. At the same time, she tries to win God's favor through her faith and self-denial, for nothing at all serves God so well as mortification and he rewards tears with his mercy. I know you are impatient to hear the rest of the story because you are anxious for this girl but equally for her lover, and fear that his ardor will end by destroying both. Take heart. His ardor becomes an ally of faith and the lover who seeks to win the maiden's hand is himself won over by Christ. Thus the flame of the passions is stamped out and that of truth set ablaze. How? In what way? I have now reached the most gratifying part of the tale. The young girl conquers; the demon is conquered. The tempter goes up to the lover; he concedes defeat. He is scorned; he is furious at the slight; he takes his revenge upon the one who slights him. What is his revenge? He ensconces himself in his erstwhile servant that evil might dislodge evil and frenzy be cured by frenzy. He rebounds from the girl like an engine of war from a mighty rampart, put to flight by her words and prayers; and he wrestles with the one who had sent him, miraculously rallying against his attacker and choking him like a latter-day Saul.[33]

12. What does he do next, the mad lover, his madness now checked? He seeks a release from his wickedness; he finds it: hardship is ever the mother of invention. How does he win his release? He takes refuge in the maiden's God, as Saul once did in David's melodious harp.[34] He goes to her pastor and, just as he was cleansed of his passion by the blow, so he is cleansed of the evil spirit by his faith in Christ and he transfers his passion to him. For a long time his change of heart is considered suspect, and he is turned away because it seemed a thing in the realm of the odd and incredible that Cyprian of all people

33. Cf. 1 Sm 16.14.
34. 1 Sm 16.14–23.

should ever be counted a Christian. Yet transfer it he does and the proof of his conversion is clear to see: he takes his books of magic and exposes them to public display; he stands triumphant over his evil and pathetic store; he preaches against the foolishness they contain, he makes a flame leap up brightly from them, he destroys in the fire their vast deceit that had been powerless to support a single spark of carnal desire; he parts company with the demons, he assimilates himself to God. How mighty is the power of grace that it can reveal God through a base passion and spirit! He becomes a holy sheep in a holy flock and even, as I have heard, a church menial, much given to prayer that he might rid himself of his former brazenness and school himself to humility. After that he is a pastor; indeed, the greatest and most respected of pastors. He does not preside merely over the church of the Carthaginians and of Africa which, thanks to him and his efforts, is famous to this day, but also over the entire western region and in effect even over the east itself, and the south, and the north, everywhere that he came to be admired. So does Cyprian become ours.

13. This is the handiwork of the God of signs and miracles; this the work of him who brought Joseph, sold through the conniving of his brothers, to Egypt[35] and tested him through a woman[36] and glorified him through the distribution of grain and gave him the power to interpret dreams so that he might gain a position of trust in a foreign land and be honored by Pharaoh[37] and become the father of countless thousands for whose sake Egypt is plagued,[38] the sea is parted,[39] the bread rains down,[40] the sun stands still,[41] the promised land is given for an inheritance.[42] The divine wisdom knows how to lay the foundations of great events far in advance and to use opposites to produce opposites in order to rouse even greater wonderment. Similarly, the examples of Cyprian's worthiness that we have mentioned are a sufficient measure of his absolutely sterling reputation. Yet those that remain are so numerous and of

---

35. Gn 37.28.
36. Gn 39.7–20.
37. Gn 40–41.
38. Ex 7–11.
39. Ex 14.21.
40. Ex 16.4.
41. Jos 10.13.
42. Jos 13.1.

such a quality that even if the testimony already cited failed to establish a laudatory record of achievement, the subsequent ones are enough to raise him above all competitors. Let me briefly enumerate the most prominent: his contempt for money; his thoroughly unpretentious bearing; the discipline and purification he imposed on his body so as to counter his former impulses; his ascetic mode of dress; a social demeanor dignified yet kindly, steering a middle course between over-familiarity and snobbishness; his sleeping on the ground; his vigils, this man who, although he learned such habits late in life, far eclipsed his predecessors; his gift for language, which he used to mold the character of one and all and to clear away doctrinal ignorance and enhance men's lives and restore to its former grandeur the divinity of the sovereign and royal Trinity, which was being fragmented while some were even fusing it together, because he stayed within the bounds of pious union as well as connumeration. Although I could go on indefinitely, I shall compress my remarks and end my talk with the end of his life.

14. Decius[43] was raging against us and devising all sorts of torments, and some of his horrors were already upon us while others were yet to come. He had two objectives, both equally important: to crush Christians and to outdo previous persecutors—or perhaps I should say, to crush and force to capitulate either all Christians or Cyprian alone. When he realized just how eminent a personage Cyprian was, for his piety as well as his good name, he saw that his own triumph would be that much more brilliant and remarkable should he prevail over him. In the one case he would be prevailing over Christians alone; in the other, over the religion itself and its doctrines. And so it marked excellent strategy, he thought, first, to cut out the tongue that was sustaining them and then, when they had been stripped of their powers of speech and reason, to imprison them. His scheme was impious and perverse, but not completely irrational given his purpose and design, as the sequel showed. For after Cyprian had manfully and heroically repulsed every attack and attempt made upon him, just as a rock

---

43. Cyprian of Carthage went into voluntary exile during the persecution of Decius (249–51).

on the shore does the onslaught of the waves, and Decius finally condemns him to exile, our hero, disdaining his own personal fortunes and taking no satisfaction in the fact that he himself was being spared, did not think the sentence provided safety for his person so much as his being muzzled and abandoning the others in their hour of need constituted a danger to his soul. Now there would be no one to guide and encourage them in their struggle. For he believed that words play no small role in redoubling the courage of those who strip for competition in the arena of virtue.

15. This is why, though absent in body, he was present in spirit and joined the others in their struggle. Not able to help them with the spoken word, he does so with his pen. How? He coaches them from afar by writing speeches designed to motivate them and composing tales of Christian piety. In fact, through his letters he single-handedly inspires almost more people to suffer martyrdom than did all those who were with them at the time of their ordeal by their bodily presence. He urges them to value not country, not family, not possessions, not power, not any other of the lowly things of this earth before the truth and the prizes for valor stored up in heaven for those who battle for the sake of the good, telling them that the noblest of enterprises is to purchase the kingdom of heaven for the price of a little blood and to trade ephemeral goods for eternal glory; that there is one country for those of lofty character, the Jerusalem of the mind, not these earthly nations set apart in their little borders with their many changing inhabitants; that there is only one distinction of ancestry, and that is to preserve the divine image and to become as much like the archetype as is possible for prisoners of the flesh, who can receive only a faint emanation of the good; that there is only one dominion, power over the devil, and the impregnability of a soul that will never taste defeat in her struggles to defend piety when vice contends with virtue and world with world, the one perishable, the other abiding, and vicious referee with noble contestants, and Belial takes up position against Christ.[44] For these reasons he kept trying to

---

44. 2 Cor 6.15.

persuade them to scorn the swords, to regard the fire as refreshing, to consider the most ferocious beasts gentle, to think of starvation as the ultimate feast, and to disregard their relatives' tears and wails and groans as the devil's bait and obstacles on the road to God. These are the things, he said, that mark noble and manly souls and sound purpose. Indeed, the man who said and wrote these words was himself a firsthand example of them, who counted all things as refuse *in order that* he might gain *Christ*.[45]

16. Arming them for the fray with words and sentiments like these, Cyprian raised many to martyrdom. And what reward does he receive for his efforts? How lavish and bountiful it is! Decapitated by a sword, the crowning glory of his many torments, he becomes a martyr and joins those he had sent on before him. Thus does he join Christ; thus is he translated unto Christ, Cyprian, a great man before he found religion, a greater one afterwards, mighty as both persecutor and crowned victor, awe-inspiring for his conversion as much as for his virtue. For it is less glorious to have maintained an exemplary character than to embark on a new course that is pious and godly. The one is a matter of habit, the other of conscious resolve; the one is a common occurrence; of the other, the examples are few.

17. Now of all his miracles consider how truly miraculous this next one is! The martyr will be gratified if we devote a little more time to our sermon. Such, then, is our hero's way of life; such his manner of martyrdom. And when he comes to the end of his life—if it is right to speak of his passing in these terms instead of calling it his departure unto God, or fulfillment of his desire, or release from his chains, or laying down of his burden—there occurs on this occasion, too, a miracle that ranks with the previous ones. Cyprian's name was known to everyone, and not only to Christians but even to those ranged against us, since virtue is something that everyone alike can respect; but his body vanished. The treasure was kept for quite some time by a fervently devout woman. I do not know whether she had custody of the martyr because God was rewarding her piety or be-

---

45. Phil 3.8.

cause he was testing our own devotion to see whether we could endure the forfeiture and loss of his holy remains. But once the God of martyrs chose not to make the blessing for all mankind the private preserve of a single person or to penalize the common good by showing favor to her, he reveals the location of the body. This honor too he bestows upon a worthy woman. His purpose was that womankind be sanctified also. Just as it was womankind who gave birth to Christ and who announced his resurrection from the dead to his disciples,[46] so too now with Cyprian: a woman brought him to light and another surrendered him to the common benefit of all. This is the final episode in his glorious career. In this way the man unworthy of concealment is brought into the public view. It was indeed unacceptable to remain indifferent to the abduction of one whose excellence placed him above the rites by which we honor the bodies of our deceased.

18. This, then, is the extent of what I have to say. Surely there is no need to add more. For even if we spoke at greater length we should not do justice to his outstanding qualities and the estimation in which each of us holds the man. What we have recounted is only the minimum needed to pay him the honor that is his due. The rest you should supply yourselves so that you too may offer your own gift to the martyr by exorcising demons, eradicating sickness, prophesying what is to come. In all these matters even Cyprian's dust is efficacious when joined to faith, as those who have had the experience know, who have both passed down the miracle to us and will transmit it to the time to come. Or rather, present the gifts that are greater than these, the kind that are appropriate for those who would truly honor him: mortification of the flesh, elevation of the soul, avoidance of vice, enhancement of virtue; young women: the rejection of sensuality; matrons: the beauty of virtue rather than of body; young men: a manly suppressing of the passions; old men: sound judgment; civil authorities: sound government; military authorities: kindness; men of letters: reason and eloquence; priests (if I may include our own vocation): the conscientious

---

46. Lk 24.9.

performance of your sacred duties; laity: ready obedience; those in mourning: comfort; successful men: fear; the rich: generosity; the poor: gratitude; all: a stand against the cruel and vicious persecutor that he may neither attack us openly, nor lie in wait to wound us with his arrows, nor as darkness war against us, nor as an angel of light play tricks on us and carry us off to the pit of perdition.

19. It is a terrible thing to become a slave to one's eyes or be wounded by the tongue or held in thrall by the ears or be fired with hot anger or numbed through one's sense of taste or enervated through touch, thus turning the weapons of salvation into weapons of death when we should be arming ourselves with the *shield of faith*[47] to resist the devil's treachery and, after our victory in Christ and our contending successfully alongside the martyrs, to hear that great voice proclaim: *Come, O blessed of my Father, inherit the kingdom* promised *to you*,[48] wherein is *the dwelling of all that rejoice*,[49] and dance the dance everlasting, wherein is the *sound of those who keep festival* and *voice of exultation*[50] and a purer and more perfect illumination of Godhead, the enjoyment of which is now shrouded in riddles and shadows. These are the honors that give Cyprian more pleasure than all the others combined; these the virtues to which he devoted his life when he was with us and which, now that he is gone, he urges upon all through our voice. Make sure you do not spurn it if you have any regard for his perseverance and for his struggles on behalf of the truth, and for me his emissary. Here are the first fruits of my sermon, divine and holy man; here is the reward for both your words and your contest: no Olympian olive or Delphic apples to play with, no Isthmian pine, no Nemean celery, the prizes those wretched ephebes received,[51] but words, the most fitting reward of all for the devotees of the Word; and

---

47. Eph 6.16.
48. Mt 25.34.
49. Ps 87.7 (LXX 86.7) LXX.
50. Ps 42.4 (LXX 41.5) LXX.
51. The prize for victory in ancient athletic contests was a wreath or garland of vegetation such as wild celery; see Pausanias 8.48.2. Note that winners in the Pythian Games, held at Dephi in honor of Apollo, are usually said to have received a crown of bay leaves; for the use of apples, see A. R. Littlewood, "The Symbolism of the Apple in Byzantine Literature," *Jahrbuch der österreichischen Byzantinistik* 23 (1974): 41, n. 44.

if the reward is commensurate also with your own struggles and words, that is the gift of the Word. May you watch over us from above in your mercy and give direction to our lives and words; and may you shepherd this holy flock, or help its shepherd, by warding off from it the ravening wolves who sniff after syllables and phrases and by guiding it as much as possible for the best in all else; and by granting to us in greater fullness and clarity the radiance of the Holy Trinity at whose side you now stand, which we worship, which we glorify, whose existence is intimately bound up with our own through our worship of the Father in the Son and of the Son in the Holy Spirit, in whose presence may we in aftertime enter *pure and blameless*,[52] and of which in perfection perfectly partake, in Christ himself our Lord, to whom be all glory, honor, and power forever and ever. Amen.

52. Phil 1.10.

ORATION 25

In praise of Hero the Philosopher.[1]

 SHALL PRAISE THE PHILOSOPHER, even though I am not feeling well, because it is the philosophic thing to do. The praise, moreover, will be highly deserved since he is truly a lover of wisdom while I am but her devoted servant. I therefore have in fact good reason to offer praise: if in no other way, I can at the very least show my philosophic bent by expressing my admiration for a philosopher. My reasoning is that we must either engage in philosophy ourselves, or else hold it in high regard. Otherwise, we may very well find ourselves completely cut off from the good and adjudged guilty of unreason even though we were endowed with reason at birth and through word avidly pursue the Word. Let the man accept our praise, as he does everything else, in a philosophic spirit and receive our accolades with good grace. Since we know that the philosopher shrinks from public recognition and, further, that no words of ours could add anything to the facts and might even, because of their inadequacy, diminish his standing, our object in praising him is not to indulge him but to improve ourselves. The goal is one that philosophy will not now reject since her earnest efforts are in fact directed towards a betterment of our lives. And first among her benefactions is the praise of good things, for praise is the sponsor of ardent devotion, and devotion, of virtue, and virtue, of blessed-

---

1. PG 35.1197A–1226B. Delivered 380 in Constantinople. Hero is a pseudonym for Maximus, a Cynic convert to Christianity, who ingratiated himself with Gregory and then betrayed his trust by attempting to have himself consecrated bishop of Constantinople in Gregory's own church of Anastasia. *Or.* 25 was written before the breach, on the occasion of Maximus's return to his native Alexandria.

ness, the pinnacle of our aspirations and the one to which the earnest man directs all his actions.

2. Come then, step forward, best and most consummate of philosophers and, I shall add, witnesses of the truth. Come, you who have exposed the sham wisdom that is based on words and seeks to charm through fancy language, unable or unwilling to go beyond; you who have mastered all virtue, practical as well as theoretical; a Christian philosopher in an alien garb[2] (but perhaps not alien at all since angels, when they are represented in bodily form, are shown wearing dazzling white garments, a way of symbolizing, I believe, their natural purity). Come, wise man and lover of wisdom (for up to what point can one love wisdom, if wisdom is nowhere to be found?) and Dog,[3] not in shamelessness but in your openness, not in ravenous ways but in your hand-to-mouth existence, not in barking but in your defense of the good and your vigilant watch over souls and eagerly greeting all that is akin to virtue and snarling at every stranger to it. Come, stand at my side near the holy objects and this eucharistic table as I celebrate through them the mystery of deification. It is to them that your words and your way of life and your rigorous program of purification are drawing you. Come, I shall crown you with our laurels and with joyous voice proclaim you victor, not in the center of Olympia or some small Greek theater, but in the presence of God and angels and the full complement of the church; not in the pancration[4] contest or in boxing or the double course[5] or any of those petty competitions with their petty prizes, but over the deceit of heresies, and not by way of honoring one of those heroes or daimones whose catastro-

---

2. The text of SC 284 includes a variant reading that speaks of Nazirites, ancient Jews who, like Samson, dedicated themselves to God by vowing to abstain from cutting their hair, among other practices. See Nm 6.1–21; Jgs 13.4–7; Acts 21.23–26. The term could also apply to Christian ascetics, as in Gregory's *Or.* 42.26 (PG 46.489C). Here, the similarity with the behavior of some Cynics is being stressed.

3. The term Cynicism derives from the Greek word for dog, κύων. The tradition chose this animal as its symbol for a life to be lived according to nature, without sham or hypocrisy.

4. This competition involved both boxing and wrestling.

5. A foot race that extended down one side of the stadium, round the goal, and back.

phes are celebrated in myth (for that is what their religious rites consist of, which have enlisted time to support their folly and repetition to give it legitimacy), but in honor of the living God who through his own suffering teaches us suffering, of which also our reward is the kingdom of heaven, and to become a god above human suffering.

3. And what will our proclamation say? Here, if you prefer, is a shorter and simpler version: This man is the unerring champion of the truth and defender of the Trinity unto the death, and, through his eagerness to undergo suffering, persecutor of those who persecute for the purpose of inflicting it, for nothing so worsts a persecutor as an eager victim. But if you prefer the fuller and more expansive version: This man is the best and the noblest of the noble. And when I speak of nobility, I am not using the word in its popular sense. Far from it! It does not become us, nor is it in keeping with a philosophical temper, to be impressed in this way with the nobility that issues from legends and tombs and an hauteur long decayed, nor that which attaches to family or conferred titles, a boon derived from the labors of night and the hands of princes who are perhaps not even of noble birth themselves and who dispense it like any other prize; but rather with the nobility that is characterized by piety and a moral life and the ascent to the first good, the source of our being. His claim to this nobility is proved by a single piece of evidence: our nobleman is not merely a Christian athlete but in addition comes from a family of martyrs. Hence the model of virtue came from his own home. Intellectually, he is a citizen of the world at large, for Cynicism does not at all recognize limitations imposed by a narrow geography; physically, he is a citizen of the city of the Alexandrians, which is rated with yours, or as a close second to it. Although she excels every other city in every respect, she is particularly distinguished for her fervor, and of this the finest expression is her Christianity and her disposition towards it that, though originally proceeding from choice, is now established as her natural state. For fervor joined to true piety produces devotion, and devotion is what gives faith its strength.

4. Brought up and educated in this way, as befitted a person

of such background and promise, when it came time for him to choose a vocation—the foundation, in my view, of success or failure in life—he set his sights on something grand and daring and higher than the ordinary. He shows more disdain for luxury and wealth and power than those who possess these things in greater abundance show towards everyone else. Luxury he rejects out of hand as the prime hardship, wealth as the ultimate poverty, power as the supreme impotence, on the grounds that there is nothing good about a thing that does not make its possessors better, and in most cases actually makes them worse, or fails to remain in their possession to the end. He installs philosophy as mistress over his passions and vigorously pursues the good and detaches himself from matter before he is released from it; and he rises above the visible world thanks to his instinctive greatness and nobility of character and joins himself to the world that abides. So disposed, he refuses to waste any time over which philosophy he should choose, the pagan, which plays with shadows of the truth under the cloak and guise of philosophy, or ours, which, though to all appearances lowly, is yet inwardly sublime and leads to God; and so he chooses our way without reservation, and does not allow himself to be seduced by unworthy appeals or taken in by the verbal niceties on which the practitioners of Hellenism pride themselves. Rather, he applies his philosophical effort above all to identifying from among our ways the one that was both preferable and likewise more advantageous to him and to Christians as a whole. For he regarded it as the mark of the most perfect and philosophical soul to merge in all respects the public with the private spheres of life on the ground that each of us is born not for himself alone, but also for everyone who shares the same nature and takes his being from the same source and to the same ends.

5. And he saw that the solitary and reclusive life, separate and isolated from the crowd, possessed a grandeur and sublimity that transcended ordinary mortal existence, though its benefits did not reach beyond those who lived it, since such a life turned away from the fellowship and kindness that belong to charity, which he knew to be among the first of the virtues; and that the solitary life was in addition ineffectual, since it was not

tempered by practical considerations and could not be evaluated in terms of anything else. Active participation in society, on the other hand, besides providing the test of virtue, extended its benefits also to the mass of humanity and closely resembled the divine dispensation that both created the universe and bound it together in love and that, by union and association with us, recalled the human race, which had fallen from grace as a result of the evil that had come upon it. With these choices in mind, and thinking it at the same time a matter of honor to castigate the Hellenic smugness of those who make a pretense of solemnity with their robes and beards, what does he do? How does he engage in philosophy? He takes up a middle position between their braggadocio and our wisdom and assumes their trappings and outward appearance while adopting our truth and sublimity.

6. This is why he rejects and banishes as far away as possible the Peripatetics and the Academics and the austere Stoa and Epicurus with his mindless world and atoms and hedonism after crowning them with fillets of wool, just as one of them had done with the poet.[6] As for the Cynics, finding their godlessness utterly repugnant but their unpretentiousness appealing, he is what you now see, a dog opposed to real dogs, a lover of wisdom against those who lack it, and a Christian working for everyone's well-being. Through his outward resemblance he quashes their arrogant self-righteousness, and by his novel dress, the studied simplicity of some in our own camp. In this way he provides living proof that piety does not reside in superficial details nor a philosophical temperament in a gloomy countenance but rather in steadfastness of soul and purity of mind and an inclination towards virtue that is genuine regardless of the clothes we wear and the company we keep. This holds true whether that company is ourselves alone and we insulate our minds from the senses or whether it is the crowd of our fellow-creatures amid whom we maintain an inner solitude, practicing our philosophy among non-philosophers (just like Noah's ark, which, though in the flood, was unscathed by it,[7] and Moses' *great sight*,

6. Plato, *Republic* 3.398a.
7. Gn 7.23.

the bush on the mountain, which the fire burned but did not consume),[8] neither adversely affected ourselves in any way by contact with the mass any more than adamant is by those who strike it, but by our personal example making others better to the utmost of our ability. Of this philosophy the fruit does not lie in ideal states conjured up with words (*scindapses,* as it were, to use their own expression, and *tragelaphs,* that is, just so many meaningless sounds), or in what they call categories and logical reductions and syntheses, or complete and incomplete predicates and rhetorical niceties, or mathematical lines of some sort that exist nowhere, or astronomical conjunctions and configurations dreamed up in defiance of God's providence. These things he regarded as trifling and secondary, and he played with them merely to avoid being played with by those who sport a knowledge of them.

7. What, then, was his primary goal? To plead the cause of justice before magistrates, to speak his mind freely and unselfconsciously in the presence of kings just as divine David had,[9] to contain the turmoil of a disgruntled populace, the peremptoriness of potentates, the pain of houses divided against themselves, the narrow-mindedness of the ignorant, the self-importance of the educated, the wealth that is full of pride, the excess that breeds arrogance, the poverty that invites crime, the anger that goes too far and takes judgment with it, immoderate pleasure, uncontrollable laughter; to put an end to the anguish of grief, the waywardness of youth, the peevishness of old age, the widow's loneliness, the orphan's despair. Will not anyone of sense much prefer these pursuits to syllogisms and linear measurements and star-gazing once he realizes that if we all spent our time studying logic or geometry or astronomy the quality of our life would not for all that be improved one iota (indeed, our society would completely fall apart); while if, on the other hand, the concerns I have listed are passed over, the result is utter confusion and chaos? Need we add how much better and superior these endeavors are to Antisthenes' sophisticated non-

8. Ex 3.2–3.
9. Ps 119.46 (LXX 118.46).

sense, Diogenes' dainty diet, and Crates' free love?[10] But, in deference to their common name we spare them too, so that they might have the brief pleasure of being linked to him. As for ourselves, we shall not linger over his other qualities, his prudence, his self-control, his humility, his affability, his gregariousness, his kindliness, all the other virtues wherein he surpassed his fellows, but proceed directly to the one that is last in sequence but first in importance.

8. There was a time when we enjoyed a lull from heresies, when the likes of Simon and Marcion and Valentinus and Basilides and Cerdon and Cerinthus and Carpocrates,[11] who had for the longest time hacked away at the God of the universe and waged war on the Creator in the name of the Good, were in the end consigned to that very abyss and silence[12] of theirs along with all their preposterous twaddle, just as they deserved. And Montanus's diabolical spirit and Manes' darkness and Novatian's insolence, or purity, and Sabellius's sinister advocacy of monarchianism yielded and gave way, Novatian's views finding a place in his opponents' camp, while those of Sabellius were thoroughly discredited and rejected as indefensible;[13] there were no further plagues upon the Church. Indeed, the persecutions with their attendant suffering actually enhanced her glory. After a short interval, however, a second storm breaks over the Church, the typhoon of iniquity, the complement of ungodliness, the legion of devils,[14] the mouthpiece of the Antichrist,

---

10. Antisthenes was a follower of Socrates and the traditional founder of Cynicism. Diogenes' diet was essentially vegetarian. Crates' marriage to Hipparchia was called κυνογαμία, "dog-marriage," a word sometimes changed into κοινογαμία as here, to describe the real or imagined promiscuity of some Cynics.

11. On these Gnostic figures of the second and third century an easily accessible review among many is K. Rudolph, *Gnosis. The Nature and History of Gnosticism*, trans. and ed. R. Wilson (San Francisco: Harper, 1983).

12. Βύθος (abyss) and σιγή (silence) are the two aeons that form the first syzygy in Gnosticism, one masculine and the other feminine. Cf. Irenaeus, *Against Heresies* 1.1.1.

13. On these various Christian heretics, along with Manes, who has of course lent his name to Manichaeism, consult the entries in the *Encyclopedia of Early Christianity*, ed. E. Ferguson, 2d ed. (New York: Garland, 1997).

14. Cf. Lk 8.30.

the mind that *loftily* threatened *oppression*,[15] the mutilation of the Godhead. Dreadful was its attack, more dreadful still the result, and worthy of the betrayal that the infamous Judas dared against our Lord: Arius, rightly known by the madness that bears his name.[16] He got his start in the city of the Alexandrians, where he perfected his mischief, and then, overrunning most of the world like a wild flame from a spark that is tiny at first, is finally extinguished by our Fathers and that pious company who then met at Nicaea and stabilized the doctrine of divinity with prescribed terms and definitions.

9. Once again there is a diabolical regime, and once again the evil erupts and, like a festering sore, comes to a head and bursts open, and ravening wolves clutch at us from all sides and rip the Church apart as priests take up arms against priests, and citizens attack citizens with full fury, and an emperor gives free rein to impiety and issues laws against the true faith, having as his trusted advisers creatures who are neither men nor women.[17] Who could find words to do justice to the tragic events of that time? the banishments, the confiscations, the proscriptions, the forced migrations to the desert, where untold thousands and even whole cities suffered in the open, pounded by rain and winter snows? their flight from there, since not even in the desert did they find a safe haven? the terrors more dreadful than these: the tortures, the executions, the public humiliations of bishops, monks, men, women, young, old? the officials who ministered to impiety by devising the horrors and adding to them, men who were often content to be credited simply with having proved themselves more ruthless than the emperor required?

10. The fierce persecution had barely ended—Persia found in our favor and executed the guilty party, thereby avenging the blood of many with the blood of a single individual[18]—when its

15. Ps 73.8 (LXX 72.8).
16. The Patristic term Ἀρειομανίτης, one addicted to the madness of Arius. Cf. *Or.* 36.1 and n. 6.
17. The government of Constantius II (337–61) was notorious for the number of eunuchs who ran it.
18. Julian the Apostate (361–63) died in the course of his Persian campaign.

disgraceful successor[19] begins. Under the impious mask of protecting Christians it proceeds to harass the true Christians and becomes more trying than the one before insofar as, formerly, the struggle for martyrdom brought with it recognition and glory, whereas now the suffering actually meets with indifference, at least among the biased critics of the ordeals. May I relate a single incident from that time that will bring a tear to the assembly, perhaps even to the most hard-bitten and dispassionate person himself? There are many who can confirm my tale since, in fact, the story of these tragic events reached many; and I believe future ages as well will treasure the account of what happened. A ship puts out to sea having on board an elder of the Church, one who was risking his life not at all for some base purpose but for his faith, and on a vessel with the object not to provide him with safe passage but rather to do away with him.[20] He was a pious man and gladly went on board. But fire was his fellow-passenger, and the persecutor is gleeful at the novelty of the torment. Oh, what a tragic sight! The ship leaves port. There is a crowd of spectators on the shore, some cheering, others weeping. How can I describe so great an event in a few words? The fire catches; ship and its burden go up in smoke together; fire and water join forces, opposites combining to make up the torment of a godly man, two elements divide up his one body; and a strange column of fire rises above the sea. By chance someone approached it, thinking it harmless and benign, but as he approached, he found an incredible and pathetic sight: a voyage without a pilot, a shipwreck without a storm; and the elder was now ashes, or rather, not even ashes, for he had been scattered upon the waters. And his priestly office did not even avail to secure him at least a more dignified demise or,

---

19. The narrative continues to the Arian Emperor Valens (364–78), omitting the short reign of Jovian (363–64).
20. A scholion cited in PG 35.1211D, n. 36 identifies four victims in all, the presbyters Heliodorus and Theodoulus as well as two readers and cantors. Socrates, *Ecclesiastical History* 4.16 and Sozomen, *Ecclesiastical History* 6.14 report an incident from the reign of Valens, who ordered his prefect Modestus to carry out the shipboard incineration of some eighty clerics, including Urbanus, Theodore, and Mendemus. Cf. also Xenophon, *An Ephesian Tale* 1.14.1, where pirates dispose of their victims in a similar fashion.

if not demise, at any rate burial, which even the impious claim as their due. Such was the launching of the impious one; such the end of the pious one; and nowhere does the fire from above nor the one that punishes burn brighter than such a beacon.

11. But why do I digress? It is now time to move on to your actual martyrdom and your struggles in defense of piety with which like a handsome seal you capped all your earlier achievements. The pernicious heresy I am describing was then at its height in your city,[21] where it also had its inception. But after the Trinity removes unto itself the man who had dedicated his life to it and had faced danger for it, the most saintly light of the world and priest preeminent among priests, the man who taught and guided you in your confession by his own efforts on behalf of piety, the great voice, the pillar of the Faith, Christ's second lamp and forerunner, if I may so phrase it, who fell asleep at a ripe old age full of days spent in the Lord after surviving the libels and battles, the infamous affair of the hand,[22] the dead who were really alive (I am sure that you all recognize Athanasius from my description), a second plague and scourge from Egypt insinuates itself into the Church in the person of the betrayer of the truth, the shepherd of wolves, the thief trampling through the fold,[23] the second Arius, the thick and bitter effluent,[24] the torrent raging with more violence than its godless source.[25] I am reluctant to mention the bloody crimes by which at the time the brute seizes the holy throne and the ceremonies preceding his nefarious installation.[26] Still, as you your-

---

21. Alexandria.
22. Athanasius's opponents had managed to secure a human hand, which they said belonged to Arsenius, a Meletian bishop, at the same time that they kept its presumed owner in hiding and circulated the claim that Athanasius had used it in the performance of certain magical rites. At the Synod of Tyre in 335, Athanasius put the lie to his accusers by producing Arsenius himself intact. The story is told many times in Patristic sources, as for example by Gregory himself in *Or.* 21.25 (PG 35.1097B).
23. Jn 10.1–2.
24. Cf. Hb 2.15.
25. Lucius of Samosata. Gregory plays on λύκος, wolf.
26. Lucius was installed as head of the Alexandrian Church, thanks in part to the machinations of his Arian supporter, Euzoius, bishop of Antioch, and the local connivance of the prefect Palladius (see n. 29, below), who successfully manipulated elements of the populace and the military on Lucius's behalf.

selves have both done in the past and continue to do, I voice my grief over a few of many heinous acts, using the words of the divine David: *O God, the heathen have come into thy inheritance; they have defiled thy holy temple;* and, further on, *They have given the bodies of thy servants to be food for the birds and scraps for beasts to tear apart;*[27] and I shall add these verses of his too from a second, different song of lamentation: *Because of all that the enemy has done wickedly in thy holy place. And they that hate thee have boasted in the midst of thy feast.*[28] Did they not boast? Did they not defile your holy temple with sundry evils and varied disasters?

12. The prefect[29] at the time was a godless man with no regard for the law and—the worst of his arrogance—not even a Christian; instead, he rushed from his idols to the temple of God, from his filthy blood-sacrifices to conduct even more loathsome and foul, that is, to using the outrages upon us as a kind of ritual act of devotion to his demons. A force was deployed ready and spoiling for a fight, a savage and surly mob of an army arrayed against men peaceful and unarmed. The priest[30] who succeeded the saint had legitimately been anointed in the order of the Spirit and was respected for his years and his understanding. He was driven out and Tabeel[31] now reigned, heir to what was not his. Arms are taken up against saints; foul hands raised against sanctuaries; against Psalms the din of trumpets. Note, if you will, what ensued: men struck down in holy places; women trampled underfoot, some of them even carrying the burden of nature; infants born prematurely or, to be more accurate, abortively; young girls pitifully dragged off, more shamefully abused (I am ashamed for both men's and women's sake to expose their private shame by describing the

---

27. Ps 79.1–2 (LXX 78.1–2).
28. Ps 74.3–4 (LXX 73.3–4) LXX.
29. Aelius Palladius was prefect of Egypt 371–74, i.e., under the Arian Valens, whose policies he carried out.
30. Peter, bishop of Alexandria from May 373 to February 14, 381, was the successor of Athanasius.
31. Is 7.6. Tabeel is the Tobiah of Neh 2.10, 19, et al., an Amorite official probably in Persian service, who sought to prevent the restoration of the walls of Jerusalem but was essentially thwarted by Nehemiah. The reference here is unquestionably to Valens and his prefect.

details, as I am ashamed that they were exposed even then), some of them throwing themselves down the wells inside the sanctuary, others hurling themselves from railings, shocked by the scene before their eyes, others swooning in heaps upon those already prostrate, murder upon murder, corpse upon corpse, sacred objects trampled under profane feet, altars desecrated by obscene songs and gestures and, as I learn—how will the tongue endure to say the words?—by dancers writhing upon them; blasphemous tongues screaming from holy pulpits, holy mysteries made a laughing-stock, the sound of the psalms heard no more, shrieks rending the air instead, rivers of blood, fountains *of tears*, priests arrested, monks attacked: the very image of the assault the Assyrians once launched against holy Jerusalem, an image that neither words can adequately describe nor ear take in, and that finds a fitting lament only in Jeremiah's cry from the heart, who asks for fountains *of tears*[32] and from the walls makes men weep for such calamities and lays mourning on the roads *to Zion*, which carry no one to the appointed feasts.[33]

13. The East witnessed these tragic events but there was lamentation in the West, too, where the fugitive priest[34] noised abroad the evidence of the madness. How? He produced in evidence before the church of the Romans not the bodies of the dead but their blood-stained clothes and reduces everyone to tears with his voiceless accusation in order both to dramatize the suffering and to find someone to help them in their troubles, as in fact we know he did, for that which is strong tends to be especially sympathetic to that which is weak and to range itself on the side of the less fortunate with a ready good will. All pious persons without exception react this way, but you[35] are even more deeply touched to the degree that your zeal is more fervent and your faith more complete. This is why you fight on behalf of the Word and why the forces of impiety fight against you and why in addition to many other valiant efforts on behalf of the good by both word and deed, your teaching, admonish-

32. Jer 9.1.
34. Peter.

33. Lam 1.4.
35. Hero/Maximus.

ing, chiding, questioning, rebuking, confuting ordinary citizens, officials, in private, in public, at every opportunity and in every place, you finally fall into the clutches of that mad and impious regime—What a noble fate! How sacred your wounds!—and your blameless body is flayed with whips; but, as if an onlooker at someone else's ordeal you are affected by the sight yet do not waver in your resolve; you stand as a tower of courage for all to see; and even in your silence (your tongue could no longer utter a sound) you become a teacher of patient endurance.

14. What followed after that? You are exiled from your homeland, you who do not recognize any homeland, your own or anyone else's; the object being, I think, that others too might learn piety from your personal example. The Oasis[36] becomes your place of refuge, a desolate and deserted spot that is now a shrine thanks to its association with you. Share with us the blessings of your exile as well since you have shared with us those of your return. Make your return a pageant for us. While you were there, whom did you instruct in philosophy? Whom did you cleanse of godless thoughts? Whom lead to piety? I picture to myself the school you had there, the ceremonies and festivities of which you were the focus. Tell us this too: Was there any relief for your broken body? Or did you in fact lead a life of need? Did you have any to share your struggles? Or did you suffer destitute in this respect as well? Did you miss your sisters, your partners in both chastity and fortitude? Or did you surmount your need for their companionship also? Did the thought of your mother, old and alone, make you waver? Or did you in fact draw great strength from the knowledge that piety was the greatest and most secure provision that you left with them? And now that you have happily returned to us and you who longed for us have been restored to those who longed for you by him who honors *those who honor* him[37] and provokes those who provoke

---

36. The Great or Kharga Oasis, as it is known today, is the southernmost in a series of oases in the Western Desert of Egypt. Because of its inaccessibility, it was used as a place both of refuge and banishment in late antiquity. See Zosimus 5.9, ed. F. Paschoud (Paris, 1986), pp. 109–11, n. 19.

37. 1 Sm 2.30.

him,[38] who fulfills *the desire of all who fear him*[39] and breathes resurrection unto the dead, who against all expectation restored Lazarus after four days[40] and you after four years, and lays *bones upon bones, and joint upon joint,* to use the words of the vision of Ezekiel,[41] the most wondrous and sublime of prophets, I would have you take up again your former ways and candid manner of speaking so that no one will think that you have been broken by your ordeal or that out of cowardice you abandon your philosophic habit.

15. Confound the superstition of the Greeks, as you did once before, and their polytheistic denial of God, along with their gods old and new and their disgusting myths and more disgusting sacrifices by which they attempt to purify slime with slime, as I have heard one of them say[42] (that is, use the bodies of dumb animals to purify their own), and the misshapen and monstrous figments that they venerate. If that is their notion of divinity, how perverse! And if, on the other hand, they intend them as illustrations, how absurd! Let them provide an explanation of their reasoning and the divine truth underlying this grotesquerie! Even superficial portrayals of the beautiful should be free of ugliness. But if they say that something else besides is involved, let them tell us what it is and from what books or theologians it derives. Confound too heresies and their violent outbreaks, and all the more vigorously since you have suffered from them in the past. The philosophical spirit is made more noble by suffering; hardened by trials, like hot steel plunged into cold water. Define too for us our orthodox faith by teaching us to recognize one God, unbegotten, the Father, and one begotten Lord, his Son, referred to as God when he is mentioned separately, but Lord when he is named in conjunction with the Father, the one term on account of his nature, the oth-

38. Dt 32.21. 39. Ps 145.19 (LXX 144.19).
40. Jn 11.39. 41. Ezek 37.7.
42. Apollonius of Tyana, *Ep.* 27: "Heraclitus was wise, but not even he could persuade the Ephesians not to purify slime with slime." See R. J. Penella, *The Letters of Apollonius of Tyana. A Critical Text with Prolegomena, Translation and Commentary* (Leiden: Brill, 1979), pp. 46–47, 105; additional references in M. Marcovich, *Heraclitus. Greek Text with a Short Commentary,* editio maior (1967, reprinted Sankt Augustin: Academia-Verl., 2001), pp. 455–63.

er on account of his monarchy; and one Holy Spirit proceeding, or, if you will, going forth from the Father, God to those with the capacity to apprehend things that are interrelated, but in fact resisted by the impious though so recognized by their betters and actually so predicated by the more spiritual. Neither should we place the Father beneath first principle, so as to avoid positing a first of the first, thus necessarily destroying primary existence; nor say that the Son or the Holy Spirit is without beginning. Thus we shall avoid depriving the Father of his special characteristic. Paradoxically, they are not without beginning, and, in a sense, they are: they are not in terms of causation, since they are indeed from God although they are not subsequent to him, just as light is not subsequent to the sun, but they are without beginning in terms of time since they are not subject to it. Otherwise, that which is transitory would be antecedent to things that abide, and that which has no independent existence to things that do.

16. Neither should we posit three first principles if we want to avoid the polytheism of the Greeks, nor a single one, Judaic in its narrowness as well as grudging and ineffectual, whether by positing a self-absorbing deity (the preferred view of those who have the Son issue from the Father only to be absorbed into him again) or by disallowing their natures and stripping them of Godhead, as our current experts like to do, as though the Godhead feared some rival opposition from them or could produce nothing higher than creatures. Likewise, we should not claim that the Son is unbegotten, for the Father is one; nor the Holy Spirit is Son, for the Only-Begotten Son is one. In this way, the divinity of each will be defined in terms of the property that is unique to each, in the case of the Son, his Sonship, in the case of the Holy Spirit, its procession and not sonship. We should believe that the Father is truly a father, far more truly father, in fact, than we humans are, in that he is uniquely, that is, distinctively so, unlike corporal beings; and that he is one alone, that is, without mate, and Father of one alone, his Only-Begotten; and that he is a Father only, not formerly a son; and that he is wholly Father, and father of one wholly his son, as cannot be affirmed of human beings; and that he has been Father

from the beginning and did not become Father in the course of things. We should believe that the Son is truly a Son in that he is the only Son of one only Father and only in one way and only a Son. He is not also Father but is wholly Son, and Son of one who is wholly Father, and has been Son from the beginning, since there was never a time when he began to be a Son, for his divinity is not due to a change of purpose nor his deification to progress in time; otherwise, there would be a time when the one was not a Father and the other not a Son. We should also believe that the Holy Spirit is truly holy in that there is no other like it in quality or manner and in that its holiness is not conferred but is holiness in the absolute, and in that it is not more or less nor did it begin or will it end in time. For what the Father and Son and Holy Spirit have in common is their divinity and the fact that they were not created, while for the Son and the Holy Spirit it is the fact that they are from the Father. In turn, the special characteristic of the Father is his ingenerateness, of the Son his generation, and of the Holy Spirit its procession. But if you seek after the means, what will you leave to them—in the words of Scripture, they alone know and are known by one another[43]—or also for those of us who will one day receive illumination from on high?

17. First get to be one of the things that we have talked about, or someone of like sort, and then you will come to know in the same measure as they are known by one another.[44] But for now, we ask you to teach us to see just this much, that unity is worshipped in Trinity and Trinity in unity, both its union and its distinction miraculous. Do not worry about the passions when you confess generation: the divine is impassible even if it has generated. This I can assure you: its generation takes place in a divine, not a human, fashion since its existence is not human either. Do worry about time and creation: He is not God if he was created; otherwise, you mount a useless defense of God and do away with him altogether by making what belongs to the same Godhead—and in fact frees you from servitude if you sincerely profess his lordship—a servant like yourself. Do not wor-

43. Mt 11.27.
44. 1 Cor 13.12.

ry about the procession: the all-abounding Deity is under no compulsion either to bring forth, or not to bring forth, in a similar way. Do worry about estrangement and the ominous fate that lies in store not for those who acknowledge the divinity of the Spirit, but for those who impiously discount it.

18. Neither show a perverse reverence for divine monarchy by contracting or truncating deity, nor feel embarrassed when you are accused of worshipping three gods. Someone else is equally liable to a charge of worshipping two. For you will either manage to rebut the charge in common with him or you will be in common difficulty; or else his deity will founder along with his arguments while yours will remain intact. Even if your powers of reasoning are not up to the task, it is still better to falter with rational arguments directed by the Spirit than to adopt easy but impious solutions out of indolence. Be contemptuous of objections and counter-arguments, and the newfangled piety and piddling wisdom; more contemptuous than of spiders' webs, which can snare a fly but are easily snagged by a wasp, not to mention a finger or anything with some mass behind it. Be our instructor in our learning to fear one thing alone: seeing our faith dissolve in sophistics. It is not terrible to be bested in argument, since skillful argumentation is not a universal attainment. What is terrible is experiencing the loss of one's God, because hope is universal to all. These matters you will, of course, pursue on your own more intently as well as more thoroughly. Your wounds are my assurance, and your body, which has labored in the defense of piety. And we shall join you ourselves to the extent of our ability.

19. And when you embark on your noble journey, remember, if you will, the Trinity that dwells in tents—if God can at all be said to dwell in things made by human hands—and this small harvest, one not from seeds of piety that are small, to be sure, but one still thin and immature and being gathered a little at a time. For we are become *as* those gathering *straw in harvest* (if the prophet's words are here apropos) and *grape-gleanings in the vintage, when there is no cluster.*[45] Do you see how small our

---

45. Mi 7.1 LXX.

gathering is? For this very reason help make our threshing floor richer and our wine-vat more full.[46] Speak of our calling as well as of our remarkable visit here, undertaken not for common enjoyment but as a way of participating in suffering, so that by sharing affliction we may also share the glory. You have in this people a prayerful ally and comrade in your travels, the flock that is small in number but not in piety, whose smallness I respect more than others' size. These are the words of the Holy Spirit; with it you will go through fire[47] and lull to sleep the wild beasts and turn princes to moderation. With this intent set out; with this intent be on your way and come back to us again, richly enriched, laureate a second time, to sing with us the hymn of victory now and in the future in Christ Jesus our Lord, to whom be the glory forever. Amen.

46. Jl 2.24.
47. Ps 66.12 (LXX 65.12).

ORATION 26

On himself upon returning from the country after the Maximus affair.[1]

I MISSED YOU, my children, and was missed by you to an equal degree. I have every confidence that this is so; if you require further assurance, indeed *I protest, brethren, by my pride in you which I have in Christ Jesus our Lord.*[2] This oath that I use was made by the Holy Spirit, who impelled me to return to you that we might prepare for the Lord *a people for his own possession.*[3] Note how great an assurance this is: I both convince you of my affection toward you at the same time that I declare my confidence in yours for me. This is not at all surprising. Those who share a common bond in the Spirit also share common experience; and those who share common experience give it also a common credence. An experience one has not had himself one also will not credit to another; whereas he who has had such is more inclined to respond in a positive way; he becomes in his own person the mirror-image of another, an invisible witness of an invisible sentiment. This is why I could not bear to be away from you any longer, thoroughly distressed and grieved though I was by the affairs of the world; not only by the vexations of city life, crowds, noise, bazaars, theaters, excesses, abuses, leaders and minions, winners and losers, mourners and mourned, people in tears, in smiles, marrying, burying, praised,

---

1. PG 35.1228A–52C. Delivered 380 in Constantinople. In the turmoil following Maximus's attempt to seize the patriarchal throne (see below, sections 14–18), Gregory withdrew to the countryside while Maximus went west in search of recognition, first from Theodosius in Thessalonica and later from Pope Damasus and St. Ambrose in Italy, who initially supported him until further information forced them to withdraw their support. See further *Or.* 25 and *De vita sua* 750–1112.
2. 1 Cor 15.31.
3. Dt 7.6; Ti 2.14.

reviled, the mass of corruption, the seethe of the world, the fortunes that shift as if caught up in Euripus and the winds; but also recently by matters before us more venerable and hallowed, I mean those involving the sanctuary and holy table. Although they are supposed to be our responsibility, since we are one of those whose role it is to approach God, I am afraid we might make poor use of our privilege and react like straw unable to endure the flame.[4]

2. Nevertheless, I have returned to you, forced to run away, but not to run back; indeed, I have done so most eagerly (my feet had a mind of their own, as the saying goes),[5] the Holy Spirit leading the way as though I were a stream that has to be forced to flow uphill but needs no encouragement to rush the other way. A single day is truly an entire lifetime to those weary with desire. Jacob's predicament is, I believe, different. He spent fourteen years in the service of Laban the Syrian for the two maidens, yet he did not weary. All his days, the Bible says, *seemed but* one day, because of *the love* he had for them,[6] perhaps because his heart's desire was there before his eyes, or because it is not onerous to weary for the sake of love, even though deferral brings pain. Thus we are slow to desire what is within easy reach, as one of the ancients has said.[7] At any rate, when I was with you, I scarcely realized the extent of my affection for you; but when I parted from you, I came to know longing, that sweet tyrant. This is not strange at all, for if even a cowherd grieves so much over a calf that has wandered from the herd, and a shepherd over a lamb missing from a flock of ten, and a bird over the nestlings she has left for a little while, that the herdsmen take up their pipes and climb to some vantage point, swelling their reeds with their distress and calling to the strays as if they were rational creatures who, if they should heed the call, give more joy than all the others put together who have caused them

---

4. Cf. Is 5.24; Jl 2.5.
5. An allusion to Hephaestus's tripods in Homer, *Iliad* 18.376; cf. also Plato Comicus, fr. 188.
6. Gn 29.20.
7. Cf. Dio Chrysostom 9.4; Demetrius *De elocutione* 100. J. Mossay in SC 284, p. 229, n. 1 cites Pliny, *Ep.* 8.20, though it must be understood that Gregory does not use Latin sources.

no anxiety[8] while the bird flies squawking to the nest and settles on her squawking young and enfolds them in her wings;[9] if so, how great a store might a goodly pastor set by his rational brood, especially since he has faced a certain danger on their behalf and consequently cherishes them even more?

3. How I fear the ravening wolves who, watching and waiting for our darkest hour, might tear the flock apart with their divisive and inflammatory words, for, unable to prevail openly, they watch to see when we are hard pressed. And I fear robbers and thieves who might climb into the sheepfold and either brazenly carry off or furtively steal so as to kill and slaughter and destroy,[10] *seizing prey, devouring souls,* as one of the prophets says.[11] And I fear the side-door that someone who was one of us yesterday and the day before might find unlocked, enter as if it were his own, and then turn intruder and do us harm. Many and varied are the wiles of the one who plots such villainies, and no master craftsman is so expert in any item of his varied repertoire as the Devil is in his nefarious skill. And finally, I fear also the dogs who force their way into the pastorate and in their absurdity contribute nothing to the office other than a tonsure of the hair upon which they once lavished their vile attentions. They have neither remained dogs nor become shepherds except to ravage, scatter, and destroy the labor of others. It is always easier, you see, to destroy than to preserve, and *man is born to trouble,*[12] says Job, just as a ship is built and a house constructed, but anyone in the world can kill, or wreck, or set on fire. So let there be no feeling of accomplishment even now on the part of those who sicked dogs upon the flock and who could not claim to have brought in or saved one single sheep. They never learned to do good because they practiced evil. And if they trouble the flock, why, this is something even a small storm, something even a minor malady, something even one wild animal making a surprise attack, can do. So let those who take glory in their own shame cease and desist; let them put an end to their wickedness, if they can, and worship and bow down and

8. Cf. Mt 18.12–13; Lk 15.4–7.
9. Cf. Mt 23.37.
10. Jn 10.10.
11. Ezek 22.25 LXX.
12. Jb 5.7.

weep *before the Lord* their *maker*[13] and be joined to the flock, all who are not completely beyond the pale.

4. These are the concerns of your fearful and worried pastor. This is why I am being criticized for my caution as though it were the dereliction of duty. I am not one of those shepherds who eat *the fat*, and clothe themselves *with the wool* and slaughter *the fatlings*,[14] and drive their flock to the point of exhaustion or sell them and say, *Blessed be the Lord, I have become rich*,[15] who shepherd themselves, not their sheep, if you recall at all how the prophets denounce bad shepherds; but I am rather one of those who can say with Paul, *Who is weak, and I am not weak? Who is made to fall*, and indignation and concern are not mine? *For I seek not what is yours, but you;*[16] and, *by day* the heat *consumed me, and the cold* afflicted me *by night*,[17] in the words of the shepherd-patriarch whose sheep were marked and had learned to conceive in the heavenly troughs.[18] This, then, is why I have come to you, who are similarly affected. And now that I am here, let us give each other an account of what we have accomplished in the meantime. For it is a good thing to suppose that an account is required of us not only for what we say and do but also for every moment, down to the very last and briefest part of each hour. So tell me your activities and I in turn shall lay bare the thoughts I had when I was communing with myself in solitude.

5. What ideas on matters sublime did you either maintain as you received them from me or introduce on your own concerning either divinity or the other doctrines that I lavished on you so often? I demand not only the loan, but the interest as well; not only the talent, but also the profit, lest anyone bury and hide what was entrusted to him and falsely accuse the giver of churlishly coveting what is not his own.[19] What harvest of praiseworthy deeds have you produced either without the knowledge of the left hand[20] or in such a way that *your light* shines *before men*,[21] so that *the tree* might be known by its fruit[22] and the

---

13. Ps 95.6 (LXX 94.6).
14. Ezek 34.3.
15. Zec 11.5.
16. 2 Cor 11.29, 12.14.
17. Gn 31.40.
18. Gn 30.25–43.
19. Mt 25.18–27.
20. Mt 6.3.
21. Mt 5.16.
22. Mt 7.16–20.

teacher might be seen in his students and that it might be said by anyone of those who pay attention to our affairs (there are many, some with genuine interest, others out of mere curiosity) *that God is really among you*[23] and that he is the subject not only of sound preaching, but of sound worship as well? For just as there can be no righteous action without faith—most people, after all, pursue the good both to win acclaim and because it is in their nature to do so—so *faith apart from works* is *dead*[24] also. And do not let yourselves be deceived by the hollow words of anyone of those who readily make any concession in order to gain their sole objective, the promotion of their impious doctrines and pay a vile reward for a vile business. By your works, then, show your faith, the rich produce of your region: that we have not sown on barren ground and that there is a sheaf in you that can yield flour and is worth storing, so that we may cultivate you even more eagerly. Who bears fruit *a hundredfold?* Who *sixtyfold?* Who, finally, even *thirtyfold?*[25] Or, conversely, who goes from the thirty to sixty—the Gospels give us this sequence, too—and at last reaches the *hundred* mark[26] so that *advancing* he might *become great* like Isaac,[27] going *from strength to strength,*[28] singing the gradual Psalms and *in his heart* purposing *to go up?*[29]

6. *I seek the fruit which increases to your credit.*[30] The gain is yours, not mine, except that because it is yours, it is ours, too, the benefit glancing from you to us just like the reflected rays of the sun. Did you feed the poor? Did you show hospitality? Did you wash the feet of the saints?[31] Did you, while taking pleasure in the belly that is destroyed[32] (one must make allowances for this) find the commandments a source of pleasure as well? Understand that there is no pleasure better than this, nor one more lasting for those who choose so to live. Did you, to the best of your ability, ease the lot of those who serve the altar, those blessed with poverty—if I may so put it—that they might without distraction better attend the altar and be enabled by

23. 1 Cor 14.25.
25. Mt 13.8, 23.
27. Gn 26.13 LXX.
29. Ps 84.5 (LXX 83.6) LXX.
31. 1 Tm 5.10.

24. Jas 2.26.
26. Mk 4.8, 20.
28. Ps 84.7 (LXX 83.8).
30. Phil 4.17.
32. 1 Cor 6.13.

your generosity to offer gifts in return themselves, since it is shameful both for us to make these requests and for you not to supply them? But I have not admonished you in this way *to secure any such provision (for I would rather die than* be deprived of *my ground for boasting* and lose my reward for preaching the Gospel by reaping advantage from it here on earth. To preach the Gospel is a matter of necessity: the honor lies in doing so *free of charge*)[33] but so that you may learn to serve Christ by serving even one of the least.[34] For just as, for my sake, he became everything that I am, except for sin, in the same way he accepts as his own even my smallest acts of kindness, whether you give of your shelter; whether of your clothing; whether you visit the prisons; whether you tend the sick; whether you just perform the most ordinary gesture of refreshing with a cup of cool water the tongue of a man parched with thirst, just as the rich man tormented in the flame asked of the beggar Lazarus but, in a measure of return for a life of indulgence on this earth and his neglect of Lazarus, who was hungry and full of sores, asked of Lazarus in the other and did not receive.[35]

7. This, then, is what we require of you; and I know that you are not discomfited at the prospect of having an account asked of you either by us, or on the last day when all our affairs are gathered up. As Scripture says, *And I am coming to gather* your intentions and your actions;[36] and, *Behold* man, *and his work,* and *his reward with him.*[37] But now to our own affairs and the thoughts we bring back to you from our retreat. It was not only Elijah who chose to lead a solitary existence at Carmel[38] and John, in the desert,[39] but Jesus himself regularly spent his life partly serving the public and partly in prayers offered in the leisure of his desert solitudes.[40] What standard was he setting for us? In my view, it is that we should devote a measure of our life to solitude as well so that we may commune with God untrou-

---

33. 1 Cor 9.15–18.
34. Mt 25.40.
35. Lk 16.24–31.
36. Is 66.18.
37. Is 40.10 LXX.
38. 1 Kgs 18.19.
39. Mk 1.4; Lk 1.80. Cf. *Or.* 10.1, delivered in 372 on the occasion of a similar return from a retreat into solitude. Some of the themes of this earlier address are repeated here.
40. Lk 5.15–16.

bled and, for a short time, recall our minds from the vagaries of the world. For he himself did not require a retreat—being God, who fills all things, he could not limit himself to any one place—his purpose, rather, was that we might learn that there is a proper time for action and one for an activity more sublime. What, then, are the results of my solitude? Like a good merchant who finds a profit to be made everywhere, I should like to show you a sample of my wares from this source, too.

8. Right about sunset, I used to go for a walk by myself along the seashore. This is what I have always done when I want to relax and take my mind off my troubles. Not even a bowstring can keep its tension if it is always stretched tight. It must be loosened a little from its notches if it is to be tightened again and not prove useless to the bowman and of no help in the hour of need. So I took walks, and while my feet were carrying me along, I kept my eyes fixed on the sea. I found no delight in it, though at other times, when its calm surface turns a deep red and it laps against the shore in sweet and gentle play, it is most delightful. But at that particular time (I take delight in adding the words of Scripture) the sea *rose* in agitation *because a strong wind was blowing*.[41] And, as usually happens in such storms, some of the waves began to swell far out at sea and, after gradually reaching a crest, rippled to the shore and died, while others crashed over the nearby rocks and were sent flying backwards and dissipated in foam and fine mist. On that spot rocks and wrack and cockles and the tiniest of oysters were dislodged and spewed forth, and some of them washed back out to sea as the waves receded. But the rocks remained unshaken and unmoved just as if nothing disturbed them except for the waves clashing against them.

9. Clearly, there was something of significance and value for me here. And, since I am the sort who tries to find a personal message in everything, especially when some incident happens to set my mind churning as was the case that day, I did not take in the sight casually. What I saw was a revelation to me. Truly, I said, is not our life, and human affairs in general, an ocean that

---

41. Jn 6.18.

contains much bitterness and instability? And are not the winds the temptations that befall us and all the unexpected turns of events that occur? I believe that the most marvelous David also had this very thought in mind when he said, *Save me, O Lord! For the waters have come up to my neck;*[42] and, *Deliver me from the deep waters;*[43] for *I have come into deep waters, and the flood sweeps over me.*[44] It seemed to me that people subjected to temptation fall into two groups. Some are swept away like objects that are exceedingly light and lifeless without putting up the least resistance to the assaults made against them; they have not in themselves the means to resist, no ballast of prudence and reason to withstand the accidents of fate. Others are *a rock* worthy of that Rock on which we stand and which we worship,[45] that is, all those who adopt a philosophic mode of life and rise above the lowly masses. They stand firm before all attacks, steadfast and unshaken, while those who are shaken, on the other hand, they either laugh at or feel sorry for, depending upon whether they view the matter from the perspective of philosophy or philanthropy. Where they themselves are concerned, however, they consider it disgraceful, first of all, to make light of dangers so long as they are remote, or rather not to regard them as dangers at all but then, when they hit close to home, to be overwhelmed by them and to think of them as what? permanent when they are in fact temporary. Second, [they consider it disgraceful] to adopt a philosophical temper when circumstances are far from pressing, but to show oneself devoid of any philosophical disposition when it is needed, like a man who has a very high opinion of himself as an athlete yet never goes down into the arena, or one who thinks of himself as a respected pilot and vaunts his skill during a calm but lets go of the tiller in a storm.

10. Once I had arrived at this line of reasoning, I hit upon still another image that fits our present circumstances quite well. Perhaps you will think me a garrulous old storyteller if I let you too know about it. But you really should know it, since I no-

---

42. Ps 69.1 (LXX 68.2).
44. Ps 69.2 (LXX 68.3).
43. Ps 69.14 (LXX 68.15).
45. Cf. Mt 7.24–25, 16.18.

tice that even Scripture often uses such devices as a way of clarifying its meaning. There is a mythical plant that blooms when cut and grapples with the steel; if we may speak paradoxically of a paradoxical matter, it comes to life in death and grows by being cut and is strengthened by being diminished.[46] So the story goes, and the free play of imagination; and the philosopher, I believe, is clearly a similar kind of creature. He increases in stature through afflictions and makes trouble the stuff of virtue and wins glory through adversity, neither exalted by the weapons *of righteousness* on the right hand nor brought low by those on the left,[47] but always the same in the midst of change or found to be even more valued, like gold in a furnace. Let us look at it this way. Is he from a good family? He will display a character to match his blood-line and so win esteem on two counts, both his lineage and his own presence. Is he of humble origin, a figurine made of poor clay (not that there is a large difference between one kind of clay and another)? He will offer instead nobility of mind, the means by which each person shapes himself for better or worse. The other kind of nobility, to which one is born or appointed, he will reject as counterfeit and worthless. In other words, we have three types: one has its origin on high; by it we are all equally high-born since we are made *in the image of God*;[48] the second, deriving from the flesh and involving corruption, to my mind hardly entitles anyone to be called noble; and the third is determined on the basis of virtue and vice, and our claim will be greater or less depending in my view on the extent to which we either preserve or destroy the image. This is the nobility that the true wise man and lover of wisdom will embrace. The fourth type, which is drawn from documents and decrees, I shall consider worth discussing the day that I define beauty as made up of pretty colors or show respect to a monkey because he has been appointed a lion.

11. Is he young? He will fight down his passions like a man and the true enjoyment of his youth will lie not in succumbing

---

46. Cf. Horace, *Odes* 4.4.57–60, where the plant in question is the *ilex*, or holm oak.
47. 2 Cor 6.7.
48. Gn 1.27.

to the temptations of the young but in displaying mature judgment in a body at its most vigorous; and victory will mean more to him than it does to those who are crowned at Olympia because it will be won in the public arena of the entire world and is one that cannot be bought at any price. Is he inclining towards old age? But his soul will not age with him. He will welcome the hour of his release as the time appointed for the liberation vouchsafed to him; he will go in gladness to the world beyond, where no one is too young and no one old, but all are perfect in the age of the spirit. Is he physically attractive? The beauty of his body will be a dazzling reflection of the beauty of his soul, one of the other. Have the years left his bloom untouched? He focuses on the inner man and is oblivious to the stares. Is he unattractive in appearance? Yet below the surface he is fair just as the calyx with no brilliance or scent of its own conceals in itself the most fragrant and brilliant rose. Is he *the fairest of the sons of men?*[49] He gives the onlooker no opportunity at all to gawk at his outer form but diverts attention to the inner man. Does he enjoy good health? He will use it to the best purpose: he will admonish, he will rebuke, he will speak his mind, he will keep vigil, he will sleep on the ground, he will fast, everything that is carnal he will make void, he will reflect upon the things of earth and the things of heaven, with full devotion he will meditate on death.[50] Will he be ill? He will struggle against his illness, but should he be overcome, the victory will still be his and the reward the fact that his struggles are over. Is he rich? He will devote himself to giving away his wealth; he will distribute what he has to the one in need as though steward of goods not his own so that both that one may benefit from the sharing and he himself be drawn unto God with nothing but his cross and his person. Is he poor? He will be rich in God and in his scorn of the wealthy for constantly adding to their possessions but remaining constantly in want because they require more, and drinking that they might thirst the more.

12. Is he hungry? He will be fed along with the birds who

---

49. Ps 45.2 (LXX 44.3).
50. Meditation upon death is a mark of the philosopher in Plato, *Phaedo* 67e and 81a; cf. also Epicurus, fr. 470, ed. Usener, and Irenaeus, fr. 11, PG 7.1233B.

subsist though they neither sow nor plow.[51] He will live with Elijah in Zarephath: *The jar of meal shall not be spent, and the cruse of oil shall not fail;*[52] the one will gush forth like water forever and the other proliferate without stint so that the hospitable widow may be honored and provide sustenance to him who sustains her. Will he be thirsty? Springs and rivers will be his drink, a drink that does not intoxicate, nor is it rationed; though all should fail because of drought, a torrent will doubtless quench his thirst. Will he be cold? So was Paul,[53] but for how long? Even a rock can provide some cover. Let the words of Job convince you: *They cling to the rock for want of shelter.*[54] Look also if you will at the things that have to do with spiritual betterment. Will he be reviled? He will prevail by not reviling in turn. Will he be persecuted? He will endure. Will he be slandered? He will try to conciliate.[55] Will he be defamed? He will pray. Will he be struck on *the right cheek?* He will offer his left also;[56] if he had a third, he would present that one too so that he might better instruct his assailant in patience, teaching by example what he could not by words. Will he be reproached? So was Christ. It shall be an honor for him to share the experience. Whether he be called *a Samaritan* or accused of harboring demons,[57] with God beside him he shall accept whatever comes. However much he suffers, much he will never know: vinegar, gall, a crown of thorns, a scepter of reeds, a scarlet robe, a cross, nails, robbers crucified alongside him, the taunts of passersby. For God stands truly supreme in his sufferance of supreme abuse.

13. Nothing is more abiding, nothing more unassailable than the philosophic life. All things will yield before a philosopher does. There is a wild ass in the wilderness, says Job, loose and free; *he scorns the tumult of the city, hears not the shouts of the driver.* There is *a wild ox,* a free-spirited creature. *Is* he *willing to serve you? Can you bind* him *at* the *crib* and bring him under the yoke?[58] If he succeeds in shutting himself off from all the things of this world, wings like those of an eagle are fashioned for him;

---

51. Mt 6.26.
52. 1 Kgs 17.9, 14.
53. 2 Cor 11.27.
54. Jb 24.8.
55. 1 Cor 4.12–13.
56. Mt 5.39; Lk 6.29.
57. Jn 8.48.
58. Jb 39.5–12.

he will return to the house of his master; he will fly up to God.[59] Let me sum up.

God and angel, these two, are not subject to external forces. The philosopher stands as a third, free from matter, yet in it, unconfined by the limits of the body, yet in one, heavenly while on earth, impassible in the midst of passions, submissive in every respect save his will, triumphant in his triumph over those who think themselves superior. And now that our verbal portrait of the philosopher, starting from the point I mentioned, is finished, come, let us examine our own affairs in relation to him (for *I think that I have the Spirit of God*,[60] vulnerable though I am and subject to any of the frailties I have mentioned) in order that, if I am found wanting by those who hate and attack me, they may be pardoned at least for their actions, even if not their motive; while if, on the other hand, I am found to be better than my enemies and superior to them, they may either put an end to their wickedness or find a new outlet for their injustice, seeing that their present strategy is laughable, and so avoid a charge of stupidity in addition to wickedness on the ground that their unlawful activities are of no avail and they do not even know how to perpetrate the injustice on which they are intent.

14. For what exactly can they do to me? They have tried everything. Let us take a look at the ways one can be wronged by his fellows. Will they call me ignorant? There is only one kind of knowledge that I am aware of, to fear God, for *the fear of the Lord is the beginning of knowledge*;[61] and, *The end of the matter; all has been heard. Fear God.*[62] So says Solomon, the most wise. Hence they have only to prove that I have no such fear and they have won. Of the remaining knowledge,[63] part I have already rejected but I hope and pray, trusting in the Spirit, to acquire the other. Will they accuse me of poverty? It is in fact my true wealth. Would I could strip off even these miserable rags and run naked through life's thorns! Would I could strip off even this heavy dress on the spot for a lighter one! Will they call me a fugitive from my country? What a low opinion they have of us,

59. Cf. Is 40.31.
60. 1 Cor 7.40.
61. Prv 1.7.
62. Eccl 12.13.
63. Part classical, part Christian παιδεία.

these truly vicious people who despise foreigners! Do you gentlemen really believe that my country is something on a map? My country is everywhere, and nowhere.[64] Is it not you who are a foreigner and a transient? This residence of yours has nothing to commend it, in my view. If such is your attitude, take care that you are not banished from the true homeland, to which our sojourn on earth must be directed.[65] Perhaps you will criticize me for being old and in poor health. This is not entirely the result of natural and physical causes. Let me tell you a secret: my condition, if I may boast a little, is at least partly a matter of deliberate choice. I do not think your plump and pampered carcass is an attractive sight either. You should sprout some gray hair and a wan complexion so that you might give the impression, at least, of being sagacious and philosophic.

15. What else can they do? Remove me from my thrones? Which of them, past or present, have I mounted with any relish? Do I congratulate others on their accession? You certainly do not make them a pleasure for me when your own elevation is so unworthy, do you? Have not even the recent events made my position clear to you? Or was that too simply my way of testing your feeling for me, a mere flirtation, if you will? Devious people tend to project all their own faults on others, thinking one thing but saying another. How then do you account for the contrition I feel? For the curses that we called down upon ourselves before one and all? For our tears and the fact that you almost felt sorry for us even though you despised us for our intransigence? Will they strip me of my rank? When has that ever meant anything to any sensible person? Actually, as matters now stand, running away from it strikes me, at any rate, as elemental good judgment. It is because of rank that our affairs are all in disruption and upheaval; that this whole world of ours is racked by anxiety and some senseless struggle that does not even have a name; that we, who are born from God, risk falling under the power of men and losing our great and wondrous name. Would there were no such thing as rank, no precedence of place and

---

64. The Christian equivalent of the famed cosmopolitanism of the Cynics, sometimes credited to Diogenes. See Diogenes Laertius 6.63.

65. Cf. Phil 3.20; Heb 13.14.

tyrant's prerogative, so that we might know one another on the basis of virtue alone! As it is, this jostling to be on the right or the left, or in the middle, or higher or lower, or to walk in front or together, *multiplies* our *wounds without cause*[66] and has pushed many into the pit and driven them off to the place of the goats—and not just the lay public, but now also their pastors who were teachers *of Israel and* did not understand *this*.[67]

16. Will they bar me from the altars? But I know of yet another altar, one of which our visible specimens are only the symbols; one over which no chisel or workman's hand has ever passed; that has never *heard* the hammer or other tool of the craftman's trade,[68] but is the product of the mind alone and approached only through contemplation. It is before this altar that I shall stand and offer acceptable victims as sacrifice and oblation and whole burnt-offerings so far superior to those we now make as truth is to shadow. It is this altar that I believe also the divine David contemplates when he says, *And I will go in to the altar of God, who gladdens my* spiritual *youth*.[69] No one at all can drag me from this altar. Will they drive me from the city? Most certainly not from the one in heaven as well. If those who hate me had this power, they would launch a full-scale war against me. But so long as they cannot do this, they spray us with spittle or blast us with hot air or play their dream games. That is my opinion of their war. Will they take away possessions? What possessions? If you mean my own, they are welcome to cut off my wings, too, which I do not have. But if you mean the possessions of the Church, here we have the reason for the whole war. It is because of these that the thief covets *the money box*[70] and betrays God for thirty pieces of silver, that most foul deed.[71] So much was the worth, not of the betrayed, but of the betrayer.

17. Will they lock me out of my house? Will they take away my comforts? Will they turn my friends against me? We have been burdensome to very many indeed, as you see, although we did so at their invitation and have no intention of showing in-

66. Jb 9.17.
68. 1 Kgs 6.7.
70. Jn 12.6.

67. Jn 3.10.
69. Ps 43.4 (LXX 42.4).
71. Mt 26.15.

gratitude. But if in fact we have burdened them,[72] it is by not imposing on them enough rather than too much. The reason? Because a pious and God-loving house took us in just as the house of the Shunammite woman did Elisha,[73] a house unstinting in its hospitality, with members who are our kinsmen in body and spirit.[74] They are the nucleus around which this congregation was built when, not without fear and danger, it was still practicing its persecuted faith in secret. May the Lord repay it on the day of *vengeance!*[75] And if a life of luxury is our goal, I hope our enemies have the luxury of destroying us. This is the worst curse I will wish upon myself. As for our friends, some, I well know, will avoid us even though they have not had to suffer—shared injury makes for shared sympathy—as for the rest, we have long since become inured to their contempt. Some of my friends and neighbors quite openly *drew near before* me and *stood still* while others—most mercifully—*stood afar off*,[76] and all were offended *this night.*[77] Even Peter came close to denying me, and perhaps he does not even weep *bitterly* to cure his sin.[78]

18. It would appear that I am the only one with any spirit or resolve; the only one with a hopeful outlook amid troubled times; the only one with perseverance, both honored in public and privately scorned, and familiar to both the East and West thanks to the attacks against me. The sheer madness of it! *Though a host encamp against me, my heart shall not fear; though war arise against me, yet I will be confident.*[79] So far from viewing any aspect of the present situation with alarm, I take no notice of its

---

72. 2 Cor 12.13–14.
73. 2 Kgs 4.8.
74. Gregory may have stayed with relatives upon his arrival in the capital. The little church of Anastasia where he held services may either be their house or, more probably, a building close by. See further, R. Snee, "Gregory Nazianzen's Anastasia Church: Arianism, the Goths, and Hagiography," *DOP* 52 (1998): 157–86.
75. Is 61.2, 63.4.   76. Ps 38.11 (LXX 37.12) LXX.
77. Mt 26.31.
78. Mt 26.69–75. There may be an allusion to Athanasius's successor, Peter, who supported Gregory at first, but then was manipulated against him by Maximus. He finally detected Maximus's true colors and became reconciled with Gregory in the end.
79. Ps 27.3 (LXX 26.3).

impact on me and instead grieve for those who have caused me pain. You who were once members of Christ, members precious to me however ravaged you may be now, members of this flock, which you have very nearly betrayed even before it was formed, how came you to scatter and be scattered like cattle loose from the tether? How came you to set altar against altar? *How are you destroyed in a moment?*[80] How is it that the breach that laid you low made us feel the pain too? How came you to exploit simple shepherds to the ruination of their flock? I will not fault them at all for their lack of sophistication; it is you I will blame, and your wicked ways. *O Israel, who will aid thee in thy destruction?*[81] What drug should I use to help the healing? What sort of dressing should I apply? How shall I suture your gaping wounds? What tears, what words, what prayers can I use to mend your broken form? Perhaps such as these?

19. Holy Trinity, venerable and perfect, rightly united by us in worship, the successful completion of this noble task lies with you. Those who set themselves so far apart from us that the very separation has taught them the value of harmony may you restore to us once again; and ourselves in return for our trials here on earth may you reward with the blessings of heaven that are free from faction. The first and greatest of these is to be more fully and more purely enlightened by you in the matter of how, though the same, you are both conceived as unity and seen as trinity; how the unbegotten and the begotten and the one that proceeds are one nature but three distinct persons, *one God, who is above all and through all and in all,*[82] who is not surpassed, or altered, or diminished, or severed;[83] who is in part already comprehended and in part still the object of our quest, yet doubtless one day to be comprehended in all your majesty by those who while on this earth have nobly undertaken the quest through a life of contemplation; to whom be all glory, honor, and power forever. Amen.

80. Ps 73.19 (LXX 72.19).   81. Hos 13.9 LXX.
82. Eph 4.6.
83. The theological idea is that none of the three is superior or inferior to the other two, is not different in kind, and cannot be placed beneath the others or divided from them.

ORATION 32

On discipline in theological discourse and that discoursing about God is not for everyone or for every occasion.[1]

UR FESTIVAL is well attended and you have gathered here in eager anticipation. And so a splendid opportunity presents itself for me to ply my trade. Allow me then without any further ado to offer you a sampling of my wares. It is a moderate one and cannot meet the anticipation you all have, which expects more, yet it is in keeping with my ability; one does better to contribute what one can than not to make the effort at all. A person should certainly not be held responsible if he lacks an aptitude for such things; culpable, however, he is if he refuses to involve himself be it in matters divine or human. I am a poor and insignificant shepherd who have yet to win acceptance from my fellow pastors.[2] To speak with reticence, whether their behavior is attributable to *good will* and sound doctrine or whether it is a product of petty strife,[3] *I do not know. God knows*, says the divine Apostle,[4] and *the day* of revelation *will disclose it* clearly, and the last fire in which all our affairs are judged or purged.[5] Nevertheless, I shall try my best not to hide my gift, or to put my lamp *under a bushel*,[6] or bury my talent,[7] the criticisms I have often heard you make when you accused me of being lazy because you were unhappy about my silence, but to instruct you with words of truth and to make you one in Spirit.

2. Now then, my brothers, how should I set about improving[8]

---

1. PG 36.173–212D. Delivered 379 in Constantinople.
2. Gregory faced opposition not only from Arians but also from orthodox clergy who questioned the legality of his appointment.
3. Phil 1.15.
4. 2 Cor 12.2.
5. 1 Cor 3.13–15.
6. Mt 5.15.
7. Mt 25.18.
8. Cf. 2 Cor 13.9.

you? What words should I use to honor the martyrs whose festival we are celebrating today?[9] What is the first thing I should say, or the most important? What would be most profitable to you spiritually? Or most useful on the present occasion? We may make the determination in the following way. What is the most beautiful feature of our religion? Peace; and, I may add, also the most beneficial. Again, what is the most pernicious and brings it most shame? Discord. Now that I have asked and answered this question, I shall pose a second one, too. What is it that has especially destroyed peace, and what has been most conducive to its opposite? Our aim is to isolate the causative agents as we do for physical illnesses, and seal off the sources of contamination, or dry them up. Then we shall be able to put an end to the discharges that they exude as well as their effects. One cannot, after all, reach any fit understanding about the end result if he has not given proper attention to its origin. So then, do you wish to state the cause yourselves and tell about it? Or do you authorize me as your physician to diagnose and to correct it? I am of course both ready to speak if such is your pleasure, and more ready to listen to what you have to say. You are deferring to me, I can see. Perhaps you suspect, rightly or wrongly, that we are not an incompetent physician when it comes to handling such cases or unaware of how to treat souls. Do not be surprised, then, if what I am going to say seems strange. Strange it is, yet true, I assure you, and you will agree with me if you will stay to the end and listen and resist the impetuous impulse to get up and leave before the end of the sermon, a habit of which I disapprove.

3. Passionate and strong-willed natures are the cause of this uproar; I do not at all mean those who are zealous and strong-willed in any strict sense—we certainly do not condemn impassioned feeling, without which no great accomplishment in piety or any other virtue is possible—but rather those whose intensity of feeling is accompanied by folly and ignorance and its vile offshoot, rashness, for rashness is the child of ignorance. Weak natures are sluggish and equally slow to incline to virtue

---

9. The identity of these martyrs, literally, "athletes," is unknown.

or to vice; they do not suffer wide swings in mood, and their behavior resembles the movements of people who are numb. High-spirited natures, on the other hand, when guided and directed by reason, are a great resource for the promotion of virtue; yet, when knowledge and reason fail them, they are equally productive of vice. After all, even a horse must be high-spirited and full of heart if it is going to be a champion, whether on the field of combat or a race course. The same animal would be quite useless unless it had been broken to the bit and rendered tractable by rigorous training.

4. Yes, this it is that most often has shattered limbs, divided brothers, thrown cities into confusion, driven citizens mad with rage, led nations to prepare for war, turned priests and kings against one another and their people, the people against themselves and their priests, parents against children, children against parents, men against women, women against men. It has confounded all the titles that connote mutual trust and affection: servants and masters, teachers and pupils, old and young; repudiated the law of modest deference, virtue's greatest ally, and introduced instead that of unbridled self-interest. We have become not a tribe and a tribe unto itself, a rebuke once leveled against Israel; nor an Israel and a Judah, two segments of but a single nation, and a small one at that, but we have been split down the middle of our homes and families, virtually each person against himself, the entire civilized world and the whole human race where the word of God has spread. The rule of many has become the rule of none and *our bones have been scattered at the mouth of the grave;*[10] and now that we have conquered our enemies from without, it were necessary to exterminate one another and, like lunatics who claw at their own flesh, not even sense what we are doing but actually relish the pain more than others do their serene existence and reckon our distress a gain, suppose that our fragmentation offers *service to God,*[11] distinguish ourselves from others (though this kind of distinction carries with it not praise, but condemnation), and be fired up,

10. Ps 141.7 (LXX 140.7) LXX.
11. Jn 16.2.

though with a fire that does not purify but destroys. For *the word that is sharp*,[12] the sword of Christ, does not divide believers from non-believers, nor *is fire* cast or kindled[13] (that is, the fervor of the Spirit and the faith that devours and consumes the grossness of matter) but instead, we are sundered and devoured as never before.

5. It is this that has taken the one Church and split it into many parts associated with no individual Paul or Cephas or Apollos or other planter or waterer;[14] instead, it has produced countless Pauls and Apolloses and Cephases. They are the ones by whom we identify ourselves instead of by the great and new[15] name of Christ; they are the ones to whom we are said to belong. How I wish this were the extent of it! But there are also many—and I shudder to pronounce the word—Christs, not just one: we have the generated Christ, the created Christ, the one who originated with Mary, and the one resolved back into the source of his being, and the mindless human, and the one with real and the one with phenomenal existence. Similarly, we have also many Spirits: the uncreated, and the creature, and the one equal in honor, and the one defined as operation, and the one whose existence is strictly nominal. We must recognize one God, the Father, without beginning and unbegotten, and one Son, begotten of the Father, and one Spirit who takes his existence from the Father and who, while yielding to the Father his ingenerateness and to the Son his generation, is yet in all other respects their equal in nature, dignity, glory, and honor. These are the doctrines that we must acknowledge; these we must confess; on these we must take our stand, and leave their garrulous nonsense and *godless chatter*[16] to those with nothing better to do. What is it that provoked all these ideas of theirs? A passion that has no logical foundation and no connection with knowledge and a faith that sails along with no one at the helm.

6. So, with this in mind, my brothers, let us not be slothful in

---

12. Heb 4.12.   13. Lk 12.49.
14. 1 Cor 3.4–9, 22.
15. Instead of καινόν, "new," the text in SC 318 reads κοινόν, "common," a marginal correction discussed in PG 36.179D, n. 31.
16. 1 Tm 6.20; 2 Tm 2.16.

pursuit of the good, but *fervent in the Spirit*,[17] lest by slow degrees we sleep *the sleep of death*[18] and the Enemy sow his evil seed upon us in our slumber,[19] for sloth is akin to sleep; and let our zeal be untainted by selfishness and folly lest we be carried away and stray from the royal road and surely stumble in one of two ways: either our slothfulness will need a whip or our fanaticism will hurl us to destruction. Instead, by extracting from both as much as will best serve our purpose, a sense of meekness from the one, impassioned feeling from the other, let us shun the injurious aspects of both, the hesitation of the one, the recklessness of the other; in this way we can avoid both ineffectual deficiency and the dangers of excess. Unproductive sloth and undisciplined passion are equally useless things; the one, because it does not draw nigh to the good, the other, because it overshoots the mark and produces something that is righter than right, as the divine Solomon well understood: *Do not swerve,* he says, *to the right or to the left,*[20] and do not fall from opposite extremes into an equal evil, namely, sin. And yet, he does enjoin the naturally right when he says, *For God knows the ways on the right hand, but those on the left are crooked.*[21] How then does he enjoin the right while at the same time direct us away from the right? Clearly, he is talking about a kind of right that is only apparent, not actual. This is what he has in mind when he says elsewhere, *Be not righteous overmuch, and do not make yourself overwise.*[22] For passion in word and deed that goes beyond the bounds of virtue and the good has an equal impact on both justice and wisdom. Virtue is impaired alike by too much as well as too little, just as any addition to or subtraction from a rule.

7. So, let no one be wise beyond due measure or more exacting than the law requires, or brighter than the light or straighter than a rule, or more exalted than the commandment. How can this be achieved? By maintaining a sense of proportion and respecting the law of nature, by using reason as one's guide and refusing to reject a standard of order. *Look at the heav-*

---

17. Acts 18.25; Rom 12.11.
18. Ps 13.3 (LXX 12.4).
19. Mt 13.25.
20. Prv 4.27.
21. Prv 4.27a LXX.
22. Eccl 7.16.

ens above and at the earth beneath,[23] then consider how and whence the whole was formed, what it was before its arrangement and what the whole is now called.[24] It is through order that all things have been given their arrangement, and Logos who has done the arranging. It would of course have been possible for everything to come into being all at once as a unit, since he who gave existence to things nonexistent and supplied their shapes and forms as they emerged into being would not have been incapable of arranging and producing the whole at a single stroke; instead, he assigns number to things—first, second, third, and so on—so that order may be part of creation from the start.[25]

8. It was order, then, that assembled the whole. It is order that holds together the things of heaven and the things of earth; order among the things we perceive with our minds; order among those we perceive with our senses; order among the angels; order among the stars, in their movement and their magnitude and their relationship to one another and their brilliance. *There is one glory of the sun, and another glory of the moon, and another glory of the stars; for star differs from star in glory;*[26] order in the intervals and seasons of the year as they advance and recede in regular fashion and temper inclemency with their moderating action; order in the measured intervals of night and day; order in the elements from which bodies are composed. Order has set the heavens in orbital motion; has spread abroad the expanse of the air; has set the earth beneath or even above;[27] has poured forth and harnessed the liquid element; has allowed the winds to blow but not turned them loose; has confined moisture in the clouds but not withheld it, sowing it instead over the face of the whole earth in regular and equitable fashion; and these things not for a brief period, nor for a single moment or occasion, but from the beginning to the end of time, guided and conducted along the same round, on the

---

23. Is 51.6.
24. The word here translated as "arrangement" comes from the Greek κόσμος, or universe, that is, "the whole." See also *Or.* 28.22–31.
25. See *Or.* 44.4–5 and n. 16.   26. 1 Cor 15.41.
27. I.e., mountains.

one hand fixed in their existence by the Logos, yet in motion thanks to their flux. *He established them for ever and ever; he fixed their bounds which cannot be passed.*[28] This refers to their fixity, while whatever has taken or will take place involves their flux. Verily, when order prevails we have the world, the universe, and beauty inviolate. But disorder and disarray give rise to thunderbolts in the air, earthquakes on the land, tidal waves in the sea, wars in cities and homes, diseases in the body and sins in the soul, conditions all synonymous not with order, or peace, but with turbulence and disorder. And let us understand, my brethren, that even the bruited destruction that awaits us is nothing other than an excess of disorder. Order binds, disorder undoes, whenever he who has bound it together sees fit to undo the universe or make it over.

9. It was order that ordained a mode of reproduction for all living forms as well as their sustenances and the habitat suitable for each. And neither does one see dolphins ploughing furrows or the ox gliding through waves; just as one does not see the sun waxing or waning by night nor the moon blazing brightly by day. *The high mountains are a refuge for the stags, and the rock for the hares. He appointed the moon for seasons; the sun knows his going down.*[29] It is night, and mankind is curled asleep and the wild animals roam free seeking the food allotted to each by the Creator; it is day, and the animals *are gathered together* and man bustles *to his labor;*[30] and we yield to one another in orderly fashion, according to the law and regulation of nature. I shall add the most important point of all, and the most germane. It was order that formed man as a rational animal from a mixture of rational and irrational elements and bound dust to mind and mind to spirit in a mysterious and ineffable way. And, so that its creative process might appear even more remarkable, the same creature it both preserved and dissolved; for as it removed one, it introduced another in succession to take its place, as in a stream, and through dissolution made mortality immortal. It is order that set us apart from the beasts and founded cities and enacted

28. Ps 148.6.
29. Ps 104.18–19 (LXX 103.18–19) LXX.
30. Ps 104.20–23 (LXX 103.20–23) LXX.

laws and rewarded virtue and punished vice and invented arts and instituted the bond of marriage and put tenderness in our lives through the love that we feel for our children and instilled in us something that surpasses the earthly longing of the flesh, the longing for God.

10. But what need is there to run through the list? Order is the mother and mainstay of all that exists. If it could speak, it alone could claim the beautiful words of the Logos who created all things: When God gave substance and existence to the whole, *I was by him, suiting myself to him;*[31] *when he prepared his throne upon the winds, and strengthened the clouds above;* when he laid the foundations of the earth and when *he secured the fountains of the earth*[32] and *by the breath of his mouth* gave them *all* their *host.*[33] However—and here I finally reach the point of my sermon and the reason why I have gone through all these examples—in the churches, too, order has determined that there shall be one element consisting of the flock and another of their shepherds; and that the one rule and that the other be subject to rule; and that the one function as the head, so to speak, another as the feet, another as the hands, another as the eyes, and others as the other parts of the body, with a view to the happy concord and advantage of the members as a whole, be they of higher or lower status; and, just as in the human body, the limbs do not stand detached from one another but exist as one body, a whole composed of different parts; nor do they all function in the same way even if they have the same need of one another, as required for their cooperation and goodwill;[34] nor does the eye walk but leads the way; nor the foot peer ahead but moves and changes position; nor the tongue hear sounds, for that is the function of the ear; nor the ear speak, for that is the function of the tongue; and the nose is the organ of smell; and *the palate tastes* food, as Job says;[35] and the hand is the instrument for giving and receiving; and the mind directs them all

---

31. Prv 8.30 LXX.   32. Prv 8.27–29 LXX.
33. Ps 33.6 (LXX 32.6).
34. The text of SC 318 includes a variant reading omitted in PG 36.185C: καὶ ἰσοτιμίας ἐν τοῖς ἀνίσοις ("and equality among the unequal").
35. Jb 34.3.

ORATION 32   199

since it is the source of sensory perception and the locus to which sense impressions are channeled: so it is with us as well, the common body of Christ.

11. For we are all *one body in Christ* and individually *members* of Christ *and one of another*.[36] One part rules and presides while the other is guided and directed; and neither do they both have the same function, since ruling and being ruled are not the same thing, yet both become one in one Christ, being joined together[37] and knit by the same Spirit. Again, how great is the gap not only among the ruled in age, and education, and training, but what disparity among their leaders too! *And the spirits of prophets are subject to prophets:*[38] when Paul speaks, doubt not. *And God has appointed*, he says, *in the church first apostles, second prophets, third pastors* and *teachers*,[39] the first for truth, the second for foreshadowing, the third for illumination and service according to their capacity.[40] And the Spirit is one, but the gifts of the Spirit are not equal, for neither are its vessels. *To one is given through the Spirit the utterance of wisdom* and contemplation; *to another the utterance of knowledge* or revelation; to another *faith* firm and unquestioning; *to another the working of miracles* and wonders sublime; *to another gifts of healing*, gifts of *helping* (that is, protecting), gifts of administering (that is, disciplining the flesh), *various kinds of tongues, the interpretation of tongues*,[41] the greater *gifts* and the secondary, *in proportion to our faith*.[42]

12. This, my brothers, is the order we should respect, this the order we should preserve. Let one man serve as an ear, another as a tongue, a third as a hand, and another in some further capacity. Let one man teach and another learn and yet another do *honest work with his hands* that he may give to him that is poor and needy.[43] Let one man rule and preside and another be justified in his service; and let him who teaches do so in a dignified way. *Let two or three prophets speak, and each in turn; and let one in-*

36. Rom 12.5.
37. Eph 4.16.
38. 1 Cor 14.32.
39. 1 Cor 12.28; Eph 4.11.
40. These functions correspond to the three levels of the ecclesiastical hierarchy.
41. 1 Cor 12.8–10, 28.
42. Rom 12.6.
43. Eph 4.28.

terpret. But if another has been enlightened, let the first yield.[44] And let him who learns be receptive to instruction; and him who ministers do so *with cheerfulness* and him who attends, with eagerness.[45] Let us not all try to serve as a tongue, that most facile medium; let us not *all* try to be *apostles, all prophets, all interpret*.[46] Do you think talking about God is important? But it is more important to purify yourself for God, because *wisdom will not enter a deceitful soul*.[47] Indeed, we have been bidden to sow *righteousness* and reap *the fruit of life* that we may be enlightened by the light *of knowledge*.[48] And Paul would have us be known of the Lord through our love of *the Lord* and, by being known, be taught. This he sees as a better path to *knowledge* than the conceit that puffs itself up.[49]

13. Do you think teaching important? Yet learning carries no danger. Why do you make yourself a shepherd when you are a sheep? Why do you assume the role of head when it is your lot to be a foot? Why do you try to play the general when you have been assigned to the ranks? Why do you go after the high but risky profits of the sea when you can, without hazard though with less gain, farm the land? If you are a man in Christ and your *faculties* have been trained by practice[50] and the light of your knowledge is bright, seek to impart *the wisdom* that is imparted *among the mature* and that is *secret and hidden*;[51] and do so when you have reached the desired level and are so entrusted. For *what have you* that is your own doing, that was not given you and you did not receive?[52] But if, on the other hand, you are still *a child*, with toddling mind and unable to reach higher, become a Corinthian, fed on milk. Why do you need more *solid food*[53] which your fragile body can neither digest nor use? Go ahead and speak out if what you have to say is better than silence, for, as you know, it is commendable to impose order on one's tongue;[54] but try to cherish quiet when silence is preferable to

44. 1 Cor 14.27–30.
45. Rom 12.7–8.
46. 1 Cor 12.29–30.
47. Wis 1.4.
48. Hos 10.12; 2 Cor 4.6.
49. Cf. 1 Cor 8.1–3.
50. Heb 5.14.
51. 1 Cor 2.6–7.
52. 1 Cor 4.7.
53. Heb 5.12–13; 1 Cor 3.2.
54. Cf. Prv 10.19–21.

speech, and be content sometimes to speak up and sometimes to listen; sometimes to express your approval and sometimes to withhold it, though not in an ill-tempered way.

14. My brothers, you cannot know how difficult it is for us to stand here as a pompous figure of authority and lay these rules upon you, the people. But what is truly lamentable is that perhaps even most of us do not ourselves realize the weight that every thought and word and deed carries with God; and not only with God, but with the majority of men as well, who are slow to judge their own conduct but quick to scrutinize someone else's and would more easily excuse the greatest shortcomings in others than the most trifling in ourselves; and, the more ignorant they are, the more inclined to convict us of impiety than themselves of abject ignorance. You cannot know how great a gift from God is silence and not having to speak on every occasion, thus to have it within ourselves, as keepers over both our speech and our silence, to choose what to say and what to suppress. For all speech is by nature loose and inadequate and, because it is open to challenge, vulnerable, and speech about God all the more so as the subject is more important and the emotion runs higher and the venture is more difficult. What shall we fear? And where then place our trust? Human reason? Speech? The things we hear? We oscillate precariously between three poles: the difficulty of forming a conception of him, the near impossibility of expressing it in words,[55] and the still greater task of finding an ear to receive it in purity.

15. God is light, light the most sublime, of which all our light is but a momentary emanation or radiance penetrating the regions below, dazzling though it may appear. As you see, he tramples the gloom that surrounds us and *made darkness his covering around him*,[56] putting it between himself and us, just as Moses also once put a veil between himself and Israel's hardness of heart[57] so that dark nature might not win an easy glimpse of that secret beauty of which only a few are worthy and just as easily reject it because it was effortlessly acquired; and that light

55. Cf. Plato, *Timaeus* 28c; *Or.* 28.4.
56. Ps 18.11 (LXX 17.12).
57. Cf. 2 Cor 3.7–15; Ex 34.33; Rom 11.25.

might commune with light, drawing it ever upward with desire, and that a mind made pure might approach the most pure and a portion of that light reveal itself now and a portion in the time to come as a reward of virtue and of our inclination or assimilation to it while on this earth. *For,* says Scripture, *now we see in a mirror dimly, but then face to face. Now I know in part; then I shall understand fully, even as I have been fully understood.*[58] What lowly creatures we are! And how magnificent the promise to know God as fully as we have been known! These are the words of Paul, the great *preacher* of the truth, *the teacher of the Gentiles in faith,*[59] who fully preached the Gospel all about,[60] who lived in nothing other than in Christ,[61] who reached up to *the third heaven,* who beheld paradise,[62] who in order to reach perfection longed to depart.[63]

16. Moses himself scarcely saw the *back* of God because of the rock[64] (whatever may be the meaning of "back" and "rock") and this only when, after much prayer, the promise made to him was kept, except that he, Moses, the God to Pharaoh,[65] the leader of so great a multitude, the one who displayed such miraculous powers, did not see all he wished; what escaped him was more than what met his eyes. As for you, whom did you feed from the sky?[66] What water did you give from the rock?[67] What sea did you divide with your *rod?*[68] What people did you lead through the waters as if through dry land? What enemies did you drown? Whom did you lead by a pillar *of fire* and *of cloud?*[69] What Amalek did you defeat, by stretching out your hands in prayer[70] and mystically, so long before, prefiguring the cross, that you might consider it a misfortune not to see God in his perfection and as a consequence everything seem to spin and turn upside-down? From my remarks about Moses is it not clear to you that God's gifts are systematically ranked, and that there is a rule that determines their order? If you are Moses, go up into the

---

58. 1 Cor 13.12.
60. Rom 15.19.
62. 2 Cor 12.2, 4.
64. Ex 33.21–23.
66. Ex 16.13.
68. Ex 14.16.
70. Ex 17.10–12.

59. 1 Tm 2.7; 2 Tm 1.11.
61. Gal 2.20.
63. Phil 1.23.
65. Ex 7.1.
67. Ex 17.6.
69. Ex 13.21.

cloud and seek to talk to God and to hear his voice; and receive the Law, and become a lawgiver. But if you are Aaron, go up with him but stop outside the cloud and stay close by. And if you are an Ithamar or an Eleazar[71] and third from Moses or one of the elders and a member of the Seventy, stand even farther away, although you are third in rank. But if you are one of the common crowd, the mountain does not admit you; even a beast which touches there will be stoned.[72] Wait below and seek to hear only the voice and this only after you have cleansed and purified yourself, as you have been commanded.[73]

17. Let me cite a few more examples for your edification. Who consecrated the priests' hands? Moses. Who was the first to be consecrated? Aaron.[74] But even before this, who was responsible for God's affairs? And who served as spokesman for his people? Who entered the Holy of Holies? Only one. And was this a constant practice of his? Not at all. He entered but once a year, and then only at the time specified. What group carried the tabernacle? Only the Levites; and here again we find these bearers classified according to rank, some carrying the more valuable sections and others the ones less so. And also when the tabernacle had to be guarded, what group did the guarding, and how? A part took one side, another another; and nothing, not even the most trivial detail, was left unregulated or undecided.[75] But we, once we get our hands on a little glory, and often not even that, by managing to memorize at random two or three phrases of Scripture, and these hopelessly out of context (this is exactly what instant wisdom and the tower at Chalanne,[76] which we can well believe produced the babel of tongues, signify), we are forced into the impossible position of rejecting Moses and identifying with the godless scoundrels Dathan and Abiram.[77] Let us avoid their impudence and keep from imitating their folly and bringing their end upon ourselves.

18. Would you like me to put before you yet another exam-

71. Ex 28.1; Nm 3.2; et al.
73. Ex 24; cf. *Or.* 28.2.
75. Nm 2.47–53, 3.21–39.
77. Nm 16.12–33, 26.9–11.

72. Ex 19.12–13.
74. Ex 29.9.
76. Gn 11.1–9; cf. 10.10 LXX.

ple of order, this one also commendable and worthy of our notice and attention at this juncture? You observe that of Christ's disciples, all of them outstanding and worthy of election, one is called the rock and is entrusted with the foundation of the Church,[78] while another is especially loved and lays his head *on Jesus' breast*,[79] and the rest accept the preferential treatment. And when the time came to go *up* the *mountain* so that Christ might become radiant in form[80] and reveal his divinity and uncover him who lay veiled in his flesh, who go with him, since not all witnessed the miracle? Peter and James and John, who both in actuality are and are numbered before the others. And when he suffers and when he withdraws to pray shortly before the Passion, which of them are at his side? The same ones again.[81] Such is the preferential treatment that Christ gave. And consider how courteous and orderly their behavior is on another occasion. Peter asks one question,[82] Philip another,[83] Judas another,[84] Thomas another,[85] and someone else yet another; they do not all ask the same question, nor does one person ask them all, but each has a turn, one by one. Would you say that each asked what he wanted to know? Well, then, how do you explain this? Philip wants to say something but is too shy to do it on his own and enlists Andrew's help.[86] Peter wishes to ask a question but beckons to John and has him pose it instead.[87] Where is the insistence on rank here? The ambition to be first? What better way could there be for them to show that they were disciples of Christ, *the gentle and lowly in heart*,[88] the servant for the sake of us, his servants, who ascribes to the Father all glory in all things that he might provide us with a model of humble orderly behavior, a behavior for which we have so little respect that I should be happy, seeing that we display it in issues and situations of the highest consequence, if we managed to keep from being the most presumptuous of all men?

78. Mt 16.18.
79. Jn 13.23, 25.
80. Mt 17.1–8.
81. Mt 26.37.
82. Jn 13.6.
83. Jn 14.8.
84. Jn 14.22.
85. Jn 14.5.
86. Jn 12.22.
87. Jn 13.24.
88. Mt 11.29.

19. Do you realize that humility is judged not so much in small matters—this would be the case with a false, but flashy, show of virtue—as it is put to the test in great ones? In my opinion the humble-minded man is not the one who says little about himself, and this only to a few and rarely, nor the one who addresses his inferior in a humble way, but the one who shows restraint in discussing God, who knows what to say and what to keep to himself and in what to admit his ignorance, who yields to the one who has been charged with speaking and accepts the fact that another is more spiritually endowed and has made greater progress in contemplation. For it is shameful to choose a simple garb and manner of life over a more exalted one and put one's humility and awareness of one's human frailty on display through calloused knees and floods of tears in addition to fasts and vigils and regularly sleeping on the ground, toil and all sorts of mortifications, and then be an absolute tyrant who defers to no one in the slightest degree and lords it over every doctor of the Law when it comes to discoursing about God. It is here that a sense of humility puts a man on sure ground and secures his good name.

20. What then? Are we to keep silent on the subject of God? Is this what you would have us do? one of the more hotheaded interrupts. What subject are we to discuss if not this one? And what are we to make of those verses of Scripture that say, *His praise shall continually be in my mouth* and, *I will bless the Lord at all times*[89] and, *My mouth will utter truth*[90] and, *Lo! I will not refrain my lips*,[91] as well as the other passages he will cite that are likewise explicit on the issue? We should use gentle, not harsh words to answer him, thereby teaching him good order. I am not asking you to keep still, my sharp-witted friend, but to refrain from assuming a combative posture; not to obscure the truth, but to refrain from teaching contrary to the Law. I am the first among those who value wisdom and devote themselves to the study of God's words, or, at least, among those who wish to do so. May I never put anything above this pursuit or ever become a miser-

---

89. Ps 34.1 (LXX 33.2).
90. Prv 8.7.
91. Ps 40.9 (LXX 39.10) LXX.

able wretch in the eyes of wisdom herself for despising wisdom and instruction![92] But for all that I avoid excess and keep the bounds of moderation. I should rather leave something undone than overdo it, rather be timid than brash, if I cannot avoid both and achieve the mean. But you are behaving almost as if you were accusing me of trying to deny you nourishment altogether when I am merely trying to prevent over-indulgence, or as if I were singing the praises of blindness when I am simply urging you to use your sight with discretion.

21. *If you have* the word of understanding, *answer,* says Scripture, and no one will hold you back; *if not,* put a curb on your lips.[93] How much more this applies to those prepared to impart instruction! In proper time teach; if not, hold your tongue and open your ears. Seek to meditate on things divine, but stay within the proper bounds; to speak out the things of the Spirit and, if possible, nothing else; and to speak out with every breath you take, if not more, but in the consciousness of what has been assigned to you, for it is an inspiring and ennobling thing to have the thought of matters divine act as a goad ever urging you to God. Try not to trouble yourself over the precise nature of Father, the existence of his only-begotten Son, the glory and the power of the Spirit, the single divinity and splendor in the Three, the indivisible nature as well as confession, glory, and hope of those who truly believe. Try to keep to the words that you have known from childhood; leave sophisticated language to the more advanced. It is enough for you to have the foundation; leave it to the craftsman to build on it. It is enough to strengthen your *heart* with simple bread;[94] leave the rich dishes to the rich. No reasonable person can condemn you for not providing a lavish feast, only for failing to offer some bread and a drink of water,[95] whether to a disciple of Christ or anyone else, if you possibly can. Do not be hasty in your words. Wisdom bids you.[96] *If thou art poor,* measure *not thyself with a rich man,*[97] nor seek to be wiser than the wise. Self-knowledge also is wisdom, but not a high opinion of oneself; that would be like the afflic-

---

92. Wis 3.11.
93. Sir 5.12.
94. Ps 104.15 (LXX 103.15).
95. Mt 10.42.
96. Sir 4.29.
97. Prv 23.4 LXX.

tion that affects the vocal chords: they give out completely when strained to excess. It is better to be wise and yield graciously than to be ignorant and let arrogance lead one out of one's depth. Be quick to respond only whenever you are asked for your confession; beyond that, hesitate: in the first case, it is slowness to act that carries the risk; in the second, haste.

22. What is so bad, I ask you, about not dominating every discussion or not having the last say on every question or issue but instead seeing other people come out either wiser or more assertive than yourself? Thanks be to God that he both confers individual privilege and knows how to provide salvation through what we all have in common. This marvel can be seen not only in verbal ability, but also in creation itself, as you may have observed. Just as among creatures the important endowments are not the prerogative of some, but of all, and grace is not limited to one type of creature, so in the matter of faith the means of salvation are available not just to the mighty but to anyone who wishes it. What greater good is there than air, fire, water, earth, rain, fruit both cultivated and wild, shelter, clothing? We all have access to these, some unconditionally, others according to measure, and no one has power so unlimited as to usurp for himself the common boon. God *makes the sun rise* equally *and sends rain* on rich and poor.[98] The alternation between night and day is common to all; health is a common gift; we have a common limit of life, common proportion and grace of body, common faculty of the senses. Indeed, the poor man may even have an advantage in feeling more grateful for these favors and enjoying the common bounty with greater zest than the mighty do all their wealth. These blessings, then, are common and equal for all, and the clear marks of God's righteousness; gold and glittering jewels and a supply of soft and finely made garments and a swollen and salacious table and superfluous riches, the bane of those who possess them, are the trappings of few.

23. This is also how I view our faith. We have as our common property the Law; the Prophets; Testaments; the oracles therein; grace; elementary instruction; perfection; the sufferings of

---

98. Mt 5.45.

Christ; the new creation; the apostles; the Gospels; the apportionment of the Spirit; *faith, hope, love*,[99] both toward God and from God and not doled out piecemeal as the gift of manna once was to an ungrateful and unfeeling Israel,[100] but in proportion to our desire; ascent; illumination, in its earthly form, limited, in the one we hope for, clear; and, the greatest gift of all, the recognition of the Father and the Son and the Holy Spirit, and the confession of our highest hope. What is greater than these? Indeed, what more common? As for the gifts that are above these, though more precious because of their rarity, they are secondary because they are not vital, for the things without which one cannot be a Christian are more useful than those accessible to only a few.

24. One man's riches lie in contemplation; he rises above the mass and interprets *spiritual truths to those who possess the Spirit*[101] and *repeatedly* records on the table of his *heart*[102] the word that edifies all, as well as the one that edifies many and the one that edifies not all but some and no more; and he does not abide his poverty, but tries to penetrate deep into the divine. Let him go up and be led forth; and let his mind carry him even up to *the third heaven*, if he wishes, as in Paul's case.[103] Only let reason and knowledge go with him so that his exaltation does not bring him down and his wings droop and fail because of his soaring flight.[104] Who would begrudge an ascent that deserves praise? And what fall could compare with being impaled on your own exaltation and failing to recognize how low and insignificant is man's reach and how huge the gap that still remains between the highest among us all and the truly sublime?

25. Another man is intellectually weak and a poor speaker besides; clever turns of phrase, pithy remarks, and enigmas are beyond him, as are Pyrrho's objections, or suspensives, or oppo-

---

99. 1 Cor 13.13.
100. Ex 16.16–20.
101. 1 Cor 2.13.
102. Prv 22.20 LXX.
103. 2 Cor 12.2.
104. When Icarus flew too close to the sun, the wings his father Daedalus had made from wax and feathers disintegrated and he plunged to his death.

sitions,[105] as well as the refutations of Chrysippus's syllogisms,[106] or the specious strategies of Aristotle's rhetoric, or Plato's mesmerizing eloquence,[107] all fellows who have wormed their way into our Church like so many Egyptian plagues. This man too has the wherewithal to be saved, but what words will he use? Nothing is more bountiful than grace. You need not at all, Scripture tells us, ascend *into heaven* to bring Christ down from above, nor descend *into the abyss* to bring him up from among the dead by being over-curious regarding his primary nature or his ultimate Dispensation. *The word is near you,* says Scripture. This is the treasure that the mind possesses, and the tongue, the one by faith, the other by confession. What is more clear-cut than this wealth? What easier to obtain than this gift? Confess Jesus Christ and believe that he rose from the dead and you will be saved.[108] Righteousness is a matter of faith alone; but perfect salvation means, in addition, confession and the free and confident avowal of our conviction. You have set your sights on something greater than salvation: the glory and splendor of the other life. But for me, the greatest thing is being saved and avoiding the punishments in the other world. The path you have taken is untrodden and inaccessible; mine is well-worn, the one that has brought salvation to many.

26. My brothers, our faith would be the most unfair thing in the world if it applied only to sophisticates and those with a flair

---

105. Pyrrho of Elis (c. 365–275 B.C.) was the founder of Scepticism. "Objections" and "oppositions," as expressed for example in the dictum, "For every argument there is a counterargument" (Diogenes Laertius 9.74), were means to the end of suspending or withholding judgment on everything, i.e., "suspensives."

106. The Stoic philosopher Chrysippus (c. 280–207 B.C.) wrote prolifically on many subjects, including syllogisms. The Sceptic Sextus Empiricus (late 2d century A.D.) rejected the validity of syllogistic reasoning and specifically cites Chrysippus's treatise, *Introduction to Syllogisms,* in *Against the Logicians* 2.223 (=M 8.223).

107. The theological controversies of the late fourth century also involved a struggle over παιδεία, or the cultural tradition. Hence, Gregory does not object so much to Plato and Aristotle, by whom he himself was deeply influenced, as to the intellectual oneupsmanship practiced by his opponents. See F. W. Norris, *Faith Gives Fullness to Reasoning. The Five Theological Orations of Gregory Nazianzen,* with a translation by L. Wickham and F. Williams (Leiden, 1991).

108. Rom 10.6–8.

for language and logic. It would then of necessity remain beyond the reach of most persons, like gold and silver and all the other things considered valuable here below and in great popular demand; and what would be near and dear to God would be that which is placed high and touches only a few, while anything close enough to be grasped by the multitude would be scorned and rejected. When even among human beings the more fair-minded would not behave in such a way as to find pleasure only in outstanding distinctions rather than call for those within our power to achieve, you surely cannot expect that God would act at all otherwise. His wonders are many, but nothing is so specially characteristic of him as beneficence towards all men. Take care not to spurn the ordinary or go hunting after novelty to impress the mass. Let Solomon's advice be your guide: *Better is a little* with security than much with uncertainty[109] and, *Better* is a poor man *who walks in* his integrity,[110] another of his wise sayings; that is, the man poor in words and understanding, who uses simple expressions and clings to them as to a flimsy raft in his effort to survive, is better than the unctuous fool who in his ignorance takes pride in feats of logic and by his facility with words empties the cross *of Christ* of its power,[111] a marvel beyond word, and thereby through logic and its inadequacy degrades the truth.

27. Why do you fly off to heaven, earthling that you are? Why do you build *a tower* if you do not have *enough to complete it?*[112] Just why do you measure *the waters in the hollow of* your *hand* and mark off *the heavens with a span, and enclose all the earth in a measure,*[113] those primal elements that can be measured only by him who created them? Know thyself,[114] first of all. Comprehend the things that immediately concern you:[115] who you are and how you were molded and how you were formed so as to be an im-

109. Prv 15.16.
111. 1 Cor 1.17.
113. Is 40.12.
110. Prv 19.1 (28.6 LXX).
112. Lk 14.28–30.

114. The maxim, "Know thyself," was attributed to Thales (6th c. B.C.) and was inscribed on the temple of Apollo at Delphi along with other sayings by the Seven Sages such as "Nothing too much." See Diogenes Laertius 1.39; Plato, *Protagoras* 343a–b; and sec. 21, above.

115. Questions similar to the following are raised in *Or.* 28.22.

age of God yet bound to an inferior portion, and what causes you to move, what your wisdom consists of, and what is the secret of your nature; how you are confined in space while the mind knows no bound but extends to all things without moving at all; how the eye is small yet ranges so very far whether by virtue of sight receiving an impression of an object or by extending out to meet it; how the same thing both moves and is moved under the direction of the will; what cessation of movement really is; how the various senses function and how the mind uses these to relate to objects outside itself and take them in; how it receives the forms; and what is meant by the retention, or memory, of what it receives; and what by the retrieval or recall of that which is past; how word is engendered by mind and engenders word in another mind, and how thought is transmitted through word; how body is sustained through soul, and how soul through body shares in passion; how fear hobbles the soul and confidence sets it free, and grief cramps it and pleasure opens it up, envy withers and delusion bloats it and hope makes it buoyant; how anger makes it wild, and shame makes it blush as the blood either boils up or flushes forth; and how the traits of our passions are physically registered; what the rule of reason is, and how it controls all these things and checks our emotional impulses; how the incorporeal is contained by blood and breath; and how the absence of these denotes the departure of the soul. Understand these things, or a measure of them, my good man, for I have yet to mention the nature or movement of heaven and the order of the stars and the combination of elements and the variety of living creatures and the higher and lower echelons of heavenly powers and all the things into which the creative reason is distributed, and the laws of divine providence and governance. Even then, I still do not say, Be bold; but instead, Fear still to climb to the things more sublime and to those more beyond your ken.

28. Every harsh and contentious word is but training for strife on a larger scale; and just as we mold our children's characters from infancy so that they will turn from immoral behavior in later life, so too in dealing with words we must not adopt an ignorant and rash manner when small issues are involved so

as not to make it a habit in greater ones. It is easier to hold out against vice from the very start and avoid its assault than to beat it back and gain the upper hand against its advances, just as it is easier to put a rock in place at the outset and to keep it there than to push it back once it starts rolling. If you cannot control yourself and keep your sickness in check, pour energy and ambition into ventures where you run no risk. That is where you belong.

29. You do not accept this; your tongue knows no curb; you are unable to control your impulsive behavior and so are doomed to run amuck, refusing to be subject to the highest powers (though of course there is a limit even to their own knowledge) and assuming a level of self-importance that is not to your advantage. You swear that you are a decent person. Then do not condemn your brother, or call his lack of resolution a disregard of God, or be so quick to turn your back on him in disapprobation or dismissal. Instead, show humility on this earth while you can; on this earth honor your brother above yourself—you will not regret it—where to condemn in disgrace is to cast out from Christ, our only hope, and to cut down along with the weeds wheat we cannot see, wheat perhaps more precious than you.[116] Instead, set him on the right path, and do so gently and lovingly, not as an enemy or a brutish physician who knows one thing alone, how to cauterize and cut; at the same time, take note of yourself and your own infirmity. For what if your eyes are inflamed, or you have some other visual impairment and can barely make out the sun? Yes, what if you think everything is spinning because you happen to be nauseous or drunk and impute your own disorientation to others? You must live long and suffer much before you can accuse another of impiety.

30. Cutting down a tree or the brief bloom of a flower is not the same thing as cutting down a human being. You are an image of God, your interlocutor is an image of God, and you who pass judgment are yourself being judged;[117] and the one on

---

116. Mt 13.27–30.
117. Mt 7.1.

whom you are passing judgment is the servant of another[118] and under another's charge. Try so to evaluate your brother on the assumption that you too are being judged by the same standards. For this reason do not be quick to cut off or isolate a member when you do not know whether you are also crippling a healthy person somehow in the process; instead, admonish, *rebuke, exhort.*[119] You have a standard for treatment: you are a disciple of Christ, the gentle and loving, who bore *our infirmities.*[120] If he offers resistance the first time, be patient; if a second, do not give up: there is still time for a cure; if a third, show yourself a loving husbandman: still more, pray to the Lord not to cut down and despise the barren and useless fig tree, but to bring it around and tend it and put on manure all about,[121] the correction, in other words, imposed by a public admission and the shame and greater opprobrium that attend it. Who knows whether he will change and bear fruit with which to feed Jesus on his return from Bethany?[122]

31. You who have been anointed with the sweet scent of the Spirit,[123] compounded by the skill of the perfumer's art, endure a portion of your brother's noisomeness, be it real or imagined, that you may give him of your own sweet fragrance.[124] His uncleanness is not the poison of a viper that will envelop you in pain, or even kill you the moment it strikes, and so provide you with an excuse to avoid or slay the creature. Instead, cure him too, if you can; but if you cannot, you can at least rest easy in the knowledge that you have not personally participated in his depravity. His affliction is like an unpleasant odor that your own sweet fragrance may possibly overpower and dispel. You who cut off your brother, often even on suspicion alone, might readily adopt toward your kinsman and fellow-servant a sentiment similar to the one that the zealous Paul made bold to express when, out of compassion, he prayed it were possible that Israel be brought to Christ instead of him.[125] The one whom you might

---

118. Rom 14.4.
119. 2 Tm 4.2.
120. Mt 8.17.
121. Lk 13.8.
122. Mt 21.19; Mk 11.12.
123. I.e., μύρον, or scented oil, which was used to anoint the newly baptized.
124. See 2 Cor 2.15.
125. Rom 9.3.

have won with kindness by your arrogance you bring to ruin, your own limb, *for whom Christ died*. Hence, if you are strong, Paul says (he is referring to food), and if you are confident of your belief and are secure in your faith, then edify your brother as well. Do not let what you eat destroy him whom Christ honored with his common passion.[126] He is talking about a different matter, but the words of admonition apply all the same.

32. We should in fact have a rule similar to the one laid down by the Hebrew sages of old to the effect that there are some holy books that are to be kept out of the hands of the young on the grounds that minds still tender and impressionable are unable to derive any benefit from them.[127] In the same way, the right to discourse on the faith should not be granted to everyone nor always, but only to some and on some occasions; I mean, it should be given to those persons who are not completely irresponsible and uncomprehending as well as to those who can control their enthusiasm and ambition and are not more zealous than they should be for true doctrine. These groups should be put in a position where they can harm neither themselves nor others; and those persons who exercise restraint in discourse and who comport themselves in a truly decent and prudent manner should enjoy liberty of expression. We should, however, direct most people away from this path and the now raging fever of garrulity, and interest them in some other, less dangerous form of achievement where not only will irresponsible behavior work less harm but boundless fervor is more a mark of piety.

33. For if, just as there is *one Lord, one faith, one baptism, one*

---

126. Rom 14.15–15.2.
127. Origen and Jerome also refer to the prohibition cited by Gregory here and at *Or.* 2.48. Rabbinic literature from late antiquity speaks of restricting access to Ezekiel, Proverbs, Song of Songs, and Ecclesiastes but, except for the case of the boy who burned to death when his text of Ezekiel erupted in flames, age is not a factor in these discussions and it is uncertain whether access to any of the books in question was ever actually restricted. See Sid Z. Leiman, *The Canonization of Hebrew Scripture: The Talmudic and Midrashic Evidence,* Transactions of the Connecticut Academy of Arts and Sciences, vol. 47, 2d ed. (New Haven, 1991), 72–86 and 177, n. 334. I thank my colleague S. Weitzman for this reference.

God, the Father of all and through all and in all,[128] there were also only one road to salvation, the one accessible only through reasoned discourse and contemplation; and if by deviating from it, we stood to lose everything and to be cast out from God and eternal hope, nothing would be more treacherous than to give the sort of recommendations I have given, or to follow them. But if, on the other hand, just as in human affairs there are many different preferences and modes of life, some carrying greater distinction and prestige while others are less prominent and significant, in the divine realm, too, there is not one single thing that brings salvation nor only one road that leads to virtue, but several; and if the reason for the famous saying, which lies on every tongue, that in God's house there are many rooms,[129] is that the roads leading there are many, some carrying greater risk and prestige while others are more lowly and safe, why do we abandon the safer paths and converge on this single one, so dangerous and slippery, that leads I know not where? Or is it that the same diet is not appropriate for everyone, and allowance has to be made for differences in age and constitution, but the same way of life or discourse stands suitable for all? I for my part should certainly not say so nor should I agree with those who do. If, then, my words carry any weight with you, young and old, rulers of peoples and ruled, ascetics living in community or apart, bid farewell to vain and useless displays of ambition and, by yourselves alone, by your conduct and way of life, and by words less fraught with peril, draw near to God and attain the truth and vision of eternal life, in Christ Jesus our Lord, to whom be the glory forever and ever. Amen.

128. Eph 4.5–6.
129. Jn 14.2.

ORATION 35

On the Holy Martyrs and against the Arians.[1]

WHAT WORDS CAN EXPRESS all that the eyes can see? What sermon do justice to the blessings before us? Look! There lies before our eyes an incredible sight, the object, so often, of our prayers. Our yearning has been answered, and to spare. Once again, in this place, we honor the martyrs with rites too long in abeyance; once again God's priests assemble; once again there are choirs and spiritual celebrations. A great throng has gathered, eager, not to take up arms but to hold festival. The wonder of it! They have flung their weapons from their hands; they have broken their ranks; war is abandoned. No longer does the din of battle-cry fill the air; instead, glad celebrations and the exuberance of peace ring the entire city, which from of old was the mother of the martyrs but has been in the interim deprived of her children's honors. But now, in the words of the Apostle, she has *received full payment, and more.*[2] Hail, martyrs! This victorious struggle belongs to you as well; it is you who put an end to the terrible war, there can be no doubt. These hard-won successes of yours stand, moreover, in a class by themselves. It was you who raised the trophy to peace; you who drew the priests of God to your side; it is thanks to you that the devotees of the Holy Spirit preside over this gathering. What a tragic loss has been suffered by those who did not live to see this day, that they too might enjoy the blessings of peace after so much misery and sadness!

2. The deceit of heresy has vanished and gone, lifted like a fog by the Holy Spirit; and the bright day of peace has dawned clear, and in it the stars of the city sparkle resplendent in the

---

1. PG 36.257A–61D. The authenticity of this homily is doubtful.
2. Phil 4.18.

bright light of truth, no minions of dark night they, but shining all by day, aglow with the true light of righteousness. And now that, in the words of the Apostle, *the night is far gone*,³ or rather, is completely over, the world is made bright by the light of the day; gone are the night-ranging beasts, driven to seek the refuge of their caves and thickets; gone the shrieking bats of heresy, blinded by the light of truth, stealing into their holes in the rocks to hang upside down one on the head of another.⁴ Thanks to this day, the inebriate bands have left off their revelry. Robbers, burglars, thieves, and all the other works of night are blotted out by the bright dawn of peace. What horrors took place in the course of that night that enveloped everything in the dark slough of error? They should be consigned to deep silence and oblivion so that memories so unpleasant do not spoil the joy of the present occasion. What words could one use to recite the evils of that time? And yet, how could one keep silent? Does any drama portray such misery? Any myth conjure up misfortunes like these? What playwright ever made his stage resound with such affliction? The calamity beggars description; the suffering exceeds the power of its narrators.

3. The Devil's choir formed the base of operations. Here he set up his camp and ensconced his henchmen. Here he stationed the forces of falsehood, the champions of deceit, his demon host, his legions of unclean spirits, and, if I may use a heathen expression as well, it was from here that the dread army of Erinyes⁵ swooped down upon the Church (this is what I am moved to call the women who, contrary to nature and for malicious purpose, took to playing the man). One such in the days of Elijah was Jezebel. Her homicidal plots against the prophets of the Lord are held up for condemnation in the Scriptures⁶ so that, in my opinion, all subsequent generations may profit from the lesson of the shameless hussy. This time large numbers of women like the notorious Jezebel sprouted like hemlock all at

---

3. Rom 13.12.
4. Homer, *Odyssey* 24.6–8.
5. The Erinyes or Furies were goddesses of vengeance noted for their relentlessness and loathsome appearance.
6. 1 Kgs 19.1–2.

once over the land, surpassing the legendary figure in their poisonous ways. If you do not believe me, look at the record. That woman presented the dissolute Ahab with Naboth's vineyard to be used as a garden,[7] an extravagant amenity and effeminate frill; these women of ours, perpetrating the vile deed themselves without help from anyone, fought tooth and nail for the complete eradication of the Church, the living vineyard of God. What parallel can I find to describe them? What painting could portray such depravity? Once on a stuccoed wall I saw a fresco.[8] Please bear with me: my heart swells before the painful recollection of the wanton acts; or rather, you, too, share my anguish; the calamities we are describing are after all yours and mine, no one else's. What was it then about the fresco that I find analogous to our situation? There was a troupe of lewd women, their bodies writhing in various contortions of the dance. Such women are called maenads in mythology. Hair tousled by the breeze; the look in their eyes betokening madness; torches in their hands, the flames awhirl in unison with their wriggling bodies; a gust of wind hiking their skirts to strip away their modesty; legs high in the air as they leapt and cavorted; decency and decorum nowhere to be seen in the proceedings.

4. In the center of this ballet there was a poor excuse of a man, a real he-girl of indeterminate gender, womanish in appearance, an outlandish perversion of nature in an attitude of debauch, reeling as if from an orgy of drunkenness. This creature was lolling in a wagon of some sort that was being drawn amidst the bands of maenads by wild animals. He had a large bowl of neat wine at his side, and, surrounding him, a number of grotesque crossbreeds with shaggy faces gobbling and hopping about him on goat legs. This is just the image conjured up by that night. Women notorious for disgracing their sex, their stamping feet mocking all standards of feminine decency in a wanton execration of nature, were parading through the center of the town making brazen show of their corruption, armed with stones instead of shields, their eyes roving shamelessly,

---

7. 1 Kgs 21.1–7.
8. The following ecphrasis describes a bacchanalian scene with Dionysus, the god of wine, attended, as often in Greek art, by maenads and satyrs.

looking to kill. Once inside the sacred precincts they set their corybant on the holy throne. After that, wine and carousal and Pans⁹ issuing from the hermitages and night and promiscuity and everything that the Apostle enjoins us from mentioning when he says, *It is a shame even to speak of the things that they do in secret*.¹⁰ Who could describe in detail the conflagration, the stonings, the slaughter, the injuries? The ferocity with which they sought to dislodge the keepers of the holy shrines? How they clubbed a partisan of the truth in the center of the town but failed to kill him only because they thought him already dead?

But I really do not know how my sermon has meandered from true pleasure to linger on the details of this seamy episode. So it is time to resume whence we left off and rinse away the bitter brine of this digression with words that are fresh and sweet.¹¹ Scripture says, *In the day* of gladness, *adversity is forgotten*;¹² hence I return to the paean with which I started: that long dark night is over, and the rays of peace brighten the clear day with the light of truth. And so the sacred precincts have been purged clean of the stench of sacrilege and the homes of the pious echo instead with a joy that is complete, and nothing is lacking thereto. Here before us are the hosts, and the guests, and a table well-stocked with good things to eat.

9. Half-man and half-goat like the satyrs, Pan was a minor deity particularly associated with lust and disorder, as indicated by the word "panic."
10. Eph 5.12.
11. Plato, *Phaedrus* 243d.
12. Sir 11.25.

ORATION 36

On himself and to those who claim that it was he who wanted the see of Constantinople.[1]

AM MYSTIFIED. What in the world have my sermons done to you? How can you have been so taken with the sound of my voice, the voice of a stranger and one that is perhaps weak and devoid of all charm, that you give me the impression of being drawn to us like iron to a magnet?[2] Clinging to each other, one on one, you hang on me, and all of us on God *from whom are all things*[3] and to whom are all things. How wondrous is the chain forged by the Holy Spirit with indissoluble links! As to the reason, neither do I myself, to the best of my knowledge, have any greater claim to wisdom than anyone else (unless of course one assumes that my wisdom consists of precisely this, that I know that I am not wise[4] and do not approach the original, true wisdom, a judgment our latter-day wise men are far from making about themselves, since it is very easy, if one is puffed up with pride, to deceive oneself and to think that he is something when he is nothing);[5] nor was I the first to preach to you the doctrine of the true Faith that you so ardently embrace. I have merely followed in others' footsteps—yours, to be precise, since you are the true disciples of the famous Alexander,[6] the great champion and herald of the

---

1. PG 36.265A–80C. Delivered 380 in Constantinople. The text in PG 36.265A includes the phrase, "and regarding the eagerness that the people exhibited toward him," which is omitted from both the text and critical apparatus in SC 318.
2. Plato, *Ion* 533d–e.
3. 1 Cor 8.6.
4. Plato, *Apology* 23b.
5. Gal 6.3; Plato, *Apology* 41e.
6. Alexander, the orthodox bishop of Constantinople (327?–40), whose prayers are credited with causing the death of Arius in 336. Athanasius compares Arius to Judas by quoting Acts 1.18 ("falling headlong he burst open in

Trinity who drove impiety from our midst by deed as well as by words. You remember the prayer, worthy of an apostle, that destroyed the prince of impiety in places well-suited to the sewage that issued from his mouth in order that outrage might be repaid with outrage and that the wrongful death of souls might forever live in infamy thanks to a death richly deserved.

2. And so the spring that we have tapped for you is not new like the one that Moses produced in a waterless place for the refugees from Egypt.[7] We have instead opened up one that was hidden and covered over, just as the servants of the celebrated Isaac not only dug wells *of springing water* but also cleared those that the Philistines had stopped.[8] But I am not at all one of those characters known for their pleasantries and wit, the kind of man who tries to extort goodwill by flattery, as I see quite a number of my contemporaries doing who profess themselves priests. They take our simple and uncomplicated religion and turn it into something complicated, a new brand of politics transferred from the marketplace to the sanctuary, from the public arena to mystic rites forbidden to public view. The result is that we now have two platforms for theatrical performances, if I may use so bold an expression, which differ from one another to the extent that one is open to all and the other to a few, the one for laughter, the other for reverence, the one labelled theatrical, the other spiritual. *You are witnesses, and God also,*[9] says the holy Apostle, that we are not of this portion. On the contrary, I would sooner be charged with being tactless and inept than unctuous and servile. Indeed, even my most loyal supporters feel that there are occasions now and then when I ride roughshod over them if in my judgment they are behaving unreasonably. This was recently demonstrated by the unprecedented action you took with regard to us: you, the people, fired

---

the middle") and has the heresiarch's death take place in a public toilet; see the *Letter to Serapion on the Death of Arius,* PG 25.688C and cf. Gregory's *Or.* 25.8 and n. 15. A more detailed account in Socrates, *Ecclesiastical History,* 1.37–38, adds that the infamous spot was still being pointed out by passersby. See further A. Leroy-Molinghen, "La mort d'Arius," *Byzantion* 38 (1968): 105–11.

7. Ex 17.6.   8. Gn 26.18–19.
9. 1 Thes 2.10.

with anger and zeal, set me upon this throne—I do not know whether to call it the seat of a tyrant or a bishop—despite my vociferous protests; but set me you did, acting against the law because of your love for me; whereupon I so infuriated some of my more ardent supporters that their affection turned to enmity and they broke with us on the spot. For the fact is we look not to gratify but to benefit.

3. What has inspired this deep affection for us and our sermons? Are you prepared to produce the reason and set it forth yourselves and make known your personal feelings on the subject? Or, since you readily employ us as your spokesman in other concerns as well, would you prefer that we be the one to make this declaration? I gather from your silence that the charge falls on us. Very well, then, listen and see if I am correct in my assessment of the situation. Since you are the ones who called on us, I have first of all the impression that you are strengthening your own suit and for this reason pursuing me with so much attention. By a basic law of nature we favor all things that are our own, be it property, or children, or words, and with a generous goodwill indulge what we create. Second, I believe that there is nothing in our temperament that you value so much as the fact that it is not headstrong or domineering or pretentious or pompous but is instead the sober and retiring disposition of a man who is at once a public and a private person, as it were, leading a solitary and, to put it still more concisely, philosophic existence, and this mode of life is not the product of artful design or political calculation on our part but one that we cultivate spiritually and with simplicity. We do not keep out of sight in order to be sought out or to appear worthy of greater honor, like those who flash lovely pictures before our eyes and quickly snatch them away, but in order to prove by our reclusive way of life that we do not welcome high office and place no stock in such honors. Third, you see what we suffer at the hands both of the enemy from without and the plotters from within. As Daniel says, *Iniquity came forth from Babylon, from elders who were supposed to* judge Israel.[10] I think this is why you

---

10. Sus 5; Dn 13.5 Vulgate.

are outraged, disgusted, and at a loss how you can help the victim other than by offering your sympathy. And so compassion mingled with a sense of guilt has given birth to love. This, then, is the secret of your regard for me.

4. But since it is our sermons that are the *casus belli*, along with this exceptional and invidious tongue of ours which, trained in pagan we have refined with Christian learning, sweetening the bitter and undrinkable water of Marah with the tree of life,[11] your response has been most noble and generous: you cherish the very thing for which we are attacked. Why did we not embrace that vapid culture, sterile and decadent? In view of its popularity why indeed did we adopt a strange and outlandish creed and hold our ground against the voices raised in opposition, when we should have rejected our intellectual pursuits out of hand and given irrationality the name of faith? Believe me, this is the course I should have actually chosen on my own as a fisherman—the facile justification of ignorance that most people use—if instead of my eloquence I had been given the power to work miracles. Would that envy were expunged from the human race, the devourer of those who give in to it, the poison of those who bear the brunt of it, the only emotion that is both extremely unjust and just at the same time: unjust because it taxes only those who are worthwhile, just in that it gnaws away at those who indulge in it! For I am not going to call down curses upon those who originally heaped praise upon us. They did not foresee the consequences of their actions; otherwise, they might have added a touch of invective as well, just to keep envy in check.

5. It was envy that dimmed the light of Lucifer, brought down through his pride[12] for, being in origin divine, he found it intolerable not to be considered a god as well; envy too tricked Adam with a woman's charms and drove him from paradise, for he was led to believe that it was through denial of access to the tree of knowledge up to then that his claim to be a god was begrudged him.[13] Envy it was that made a fratricide of Cain be-

---

11. Ex 15.23; Origen, *Homilies on Exodus* 7.1; *Homilies on Jeremiah* 10.2.
12. Is 14.12.
13. Gn 2.16–17; 3.

cause he could not endure his brother's more acceptable sacrifice.[14] Envy it was that wiped out the failure of the world with a deluge[15] and destroyed the people of Sodom with a cataclysm of fire.[16] Envy it was that swallowed up Dathan and Abiram for their mad challenge of Moses[17] and made a leper of Miriam for grumbling about her brother.[18] Envy it was that stained the ground with the blood of prophets[19] and used women to bring down Solomon the most wise.[20] Envy it was that turned Judas, tricked by a few pieces of silver, into a traitor deserving to hang,[21] and made Herod a killer of children[22] and Pilate a killer of Christ.[23] Envy it was that winnowed and scattered Israel like chaff, a sin from which they have yet even now to emerge. Envy it was that provoked the Apostate to be our oppressor, one whose embers, although we have come safely through the flames, continue to scorch us still to this very day. Envy it was that sliced and split the beautiful body of the Church into hostile and opposing camps. Envy it was that provoked Jeroboam,[24] the slave of sin,[25] against us and sets a curb on our tongue because it cannot abide to see the Trinity gleaming and shining in the fullness of its Godhead and giving her true preachers a place of honor in your eyes. Am I perhaps overdoing it with such images? Or has the depicting word in reality portrayed with complete accuracy the bases of your love for me? This is certainly how I interpret the facts.

6. But I see that some are both appalled by the abuse to which we have been subjected and regard the dishonor shown toward us as a calamity that affects them. So let us reflect on this too for a moment. If, out of some petty human motive or desire for this office, I, with this gray head and limbs shrivelled with

14. Gn 4.1–16.
15. Gn 6.5–8.22. The Greek here literally means "an unworldly world" and involves a play on the word κόσμος, with its connotations of order and beauty.
16. Gn 19.24.
17. Nm 16.31–33.
18. Nm 12.10.
19. 2 Kgs 9.7.
20. 1 Kgs 11.1–5.
21. Mt 26.14–16, 27.3–5.
22. Mt 2.16.
23. Acts 13.28.
24. Jeroboam has variously been understood as an allusion to Maximus the Cynic or to an Arian bishop of Constantinople, either Eudoxius (360–69) or Demophilus (369–79).
25. 1 Kgs 13.33.

old age and disease, had either foisted myself upon you from the start, or if I now put up with these indignities, I should feel shame before heaven and earth, as they used to declare in the old days;[26] I should feel shame before this see and this holy assembly and this sacred and newly formed congregation, the target of such a great array of evil forces that threaten to destroy it before it can take root and to kill it before it can be born while it is still forming in the pattern of Christ; I should feel shame before my exertions and mortifications and these tattered clothes and the solitude and seclusion in which we have lived and my austere ways and the simple fare hardly sufficient for birds. But let even some be correct that we have lusted after another woman, we who did not want even the one who claimed us as her own.[27] Let even the Gibeonites steal a march on us; I know that the Holy Spirit has no use for them even as *hewers of wood and drawers of water*[28] so long as the kind of behavior and language they adopt continues to defile our sanctuaries. If, on the other hand, our motive in coming here was to espouse the cause of the Church and to provide her with all the assistance at our disposal now that she was widowed and without a husband, as any custodian or guardian would do, with the object of giving her in marriage to another[29] who, should he prove worthy of her beauty, would dower his queen with an even greater portion of virtue, are we to be commended for our devotion or condemned for ulterior motives, since we are being judged on the basis of passions not our own? It is just as though, my good man, we had come to the rescue of a ship in a storm or a city under siege or a house engulfed in flames and provided rafts or reinforcements or extinguishers. No doubt you would have brand-

26. Dt 32.1.
27. I.e., Sasima; cf. 1 Kgs 11.1–5.
28. Jos 9.
29. Cf. 2 Cor 11.2. Gregory here uses the technical legal vocabulary of guardianship or *tutela*, an institution designed to protect the property interests of women and minor children. The responsibilities of a guardian included the constitution of a dowry. See H. J. Mason, *Greek Terms for Roman Institutons. A Lexicon and Analysis*, American Society of Papyrologists, American Studies in Papyrology, vol. 13 (Toronto: Hakkert, 1974), svv. ἐπίτροπος and κηδεμών. I thank Callie Williamson for this reference.

ed us a pirate or one with some erotic designs on the household or the city, but not a champion or guardian.

7. But, someone will say, this is not the way you appear to most people. What difference does that make to me? I am more, no, exclusively, interested in the truth. This is what condemns or vindicates, makes one miserable or happy. Appearances have nothing to do with us, any more than other people's dreams. Sir, this is not the way you appear to most people, he says. Does the earth appear to stand still to the dizzy? Do the sober appear sober to the drunk, or rather to lurch headlong and spin around? Does not honey occasionally seem bitter to some when they are sick and in poor health? Yes, you can be sure, reality is different from what it appears when people are not themselves. So prove to us that those who hold these views are of sound mind and then urge us to alter our stance; or else go ahead and condemn us for not giving in but staying with our original judgment. I do not appear so to a good many, but to God I do; or rather, I do not "appear" to him at all, but stand fully revealed to him who knows *all things before they come to be*,[30] who fashions *the hearts* of us all, who understands *all* our *deeds*,[31] our impulses and the motives that govern our actions, whose notice nothing in the world can or does escape, who sees our world through eyes different from ours. *Man looks on the outward appearance, but the Lord looks on the heart.*[32] You have heard the words of Scripture; now believe. It is God who must be heeded rather than all the others put together, at least by those with sense. If you had two men advising you on the same matter, one quite astute and another rather ill-informed, would you not appear foolish if you dismissed the former and chose to follow the latter? Even Rehoboam was not commended for rejecting the counsel of the elders and adopting younger advice.[33] In a comparison between God and man will you prefer the opinions of man? You will not, if you listen to me and show good sense.

8. But, he continues, we are ashamed of the violent abuse that has been directed at you. And I for my part am ashamed of

---

30. Sus 42; Dn 13.42 Vulgate.
32. 1 Sm 16.7.
31. Ps 33.15 (LXX 32.15).
33. 1 Kgs 12.6–8.

you for feeling ashamed. After all, if this abuse is justified, it is we who should feel ashamed instead of you on our behalf, not so much because we are being subjected to indignities as because we deserve them. Yet if, on the other hand, this abuse is unwarranted, the blame lies with the perpetrators of it and it is for them rather than for us that you should feel sorry because they are the ones who truly suffer.[34] And if you had considered me most virtuous when in fact I was depraved, what in fact should I have done? Be more depraved to suit you better? This I could never have asked of myself. Similarly, if you imagine that I am erring when in fact I am doing right, I am not going to change my ways to gratify you. My life is my own, not yours, and I have as my counselor in all matters my reason and God's ordinances, which often convict me, though without an accuser; yes, and acquit me, though many condemn me. The only court we cannot avoid is the one that sits deep within us. To it alone we must look if we are to walk the straight path. Appearances, provided they are valid, we shall accept, if I may speak in human terms;[35] but if they are not, we shall dismiss them and take away nothing from reality for the sake of appearances.

9. And so it is: the man who pursues the good with some object in mind is not secure in his virtue, for once the object is gone, he will abandon the good as well, just as a man who sets sail to make a profit abandons the effort if there is no profit to be had. But the man who honors and cherishes the good for its own sake remains unswerving in his devotion to it because the object of his desire does not change; and so his experience is akin to God's and he can say with him, *I* remain the same and *do not change*.[36] He will not, therefore, alter or shift his position or vary with changing times and circumstances, constantly transforming himself and adopting many colors, just as octopuses adopt the color of the rocks on which they settle.[37] He will remain ever the same, stable in the midst of instability, unwaver-

---

34. Cf. Plato, *Apology* 30d; *Gorgias* 469b–c.
35. Rom 6.19.   36. Mal 3.6.
37. Aelian, *On the Nature of Animals* 1.32, characterizes the octopus's ability to change color as a σόφισμα, that is, a clever trick or device, a term that can also be applied to argumentation. Aelian adds that this ploy is quite useless because the moray eel sees through it quite easily.

ing even as things waver around him; a rock, in my view, not only unshaken by the onslaught of wind and wave but actually dissipating the forces that attack it. Enough on these matters. Besides, I do not have time to engage in a war of words; perhaps I have already said more than I should.

10. Now I direct my remarks to you, my flock. Become my *glory and joy* and *crown of boasting*, says Paul.[38] Be my defense against my inquisitors so that, just as craftsmen or painters asked to explain their art can acquit themselves simply by pointing to what they have built or painted—works are more powerful than words, as he says[39]—so I too by pointing to you shall rise above the calumnies. Rise above them I shall, but how? First, you must keep the confession in Father, Son, and Holy Spirit firm and intact, adding nothing, or subtracting, or diminishing its single divinity (for what is taken away takes away from the whole), and may you repudiate as the bane of the Church and poisoners of the truth those who think or say otherwise, whether by dissolving or separating the One into a sliding scale of natures; but do so not out of hatred but out of pity for their error. And second, you should insure that your conduct be in conformity with true dogma so that, deficient in neither, you may be eminent in both.

11. You emperors, show respect for the purple that you wear, for my words will have the force of law even for lawgivers. Recognize the magnitude of the responsibility entrusted to you and the importance of your sacred mission. The whole world is under your sway, ruled by the thin and narrow strip of cloth circling your brow. The things on high are God's alone; those below, your charge as well. Behave like gods toward your subjects, if I may put it so boldly. *The king's heart is in the hand of the Lord,*[40] we are both told and believe. Let this be the basis of your power, not gold and troops. You courtiers and confidants of the throne, do not let your authority exaggerate your notions of your own importance, and do not regard as deathless the things that are not. Remain loyal to your emperors, but above all to God, for whose sake you are loyal to these to whom you have been entrusted and

---

38. 1 Thes 2.19–20. 39. Cf. 1 Cor 4.20; Ti 3.14.
40. Prv 21.1.

assigned. You who pride yourselves on your noble lineage, let true nobility be seen in your character. Else I shall express a sentiment that, while distasteful, is a noble one nonetheless: then would your family truly belong to the highest nobility if those of ignoble character were not included in your register.

12. You savants and philosophers with your majestic cloaks and beards, you professors and teachers, avid for public acclaim, I do not see how you can be called wise when you do not know the prime doctrine of all. You who are busy after wealth, hear the Psalmist: *If riches increase, set not your heart on them.*[41] Recognize that you are putting your trust in something insecure. Unload some of the cargo from your ship and your voyage will be easier. Perhaps you will keep something from your enemy, upon whom all your possessions are going to devolve. You *bon vivants*, deprive your belly and endow your spirit. The pauper is close at hand; help his affliction; cough up part of your surplus for him. Why do you both suffer, you from indigestion, he from hunger; you from hangovers, he from dropsy; you sagging from one excess upon another, he staggering from disease? Let not the neglect of your Lazarus in this life cause you to share the fate of the rich man in the other.[42]

You who make up this great city, who are the first directly after that first one (or do not concede even this) show me that you are first not in vice but in virtue, not in loose living but in moral habit. How shameful it is to be a ruler of cities and conquered by indulgence at the same time; or to observe moderation in other respects, but when it comes to racetracks and theaters and arenas and hunting parties to be so addicted as to make them your life; and that she who is first among cities should be a city of pleasure-seekers when by all rights she should be a model of every virtue for the rest! Reject these things; be a city of God. May you be painted *on the palms of the hands* of the Lord,[43] and in the age to come may you join us in standing resplendent in your splendor before the great Founder of cities! This is the gospel of joy that I preach to you in Christ himself our Lord, to whom be the glory, honor, and power forever. Amen.

41. Ps 62.10 (LXX 61.11).   42. Lk 16.19–31.
43. Is 49.16.

ORATION 44

On New Sunday.[1]

HE HIGH VALUE we place on ceremonies of dedication, or rather on the opportunity of honoring new departures through them, is the product of a long and venerable tradition;[2] and in doing so not just once but often, on all anniversary occasions, so that our blessings do not fade away with the passage of time or slip into the dark pit of oblivion. *Islands* are dedicated *to* God, as we read in Isaiah, however we choose to interpret the word "islands."[3] In my view they are the newly established congregations of gentiles that have emerged from the bitter salt sea of unbelief and found a firm anchor in God. In another prophet it is *a brazen wall* that is dedicated,[4] which I understand to mean a true heart of gold, newly grounded in piety. And we are told to sing *to the Lord a new song*,[5] as much those of us who, after being dragged off by sin to Babylon's infernal chaos, then returned to the salvation of Jerusalem (there, to be sure, we could not sing a *song* of God because we were *in a foreign land*,[6] but here we have found a new song and new way of life), as those of us who steadily abided and ad-

---

1. PG 36.608A–22A. Delivered 383 in Nazianzus.
2. The first Sunday after Easter, or New Sunday, marked the "first of the days" in the Christian year and the "anniversary of salvation" for the faithful (sec. 5). Ceremonies of dedication or renewal (ἐγκαίνια) were normally associated with the consecration of places, such as a church, and the annual commemoration of their consecration. Here, Gregory extends the concept of inauguration to the spiritual dedication of the "new creature" in Christ. See also G. Galavaris, *The Illustrations of the Liturgical Homilies of Gregory Nazianzus* (Princeton, 1969), 38–40.
3. Is 41.1 LXX.
4. Jer 1.18; Is 16.11 LXX.
5. Ps 33.3 (LXX 32.3), 96.1 (LXX 95.1), 98.1 (LXX 97.1), 149.1.
6. Ps 137.4 (LXX 136.4).

vanced in virtue by the moral worth we have shown in the past and continue to show through the renewing power of the Holy Spirit.

2. *The tent of meeting* designed by God, constructed by Bezalel and erected by Moses, was celebrated by a dedication,[7] and a very sumptuous one, as was also David's accession to the throne, solemnized not in a single ceremony but rather a first when he was anointed and a second after he was proclaimed.[8] *It was the feast of the Dedication at Jerusalem; it was winter,*[9] the winter of unbelief, and Jesus was present, who is God and temple, God eternal, temple newly made, destroyed in one day and risen on the third and abiding for all time that I might be saved and restored from the fall of long ago and become a new creation, formed anew by his supreme act of loving-kindness. And David seeks to have *a clean heart* created *in* him and *a right spirit* renewed *within* him,[10] not because he did not possess these things—who, if not the great David, would?—but because he understood "new" to mean whatever is improved on a regular and current basis. But why adduce more dedicatory rites when we can turn our attention to the one we are celebrating today, one that brings us into contact with life after death? Dedication! This holiday, my brothers, is a dedication. Let us proclaim it over and over again from joy! And dedication of what? Those of you who know, tell us; those who do not, dedicate your ears.

3. There was light, unapproachable and everlasting,[11] God, light without beginning, without end, without limit, ever shining with triple splendor, light whose magnitude can be envisioned by few, no, not even them. And there were lights of the second order, effulgences of the first, the powers that surround him and the *ministering spirits*.[12] The light with which we are familiar not only came into existence later, but is also cut off by night and in turn cuts night off for an equal period of time; it is given over to the use of our eyes through its diffusion in the air, and what it bestows it receives from an external source. It makes

---

7. Nm 7.1–11; cf. Ex 35–40.
9. Jn 10.22.
11. Cf. 1 Tm 6.16.
8. 1 Sm 16.3; 2 Sm 2.4, 5.3.
10. Ps 51.10 (LXX 50.12).
12. Heb 1.14.

it possible for our eyes to see and is the first object of sight and, by flooding the things that are visible, grants them freedom. For God whose will it was to create this world, which is composed of things visible and invisible and is the great and awesome herald of his majesty, to the eternal beings is himself light,[13] and there is no other—for why, when they possess the greatest light, would they require a lesser one?—while lower beings, we among them, are the primary recipients of the power of this light here below. Indeed, it is fitting that the Great Light should have begun his creation with light, by which he disperses the darkness and the chaos and disorder that formerly prevailed.

4. Moreover, to my way of thinking, God did not originally bring forth this light to serve as a means to an end or to be a property of the sun, but made it without tangible form and independent of the sun, to which it was subsequently added for the purpose of illuminating the entire universe. For although in the case of his other creations he first produced the matter and then gave it its form, investing each with order and size and shape, in this instance, that he might work a greater wonder, he first produced the form, which in the case of the sun is light, and then adds the matter and makes this sun of ours the eye of day.[14] And so reckoning takes place in terms of days: first, second, third, and so on up to the seventh, when he rested from his labors.[15] Creation is apportioned according to these and systematically arranged by an ineffable logic, not served up all at once by the all-powerful Logos, for whom the act of thought alone or utterance is one and the same with accomplished fact. Nor is it at all surprising that man was the last creature to be brought forth, yet even so received the distinction of God's image and the touch of his hand: quite properly, for when a palace destined for a king is under construction, it must be completed before the king is escorted to it, his retinue already in full attendance. If, then, we had remained in our original state and kept the commandment, we should, by reaching the tree of life from

13. 1 Jn 1.5. 14. Gn 1.3, 14–15.
15. See below, section 5 and n. 16.

the tree of knowledge, have become what we were not. Become what? Immortal, and the intimates of God. But since *through the envy* of the evil one *death entered the world*[16] and fraudulently seduced mankind, this is why God becomes man and suffers with our suffering and through encasement in flesh becomes poor so that *by his poverty* we might become rich.[17] That is the reason for death and burial and resurrection; that is the reason for a new creature and feasting after the feast; the reason again that I hold festival, dedicating my own salvation.

5. What? Someone will say. Was not the first Sunday, the one after the holy night and the torchlight procession, the feast of dedication? No, my holiday-loving friend; your visions of high merrymaking make you confuse the two days. That one brought salvation; this one is the anniversary of the gift of salvation; that one marks the resurrection from the tomb; this one marks simply the second rebirth. The intention is this:[18] just as it is clear that the original creation was begun on a Sunday since Saturday, which signals the cessation from labor, is the seventh day after it; in the same way, the second creation also begins anew on Sunday, which is the first of the days that follow and the eighth after those that precede it, a day more sublime than the sublime and more wondrous than the wondrous, for it looks to our life in heaven. This is, I think, the meaning of the divine Solomon's enigmatic expression also, to give *a portion to seven,* that is, to this life, *or even to eight,*[19] that is, the life to come: he is alluding to our good works on earth and our reinstatement in heaven. And even the great David's Psalms entitled "For the eighth"[20] appear to be hymns for the same day, just as in another psalm that speaks in its title of the *dedication of a house*[21] the reference is to this day of dedication. The house is ourselves, we who have been found worthy to be and to be recognized and to become *God's temple.*[22]

16. Wis 2.24.
17. 2 Cor 8.9.
18. See A. Sharf, "The Eighth Day of the Week," in *Kathegetria. Essays Presented to Joan Hussey for her 80th Birthday,* ed. J. Chrysostomides (Camberley, Surrey: Porphyrogenitus, 1988), pp. 27–50, especially p. 45.
19. Eccl 11.2.   20. Ps 6.1, 11.1 LXX.
21. Ps 30.1 (29.1 LXX) LXX.   22. 1 Cor 3.16; 2 Cor 6.16.

6. You now have the rationale of dedications. Come then, dedicate yourselves and, casting off *your old nature*[23] live now *in newness of life*,[24] subjugating everything that gives rise to death, disciplining your whole person, spewing forth as abomination every vile morsel of the tree, yet remembering your old ways for the sole purpose of avoiding them. The fruit that brought me death was lovely to look at and good to eat,[25] but let us turn away from outward allure and direct our gaze to our inner selves. Do not let a desire for beauty get the better of you and make you a slave to your eyes—if possible, not even to the point of a furtive glance—but recall Eve, that exquisitely sweet but poisonous temptation. How can a man consigned to perdition by her who is his own find easy salvation in another? Do not glaze your gullet by swilling everything within reach: a delicacy initially appealing once consumed repels. Has your sense of smell unmanned you? Seek to avoid fragrant odors. Your sense of touch enervated you? Renounce things soft and dainty. Your ear done you tricks? Close the door to clever and deceptive words. Seek to open your *mouth* for the word of God that you may draw in the Spirit,[26] not suck in death. Whenever something forbidden beckons you, remember what you were and how you came to be lost. If you deviate in some small way from right reason try to regain your senses before you pass completely beyond the pale and are hurled down to death; and replace the old man with the new and turn to celebrate the dedication of your soul.

7. Let the serpent be the sole object of your wrath: it was he that caused your fall. Let your every aspiration be devoted to God, not to any sly, insidious end. Let reason preside over all and let not your better part be dragged down by the worse.[27] Hate not your brother, and this without expectation of gain; it was for his sake that Christ died and became your brother, al-

---

23. Eph 4.22.
24. Rom 6.4.
25. Gn 3.6.
26. Ps 119.131 (LXX 118.130) LXX.
27. The words translated as "wrath," "aspiration," and "reason" reflect Platonic terminology for the tripartite division of the soul found, for example, in *Republic* 441e–42a, while the imagery comes from the myth of the charioteer in *Phaedrus* 246a–47b.

though he is your Lord God. Envy not the righteous, you who have yourself been the victim of envy and been seduced into surrendering to it and for this reason laid low.[28] Be not ashamed to cry, you who endured suffering worthy of many tears and subsequently received mercy. Brush not aside the pauper, you who have received the wealth of divinity; but if not—for even this is asking much of the insatiably greedy—at least grow not rich at his expense. Despise not the stranger; it was for his sake that Christ, whose sojourners and strangers we all are, became a stranger on earth; otherwise you will be estranged from paradise as before. Share your food, your clothing, your shelter with the needy, you who have more of these than you need and wallow in them. Be not enamored of wealth unless it benefits the poor. Forgive; you have been forgiven. Show pity; it has been shown to you. Secure kindness for yourself by showing it to others while there is time. Let your entire way of life, all your existence, be a dedication for you.

8. Wives, reserve a part of yourselves also for God, since you have already been spoken for. Young maidens, grant your all to God since you are at liberty to do so. Do not sneak a pleasure more suited to slaves by giving up your freedom to cohabit with men, though men not your husbands. I do not propose to wear myself out by forever harping on the subject of pleasure; I do abhor casual liaisons. Men in power, be fearful of him who is more powerful; you on high thrones, of him on a higher one. Admire nothing that is transitory; disdain not what abides, nor clutch at anything that slips away in the holding; shun those things that inspire not envy but rather hatred; do not exalt yourself lest you be brought down the more; try not to show presumption by lording it over the wicked, but to feel distress at being inferior to the good; laugh not if your neighbor stumbles, but proceed to walk over to him with all the assurance you can muster and offer him your hand as he lies on the ground. When you are dejected do not lose the hope of a better day, nor apprehension in time of prosperity. A single year brings four seasons and a single swing of time many changes in human affairs.

28. Cf. sec. 4, above.

Let concern act as a damper on your pleasure and the hope for a better lot on your grief. This is how man is dedicated; this is how the day of dedication is celebrated; such is its lavish delight; such are its delicacies. *Thou shalt not appear* before me *empty*, saith the Lord,[29] but bringing with you all you have that is good. Present yourself now a new person, different in character, wholly changed. *Old things are passed away; behold, all things are become new.*[30] This bring as your contribution to the festival; change the good change; do so, however, not with an air of self-importance, but declaring with David, *the right hand of the Most High has changed*,[31] who is the source of all human virtue. The words do not mean that you should remain permanently in the same mold, but rather that you should be in constant change, improving, ever a new creature,[32] repenting if you should sin and pressing forward if your life be virtuous.

9. Yesterday your faith varied according to season; today know the faith of God. How long will you go limping *with two different opinions?*[33] How long will you go on planning? Sometime you must follow the urge to build! Yesterday you attached importance to being considered a somebody; today think it more important to be so in truth. How long will you live in a dream world? It is time to devote attention to reality too. Yesterday you were theatrical; today show yourself philosophical; yesterday abusive, wild; today gentle, soft-spoken; yesterday boisterous, today reserved; today a tippler, tomorrow a teetotaler; today daubed with the most exotic perfumes, debauching on ivory couches; tomorrow lying sleepless on the ground; instead of a buffoon, thoughtful; instead of a fop, ill-clad; instead of self-important and boastful, unassuming in demeanor; instead of under a gilt ceiling, in a humble cell; head bowed instead of stiff-necked with pride. If these things guide your thoughts and actions, there shall be a new heaven for you and a new earth,[34] and you will come to understand their meaning, and all else too.

---

29. Dt 16.16 LXX.
31. Ps 77.10 (LXX 76.11).
33. 1 Kgs 18.21.
30. 2 Cor 5.17 KJV.
32. 2 Cor 5.17.
34. Is 65.17 LXX.

10. But let us now be off to celebrate this holiday with one another in the spirit of the season. What a happy day! The whole of creation gathers for our festival and joins in the merriment. Just look at the wonders before our eyes! The queen of the seasons marshals her parade to honor the queen of days, distributing the sweetest and loveliest largess from her bounty. Now the sky has a greater clarity; now the sun stands higher and shines a more burnished gold; now the orb of the moon gleams more luminous and the chorus of stars twinkles more bright. Now the waves clasp the shore in peaceful embrace, the clouds the sun, the winds the air, the earth the crops, the crops our eyes. Now the streams sparkle more radiant in their course; now the rivers, released from the bonds of winter, gush without stint. And the meadow exudes a sweet perfume and the plants swell with blossoms and the grass is cropped and lambs gambol in fields now green. Now the ship puts out from the harbor accompanied by shouts from the shore that resound, yes, ever so many, with the love of God, and surges under billowing sail; and the dolphin frolics about, blowing and leaping ever so merrily, and playfully gives escort to seamen. Now the farmer, glancing heavenward to invoke the giver of crops, adjusts his plow, yokes his work-ox, and cuts a luscious furrow, joyous in his hopes. Now the shepherd and neatherd tune their pipes and play a pastoral air, whiling away the springtime amid the greenery and the rocks. Now the planter tends to his planting and the fowler prepares his twigs and, peeping under the new growth, carefully looks for the flutter of a bird. And the fisherman scans the deep, clears his net, and perches on a rock to rest.

11. Now the industrious bee, setting out from the hive with unfurled wing, flits over the meadows and plunders the blossoms with eminent skill. One works the honeycomb, fabricating the hexagonal cells and fitting their sides and corners flush with one another, a work at once of security and art; another lays up a store of honey, a sweet crop gleaned for its visitor without benefit of tillage. How I wish that we too, the apiary of Christ, would emulate such a model of industry and skill! Now the birds build a nest: one has just come back, another is settling in the new home, and yet another soars about the glade filling it with its

warbling and enfolding mankind in song. All creation sings the glory of God in wordless strain, for it is through me that God is thanked for all his works. In this way their hymn becomes our own, since it is from them that I take my song. Now the whole of the animal kingdom is smiling and all our senses are at feast. Now the noble steed, head high, cannot abide his stall but, defying the bit, romps over the plain and disports in the rivers.[35]

12. What of what remains to be said? Now the martyrs file past beneath the open sky to invite a God-loving people to shrines marked with their glory and proclaim their victorious struggles. One of those wearing the martyr's crown is also mine—yes, mine; do not be envious; though he has not actually joined me, some will know whereof I speak: Mamas the famous, both as shepherd and as martyr;[36] who in former times used to milk the hinds as they jostled one another to give the righteous man the nourishment of their unfamiliar milk, but who now tends the flock of a capital city[37] and today, for the many thousands who are thronging to it from miles around, dedicates the springtime, manifold in the beauties of virtue and worthy of shepherds and of words celebrating his triumph; in sum, a spring of the world, a spring of the spirit, a spring for souls, a spring for the body, a spring visible, a spring invisible; which may we, who have been richly blessed in this life, enjoy in the other as well, and be escorted new to the new life, in Jesus Christ our Lord, to whom be all glory, honor, and power together with the Holy Spirit, to the glory of God the Father. Amen.

35. Homer, *Iliad* 6.506–9.
36. Mamas was a local Cappadocian saint who was martyred during the reign of Aurelian (270–75).
37. I.e., Caesarea, the capital city or metropolis of Cappadocia.

INDICES

GENERAL INDEX

Academics, 161
Adrianople, xvi, 118 n. 11
Aelian, 227
Alexander of Aphrodisias, 135 n. 17
Alexander of Constantinople, 220
Alexandria, xiv, 159, 164, 166
Anastasia, Church of, xvi, 157 n. 1, 189
angel(s), 13, 38, 158
Anthimus of Tyana, xv, 37 n. 19
Antichrist, 122, 163
Antiochus IV Epiphanes, 73, 76, 83, 84
Antisthenes, 162
Apollonius of Tyana, 170 and n. 42
Aristotle, xx, 65 nn. 122–24, 209
Arius, 110, 111, 126, 164, 166, 221
Arsacius, xv
Arsenius, 166
Athanasius, 166
Athens, xiv
athletics, 129, 155, 158, 159, 229

Babylon, 16, 230
Bar Kochba, 17 n. 99
Basil of Caesarea, xiv, xv, 3 n. 1, 10 n. 65, 21, 23–25, 26, 27, 28, 30–32, 37, 43 n. 46
Basilides, 163

Caesarea, xiv, xv, xvi, 39 n. 1, 43 n. 46, 238
Caesarius, xiv
Cappadocia, xiv, xv, 37 nn. 18–19, 238 nn. 36–37
Carpocrates, 163
celibacy, 5, 41
Cerdon, 163
Cerinthus, 163
Chrysippus, 209
Church, 10, 13, 21, 37, 129, 163,
165, 166, 188, 194, 209, 217, 218, 224, 225, 228
compassion, 42, 49, 53, 57, 58, 61, 62, 67, 69, 70, 85, 87, 92, 99, 101, 104, 105, 213
Constantinople, xiii, xiv, xvii, 107 n. 1, 117, 131 n. 1, 142 n. 1, 157 n. 1, 175 n. 1, 191 n. 1, 220, 229
Constantius II, 164 n. 17
contemplation, 26, 41, 96, 115, 205, 208, 215
cosmos, 14, 196 n. 24, 224 n. 15
Crates, 163
Creator, 43, 47, 59, 66, 68, 98, 103, 112, 113, 163
cross, 16, 35, 72, 93, 127, 210
Cynic(ism), 157 n. 1, 158 n. 3, 159, 161, 187 n. 64
Cyprian, xvii, 142–54 passim

Decius, 151–52
demon(s), 146, 148, 150, 158, 167
Demophilus, 224 n. 24
Devil, 3, 10, 13, 20, 120, 127, 133, 152, 177, 217
diatribe, xix, xx, 66 n. 125, 76 n. 3
Diocletian, xvii
Diogenes, 163
Dionysus, 218
Doara, 36

Egypt, 15, 16, 166
encomium, xiii
enlargement *(auxesis)*, xx
envy *(phthonos)*, 10, 89, 120, 134, 136, 144, 223–24, 235
Epicurus, 161
Erinyes, 217
Eudoxius of Constantinople, 224 n. 24
Eulalius, 35, 38

242 GENERAL INDEX

Euripides, xxii
Euripus, 176
Eusebius, 18 n. 99
Euzoius of Antioch, 166 n. 26
Eve, 234

Galatia, xv, 126
Galen, 50 n. 69
generation *(genesis)*, 112–14, 136–39, 172, 194
God: Father, 20, 25, 28, 38, 57, 94, 106, 110, 111, 112, 113, 114, 125, 133, 136, 139, 156, 170–72, 194, 206, 208, 228, 238; Son, 20, 38, 106, 110, 111, 112, 114, 125, 127, 133, 136–37, 139, 156, 170–72, 194, 206, 208, 228; Holy Spirit, 3, 4, 6, 7, 8, 10, 11, 20, 21, 22, 23, 26, 28, 29, 31, 35, 38, 55, 61, 84, 86, 87, 90, 91, 94, 95, 99, 106, 110, 111, 114, 117, 119, 125, 131, 133, 136–37, 139–40, 156, 167, 171, 172, 173, 175, 176, 186, 191, 194, 199, 206, 208, 213, 216, 220, 225, 228, 231, 234, 238; Trinity, 12, 20, 53, 106, 123, 124, 125, 132, 133, 135, 136, 137, 139, 140, 164, 171, 224
grace, 11, 22, 127, 141, 207, 209
Gregory of Nazianzus, introduction *passim*, 3 n. 1, 21, 30 n. 1, 36 n. 1, 37 n. 18, 85 n. 1, 93, 95 n. 1. 107 n. 1, 131 n. 1, 134, 189 nn. 74 and 78, 191 n. 2, 214 n. 126, 224–25
Gregory of Nyssa, xvi, 28 n. 12, 30–31
Gregory the Elder, xiii, xiv, xv, 3, 19, 21, 23, 26, 27, 85 n. 1, 93, 96, 131 n. 1, 134

Hadrian, 17 n. 99
Hermes, 62
Hero. *See* Maximus
Hippocrates, 15 n. 82
Holy of Holies, 20, 28, 42, 109, 203
Homer, xiv, 75 n. 16, 79 n. 29, 83 n. 38, 176 n. 5, 217 n. 4, 238 n. 36
hospitality, 40, 179, 189
humility, 41, 99, 100, 103, 150, 163, 205, 212
hypostasis. *See* person

Incarnation, 103
Israel, 6, 8, 15, 16, 36, 39, 40, 57, 82, 85, 86, 188, 193, 201, 208, 213, 222, 224

Jerome, 214 n. 126
Jerusalem, 8, 17, 69, 76, 79, 118, 152, 168, 230
Josephus, 73 n. 3
Judaea, 83, 98
Judah, 8, 193
Julian, emperor, xv, 164 n. 18, 224
Julian, *peraequator*, xiv, xvi, 95 and n. 1, 105

lalia, xiii, xiii, xix
Law (Mosaic), 6, 16 n. 94, 35, 59, 61, 73, 74, 76, 77, 79, 80, 108, 120, 143, 144, 205, 207
Levites, 203
Logos, 6, 7, 8, 53, 55, 72, 101, 103, 120, 155, 156, 157, 168, 196–97, 198, 232
lovingkindness. *See* philanthropy
Lucius of Samosata, 166

Maccabees, xiii, xv, 72–84 *passim*, 102 n. 46
Maenads, 218
magic, 147, 150
Maker. *See* Creator
Mamas, 238
Manes, 163
Marcion, 163
marriage, 41, 84, 99, 163 n. 10, 225
martyr(s), 32, 34, 35, 47, 72, 73, 97, 142, 143, 144, 146, 153, 154, 159, 192, 216, 238
martyrdom, 72, 73, 79, 80, 81, 152, 165, 166
Mary, 194
Maximus (Hero), xvii, 157–74 *passim*, 175, 224 n. 24
Melitius of Antioch, 127 n. 41, 134 n. 8
Menander Rhetor, xviii, xix
mercy, 36, 42, 68, 69, 70, 71, 85, 89, 92, 122, 235
Montanus, 126, 163
mortification, 40, 148

GENERAL INDEX 243

Moses, 16, 31, 37, 39, 40, 76, 99, 108, 201, 202, 203, 221, 224, 231

narration *(diegesis)*, xx
Nazianzus, xiii, xiv, xvii, 3 n. 1, 72 n. 1, 85, 95 n. 1, 131 n. 1, 230 n. 1
Nazirites, 17, 158 n. 2
Nicaea, 164
Nonna, 74 n. 14
Novatus (Novatian), 126, 163

Oasis (Kharga), 169
Olympia, 158, 184
Origen, 214 n. 126, 223 n. 11

Palladius, Prefect of Alexandria, 166 n. 26, 167
Pan, 219
Paradise, 58
passion(s), 6, 41, 84, 113, 138, 144, 148, 149, 154, 160, 172, 183, 186, 211, 214, 225
Paulinus of Antioch, 127 n. 41, 134 n. 8
peace, 3, 5, 9, 13, 14, 15, 24, 26, 35, 37, 43, 117, 119, 128, 129, 131, 134, 192, 197
Peripatetics, 161
Persia, 164
person (hypostasis), 111, 190
Peter of Alexandria, 167
Peter of Sebaste, 28 n. 12
philanthropy, xix, 40, 68, 92, 100, 138, 143, 145, 182, 231
Phrygians, 126
Plato, xiv, xvii, xix, 95 n. 4, 184 n. 50, 201 n. 55, 208 n. 104, 209, 219 n. 11, 220 nn. 2, 4, 5, 227 n. 34, 234 n. 27
Pontus, xv, 3 n. 1
prefect *(archon)*, 85, 167
Prohaeresius, xiv
prophets, 42, 120, 143, 144, 207, 217

Providence (Pronoia), 64 n. 121, 65, 162, 211
Pyrrho of Elis, 208

Romans, 17, 101 n. 38, 168

Sabellius, 110, 126, 163
saint(s), 88, 121, 142, 179
salvation, 42, 87, 93, 104, 109, 127, 140, 207, 209, 215, 230, 233, 234
Samaria, 8
Sasima, xiv, xv, xvi, 21, 30 n. 1, 36 n. 1, 225 n. 27
satyrs, 218
Savior, 16, 21, 55, 98, 102, 103, 104
Seleucia, xvi
Seleucus IV Philopator, 83
Senate *(synkletos boule)*, 145
Simon, 163
Socrates, xvii
soldiers, 101
sorcery. *See* magic
source *(arche)*, 111, 112, 136–37, 139, 231
Stoics, 161

tax-adjuster, *(peraequator)*, 95
Thales, 210 n. 114
Tyana, xv

Valens, xv, xvi, 118 n. 11, 165 nn. 19–20
Valentinus, 163
virginity, 40, 99

wisdom, 53, 64, 88, 206
Word. *See* Logos
world-ruler *(kosmokrator)*, 54, 91 and n. 33, 109

zeal, 11, 24, 40, 98, 120, 131, 146, 195, 222

INDEX OF HOLY SCRIPTURE

Old Testament

Genesis
1.3: 44.4
1.14–15: 44.4
1.27: 26.10
2.7: 10.2
2.16–17: 36.5
3: 36.5
3.1–5: 24.9
3.1–20: 17.9
3.6: 44.6
3.15: 14.21
3.19–20: 19.14
4.1–16: 36.5
4.26: 14.2
6.3: 14.10
6.4–7: 14.23
6.5–8.22: 36.5
7.23: 6.10; 25.6
10.8: 14.23
11.1: 23.4
11.1–9: 32.17
15.6: 14.2
19.3: 14.2
19.24: 36.5
22.2–19: 17.10
26.13: 26.5
26.18–19: 36.2
29.20: 26.2
30.25–43: 26.4
31.40: 26.4
37.28: 24.13
37.33: 22.1
37.34–35: 22.1
39.7–20: 24.13
40–41: 24.13
49.17: 14.21

Exodus
3.2–3: 25.6
4.16: 11.2
7–11: 24.13
7.1: 11.2; 32.16
7.11–12.30: 6.17
13.21: 6.17; 15.6; 32.16
14.16: 32.16
14.21: 13.2; 15.6; 24.13
14.22: 6.17
15.23: 36.4
16.4: 15.6; 24.13
16.13: 6.17; 32.16
16.13–15: 13.2
16.13–35: 14.1
16.16–20: 32.23
17.6: 6.17; 32.16; 36.2
17.8–13: 11.2
17.10–12: 32.16
17.11: 6.17; 15.6
17.11–12: 13.2
19.5–6: 13.4; 14.15
19.6: 6.17
19.12–13: 32.17
19.16–18: 20.2
19.16–25: 6.17
19.21–24: 20.3
23.15: 19.9
23.22: 14.15
24: 32.16
24.2: 11.1
24.12–15: 20.2
25.4–5: 19.8
28: 19.8
28.1: 32.16
29: 10.4

29.9: 32.17
33.21–23: 32.16
34.33: 32.15

Leviticus
13.2: 14.37

Numbers
2.47–53: 32.17
3.2: 32.16
3.21–39: 32.17
7.1–11: 44.2
12.3: 14.2
12.10: 36.5
13.32–33: 14.23
16.1: 13.3
16.12–33: 32.17
16.31–33: 36.5
17.13 (LXX 17.28): 20.3
25.6–8: 14.3
25.7–13: 15.9
26.9–11: 32.17

Deuteronomy
7.6: 26.1
9.2: 14.23
16.16: 44.8
22.1–4: 14.28
32.1: 36.6
32.9: 6.17
32.15: 6.3
32.21: 25.14
33.1: 11.1

Joshua
2.1–24: 14.2
3.14–17: 6.17
3.16: 15.6

INDEX OF HOLY SCRIPTURE 245

6.20: 6.17; 13.2
9: 36.6
10.12–13: 6.17
10.13: 15.6; 24.13
13.1: 24.13

Judges
  11.30–40: 15.11
  13.22: 9.1; 20.4

1 Samuel
  1.22–2.11: 15.9
  2.12–4.18: 20.3
  2.30: 15.12; 25.14
  4.11: 22.2
  10.6: 9.2
  10.12: 9.2
  16.3: 44.2
  16.7: 36.7
  16.14–23: 9.2; 24.12
  16.23: 17.2
  17.49: 13.2

2 Samuel
  1.17–27: 22.1
  2.4: 44.2
  5.3: 44.2
  6.6–7: 20.3
  11.2: 24.9
  18.33–19.4: 22.1
  23.15–17: 14.3

1 Kings
  3.9–14: 20.5
  4.29 (LXX 2.35a, 5.9): 20.5
  6.7: 26.16
  11.1–5: 36.5
  12.6–8: 36.7
  13.33: 36.5
  17.9: 26.12
  17.9–24: 14.4
  17.14: 26.12
  18.19: 26.7
  18.21: 44.9
  18.42: 14.4
  19.1–2: 35.3
  19.14: 14.3
  19.18: 11.5
  21.1–7: 35.3

2 Kings
  1.9: 11.1
  4.8: 26.17
  9.7: 36.5

2 Chronicles
  33.12–13: 13.1; 19.8

Job
  1.6–12: 24.9
  2.8–9: 14.34
  3.11–12: 14.11
  3.19: 19.15
  5.7: 26.3
  9.17: 26.15
  10.11: 14.14
  11.7: 14.30
  11.12: 22.9
  15.25: 6.13
  20.15: 19.11
  24.8: 26.12
  25.4: 14.30
  26.2–3: 11.3
  31.40: 14.18
  34.3: 32.10
  39.5–12: 26.13

Psalms
  1.2: 6.2
  2.9: 6.17
  4.1: 17.2
  4.2: 14.21; 19.4; 23.6
  6.1: 44.5
  8.3: 20.11
  9.12: 14.35
  9.18: 14.35
  10.1 (LXX 9.22): 22.7
  10.12 (LXX 9.33): 14.35
  10.14 (LXX 9.35): 14.27
  11.1 (LXX): 44.5
  11.2 (LXX 10.2): 6.13
  11.4 (LXX 10.4): 14.35
  12.5 (LXX 11.6): 14.35

13.3 (LXX 12.4): 32.6
14.5 (LXX 13.5): 23.9
16.5 (LXX 15.5): 6.2
17.7 (LXX 16.7): 6.9
17.15 (LXX 16.15): 11.7
18.11 (LXX 17.12): 32.15
19.10 (LXX 18.11): 11.1
23.2 (LXX 22.2): 6.9
23.4 (LXX 22.4): 17.2
24.8 (LXX 23.8): 13.1
27.3 (LXX 26.3): 26.18
30.1 (LXX 29.1): 44.5
30.5 (LXX 29.6): 13.4
30.11 (LXX 29.12): 6.4
33.3 (LXX 32.3): 44.1
33.6 (LXX 32.6): 32.10
33.15 (LXX 32.15): 36.7
34.1 (LXX 33.2): 32.20
34.2 (LXX 33.3): 10.2
35.3 (LXX 34.3): 14.37; 17.3
35.14 (LXX 34.14): 6.3; 9.1
37.26 (LXX 36.26): 14.27; 14.38
38.3 (LXX 37.4): 14.6
38.5 (LXX 37.5): 14.37
38.11 (LXX 37.12): 6.3; 26.17

246 INDEX OF HOLY SCRIPTURE

(Psalms *continued*)
39.1 (LXX 38.2): 6.1
39.2 (LXX 38.3): 6.2
40.9 (LXX 39.10): 32.20
41.1 (LXX 40.2): 14.38
42.4 (LXX 41.5): 24.19
43.4 (LXX 42.4): 26.16
44.14 (LXX 43.14): 6.8
45.1 (LXX 44.2): 6.1
45.2 (LXX 44.3): 26.11
45.4 (LXX 44.5): 9.5
45.7 (LXX 44.8): 10.4
45.13 (LXX 44.14): 24.9
51.7 (LXX 50.9): 14.37
51.10 (LXX 50.12): 44.2
55.6 (LXX 54.7): 17.2
55.8 (LXX 54.9): 17.2
55.14 (LXX 54.15): 6.7
62.10 (LXX 61.11): 36.12
66.12 (LXX 65.12): 13.4; 25.19
69.1 (LXX 68.2): 26.9
69.2 (LXX 68.3): 26.9
69.9 (LXX 68.10): 14.3
69.14 (LXX 68.15): 26.9
69.31 (LXX 68.32): 6.4
73.8 (LXX 72.8): 25.8
73.18 (LXX 72.18): 9.2
73.19 (LXX 72.19): 26.18
74.3-4 (LXX 73.3-4): 25.11
76.3 (LXX 75.4): 13.1
77.2 (LXX 76.3): 10.2; 17.2
77.3 (LXX 76.4): 17.2
77.10 (LXX 76.11): 44.8
78.25 (LXX 77.25): 14.1
79.1-2 (LXX 78.1-2): 25.11
79.4 (LXX 78.4): 22.7
82.5 (LXX 81.5): 17.7
84.5 (LXX 83.6): 23.3; 26.5
84.5-6 (LXX 83.6-7): 14.21
87.7 (LXX 86.7): 11.7; 24.19; 26.5
89.14 (LXX 88.15): 14.5
89.46 (LXX 88.47): 22.7
91.13 (LXX 90.13): 23.14
95.6 (LXX 94.6): 26.3
96.1 (LXX 95.1): 44.1
98.1 (LXX 97.1): 13.1; 44.1
99.6 (LXX 98.6): 11.2
102.3-5 (LXX 101.4-6): 14.6
104.15 (LXX 103.15): 32.21
104.18-19 (LXX 103.18-19): 32.9
104.20-23 (LXX 103.20-23): 32.9
106.2 (LXX 105.2): 6.8
107.29 (LXX 106.29): 13.1
112.5 (LXX 111.5): 14.38
119.46 (LXX 118.46): 25.7
119.71 (LXX 118.71): 17.5
119.105 (LXX 118.105): 6.9
119.131 (LXX 118.130): 44.6
124.4 (LXX 123.4): 13.2
124.6-7 (LXX 123.6-7): 13.2
132.1 (LXX 131.1): 14.2
132.9 (LXX 131.9): 19.9
133.2 (LXX 132.2): 11.1
137.4 (LXX 136.4): 44.1
141.7 (LXX 140.7): 6.1; 32.4
143.4 (LXX 142.4): 10.2
145.19 (LXX 144.19): 25.14
148.5: 20.9
148.6: 32.8
149.1: 44.1
149.6: 6.2

Proverbs
1.3: 17.3
1.7: 26.14
1.9: 6.5
3.28: 14.38
3.34: 22.5
4.27: 32.6
7.4: 6.5
8.7: 32.20
8.27-29: 32.10
8.30: 32.10
9.2: 6.6

INDEX OF HOLY SCRIPTURE

15.16: 32.26
16.16 (LXX 15.27):
   14.36
17.5: 14.36
19.1 (LXX 28.6):
   32.26
19.17: 14.36
21.1: 36.11
22.2: 14.36
22.20: 32.24
23.4: 32.21
24.11: 19.11
26.11: 6.19
30.2: 20.5

Ecclesiastes
   3.1: 6.1; 22.15
   3.7: 6.1
   3.8: 22.15
   7.3: 14.13
   7.16: 32.6
   10.1: 23.4
   11.2: 14.22; 44.5
   12.13: 26.14

Song of Songs
   4.12: 11.1; 24.9

Wisdom
   1.4: 9.2; 32.12
   2.24: 44.4
   3.11: 32.20
   5.14: 19.4
   11.20: 24.1
   14.6: 6.10

Sirach
   1.2–3: 14.30
   4.29: 32.21
   5.12: 32.21
   6.14–15: 11.1
   11.25: 35.4

Isaiah
   1.6: 14.37
   1.16: 11.4
   1.18: 14.37
   3.12: 24.8
   6.5: 9.1
   7.6: 25.12
   8.18: 6.21

8.21–22: 6.14
14.12: 36.5
14.14: 6.13
16.11: 44.1
25.3: 6.9
28.17: 13.1
29.4: 14.29
30.15: 17.3
35.3: 17.2
35.10: 6.4
40.10: 26.7
40.12: 32.27
40.27: 19.9
41.1: 44.1
41.4: 13.1
42.2: 14.2
42.14: 6.7
49.16: 36.12
50.6: 14.4
51.6: 6.14; 32.7
53.5: 14.15
53.5–7: 19.13
53.7: 14.2
53.12: 14.4
58.7: 14.38
58.8–9: 14.38
58.9: 17.3
59.5: 23.14
60.4: 6.21
61.2: 26.17
62.1: 22.16
63.4: 26.17
64.4: 11.6
65.17: 44.9
66.18: 26.7

Jeremiah
   1.18: 44.1
   2.27: 6.3
   4.19: 17.1; 22.8
   4.31: 22.16
   9.1: 22.8; 25.12
   9.1–2: 17.1
   9.2: 20.2
   9.4: 10.2
   9.17: 22.8
   9.21: 11.5
   9.23: 14.20
   9.24: 14.20
   10.21: 9.6

Lamentations
   1.4: 6.18; 25.12
   1.15: 22.8
   4.2: 6.18
   4.7: 15.9
   4.10: 6.18

Ezekiel
   22.25: 26.3
   34.3: 26.4
   34.3–10: 9.6
   34.4: 13.4; 14.15
   34.5–6: 19.9
   34.16: 13.4;
      14.15
   37.7: 25.14
   43.19: 11.1

Daniel
   3–4.6: 15.6
   3.18: 11.5
   3.39: 14.40
   3.49–50: 15.11;
      24.10
   6.16–24: 15.11;
      24.10
   9.23: 11.1
   13.5: 36.3
   13.42: 36.7

Hosea
   1.1: 6.7
   1.7: 17.2
   10.12: 32.12
   13.9: 26.18
   14.9: 14.30
   14.10: 14.21

Joel
   2.24: 25.19
   3.11: 6.12

Amos
   4.5: 22.6
   5.8: 6.4; 24.7
   6.4–7: 14.24
   8.5: 14.24

Jonah
   2: 24.10

INDEX OF HOLY SCRIPTURE

Micah
  2.9–10: 9.3; 14.21
  4.6: 13.1
  7.1: 25.19

Zephaniah
  3.6–7: 17.3
  3.16–19: 17.3

Zechariah
  7.9–10: 19.11
  11.15: 6.4; 26.4

Malachi
  3.6: 36.9

1 Esdras
  4.35: 23.4

Susannah
  1–63: 24.10
  5: 36.3
  42: 36.7

2 Maccabees
  3.1–3: 15.11

  6.18–31: 15.3; 15.6
  7: 15.3
  7.20–41: 15.4

4 Maccabees
  1.7–8: 15.2
  5–7: 15.3; 15.6
  6.23: 15.6
  8–12: 15.3
  14.11–20: 15.4
  17.1: 15.10

New Testament

Matthew
  2: 19.12
  2.11: 14.40
  2.16: 36.5
  3.4: 14.4
  4.1–11: 14.3; 24.9
  5.7: 14.38
  5.9: 22.15
  5.15: 6.9; 32.1
  5.16: 26.5
  5.37: 19.11
  5.39: 26.12
  5.42: 14.27
  5.45: 14.25; 19.11; 32.22
  6.3: 26.5
  6.26: 26.12
  7.1: 11.3; 32.30
  7.4: 23.2
  7.6: 22.6
  7.13–14: 14.5
  7.16–20: 26.5
  8.8: 20.4
  8.17: 14.15; 32.30
  9.13: 14.40
  9.22: 14.37
  10.3: 24.8
  10.10: 6.2
  10.28: 6.22
  10.32: 15.12
  10.42: 32.21
  11.27: 25.16
  11.29: 14.15; 32.18
  12.19: 14.2

  13.8: 26.5
  13.25: 19.14; 32.6
  13.27–30: 32.29
  13.45–46: 6.5; 19.1
  13.46: 17.7
  14.15–21: 14.1
  14.23: 14.4
  14.25: 24.10
  14.30: 17.5
  14.30–31: 24.10
  16.18: 32.18
  17.1–8: 32.18
  17.18: 24.10
  17.24–27: 19.13
  18.12: 14.15
  18.22: 22.15
  18.23–35: 17.11
  19.8: 14.25
  19.21: 14.4; 14.39
  21.19: 32.30
  22.21: 19.11
  22.36–40: 14.5; 22.4
  23.13: 19.9
  23.37: 6.7; 6.21
  25.15: 6.9
  25.18: 10.3; 32.1
  25.18–27: 26.5
  25.32–33: 14.39
  25.34: 24.19
  25.35: 14.40
  25.40: 26.6
  26.14–16: 36.5
  26.15: 26.16

  26.31: 26.17
  26.36: 14.3
  26.53: 14.2
  26.37: 32.18
  26.69–75: 26.17
  27.3–5: 36.5

Mark
  1.4: 26.7
  3.24–27: 22.7
  4.8: 26.5
  4.20: 26.5
  5.13: 24.10
  11.12: 32.30

Luke
  1.20: 6.7
  1.80: 14.4; 26.7
  2.1–7: 19.12
  2.9: 19.12
  2.34: 17.7
  3.13–14: 19.11
  5.15–16: 26.7
  5.8: 9.1; 20.4
  6.29: 26.12
  6.35–38: 14.5
  6.38: 19.13
  6.48: 6.3
  7.3–6: 9.2
  7.36: 14.40
  8.13: 19.8
  10.18: 23.14
  10.19: 23.14
  10.30: 14.37

INDEX OF HOLY SCRIPTURE

11.33: 10.3
12.20: 14.18
12.49: 32.4
13.24: 14.5
13.34: 6.7; 6.21
14.28–30: 32.27
15.4–7: 26.2
16.9: 14.40
16.19–31: 19.11; 36.12
16.22: 19.11
16.22–25: 14.34
16.24–31: 26.6
18.13: 13.1
19.2–4: 20.4
19.8: 14.4
19.19: 20.4
21.2: 13.1; 19.8
21.19: 14.22
22.50–51: 14.2
24.9: 24.17

John
1.1: 6.7
1.29: 6.4; 14.4; 14.14
2.17: 14.3
3.10: 26.15
5.14: 14.37
5.29: 14.31
6.15: 14.4
6.18: 26.8
8.12: 6.4; 6.7
8.44: 6.13; 17.9
8.48: 26.12
9.5: 6.4; 6.7
10.1–2: 25.11
10.3: 19.9
10.7: 6.4
10.9: 6.4
10.10: 26.3
10.11: 6.4; 14.15
10.14: 15.12
10.14–15: 19.9
10.22: 44.2
11.39: 25.14
11.52: 6.7
12.3: 14.40
12.6: 14.39; 26.16
12.22: 32.18
12.32: 19.6

12.36: 11.1
13.5: 14.4
13.6: 32.18
13.23: 32.18
13.24: 32.18
13.25: 32.18
13.34: 11.7
14.2: 14.5; 32.33
14.5: 32.8
14.6: 6.4
14.8: 32.18
14.22: 32.18
14.27: 22.16
14.31: 14.21; 19.6
16.2: 32.4
16.13: 23.11
17.12: 6.21
18.10–11:14.2
19.23: 6.1
19.38–39: 14.40

Acts
7.58–60: 14.2
7.59: 15.3
13.28: 36.5
14.22: 13.4
18.25: 32.6

Romans
1.21–23: 14.33
5.2: 10.4
5.5: 6.6
5.11: 10.4
5.20: 6.9
6.4: 14.14; 44.6
6.19: 36.8
7.4: 24.8
7.13: 9.2
8.14: 14.23
8.17: 14.14; 14.23; 14.40
9.3: 14.2; 23.13; 32.31
9.33: 17.7
10.6–8: 32.25
10.8: 17.2
10.12: 20.7
11.4: 11.5
11.17–25: 14.3
11.25: 32.15
11.33–34: 14.30

12.1: 11.4; 15.3; 20.4; 32.6
12.1–2: 24.4
12.5: 14.8; 32.11
12.6: 32.11
12.7–8: 32.12
12.8: 14.38
12.11: 6.4; 11.4
12.15: 14.6
12.16: 6.4
13.1: 17.6
13.5–6: 17.6
13.12: 35.2
13.13: 6.4
14.4: 32.30
14.15–15.2: 32.31
15.5: 6.4
15.19: 10.3; 32.15
16.20: 23.14

1 Corinthians
1.17: 32.26
1.30: 6.4
2.6–7: 6.1; 32.13
2.9: 11.6
2.10: 14.28
2.13: 32.24
3.2: 32.13
3.4: 6.7
3.4–9: 32.5
3.5–6: 19.8
3.6: 13.1
3.13–15: 32.1
3.16: 44.5
3.22: 32.5
4.5: 11.3
4.7: 32.13
4.12–13: 26.12
5.6–7: 10.2
6.13: 6.6; 26.6
6.15: 14.37
7.20: 19.10
7.25–39: 14.3
7.40: 26.13
8.6: 36.1
9.15–18: 26.6
9.22: 6.6
9.27: 14.3
10.4: 6.3
12.8–10: 32.11
12.21: 6.8

(1 Corinthians *continued*)
  12.25: 6.8
  12.28: 32.11
  12.29–30: 32.12
  13.10: 20.11
  13.12: 14.23; 19.12; 25.17; 32.15
  13.13: 14.2; 32.23
  14.25: 23.4; 26.5
  14.27–30: 32.12
  14.32: 32.11
  14.33: 19.10
  15.9: 24.8
  15.31: 26.1
  15.41: 32.8

2 Corinthians
  1.22: 14.14
  3.6–8: 20.2
  4.6: 32.12
  4.16: 14.14
  5.5: 14.14
  5.17: 44.8
  6.7: 6.6; 9.3; 19.10; 26.10
  6.14: 6.11
  6.15: 24.15
  6.16: 20.4; 44.5
  7.1: 11.4
  8.9: 14.15; 44.4
  11.2: 14.3
  11.27: 26.12
  11.29: 26.4
  12.2: 32.1; 32.15; 32.24
  12.4: 32.15
  12.13–14: 26.17
  12.14: 26.4
  13.11: 6.4; 6.22; 22.1

Galatians
  2.1: 10.3
  2.10: 14.39
  2.20: 20.5; 32.15
  3.26: 14.23
  3.27: 14.14
  4.26: 15.5
  5.9: 14.15

  6.2: 6.4
  6.3: 36.1
  6.14: 14.21

Ephesians
  2.10: 14.2
  2.14: 6.8; 6.12; 6.21; 10.4; 22.1
  2.16–17: 11.7
  2.20: 6.3; 17.7; 19.16; 22.4
  2.21–22: 19.8
  3.1: 10.1
  3.6: 14.40
  4.3: 24.2
  4.4: 6.8
  4.5–6: 32.33
  4.6: 26.19
  4.11: 14.27; 17.6; 32.11
  4.16: 32.11
  4.22: 44.6
  4.28: 32.12
  5.8: 11.1
  5.12: 35.4
  5.22: 17.6
  5.23–24: 17.6
  6.5: 17.6
  6.12: 11.4
  6.14: 6.22
  6.16: 6.22; 11.5; 13.5; 24.19

Philippians
  1.6: 11.7
  1.10: 24.19
  1.15: 32.1
  1.23: 32.15
  1.27: 6.22
  2.2: 6.4; 6.22
  2.7: 14.4; 19.13
  2.8: 14.15
  2.16: 9.6
  3.8: 24.15
  3.13: 19.7
  3.21: 20.4
  4.7: 6.22; 22.1
  4.17: 26.6
  4.18: 35.1

Colossians
  1.20: 6.21
  2.12: 14.14
  2.19: 6.4
  3.1: 14.21
  3.3: 19.1
  3.5: 20.4
  3.18: 17.6
  4.6: 6.2

1 Thessalonians
  2.10: 36.2
  2.19–20: 36.10

1 Timothy
  1.13: 24.8
  2.7: 32.15
  5.10: 26.6
  6.16: 19.12
  6.20: 32.5

2 Timothy
  1.11: 32.15
  1.14: 6.22
  2.16: 32.5
  4.2: 32.30

Titus
  2.13: 9.6
  2.14: 14.15; 26.1
  3.14: 36.10

Philemon
  1.1: 10.1

Hebrews
  1.14: 44.3
  2.4: 14.27
  4.12: 32.4
  4.16: 9.5
  5.12–13: 32.13
  5.14: 32.13
  7.10: 20.9
  8.2: 10.4; 11.2; 19.8
  10.24: 19.17
  11.31: 14.2
  11.38: 14.11
  13.14: 26.14

James
  1.13: 24.9
  2.26: 26.5
  4.6: 23.5

1 Peter
  2.8: 17.7

2.9: 6.17; 13.4; 14.15
2.9–10: 22.2
4.10: 14.24
4.17: 19.9
5.4: 9.6

1 John
  1.5: 44.3
  1.17: 14.4
  4.8: 6.11; 14.2
  4.16: 6.11; 11.6; 22.4

www.ingramcontent.com/pod-product-compliance
Lightning Source LLC
Chambersburg PA
CBHW032031290426
44110CB00012B/753